Lecture Notes in Computer Science 3567

Commenced Publication in 1973
Founding and Former Series Editors:
Gerhard Goos, Juris Hartmanis, and Jan van Leeuwen

T0223707

Mike Jackson   David Nelson
Sue Stirk (Eds.)

Database: Enterprise, Skills and Innovation

22nd British National Conference on Databases, BNCOD 22
Sunderland, UK, July 5-7, 2005
Proceedings

 Springer

Volume Editors

Mike Jackson
University of Central England in Birmingham, Department of Computing
Perry Barr, Birmingham B42 2SU, UK
E-mail: mike.jackson@uce.ac.uk

David Nelson
Sue Stirk
University of Sunderland, The David Goldman Informatics Centre
School of Computing and Technology
Sir Tom Cowie Campus at St Peter's
St Peter's Way, Sunderland SR6 0DD, UK
E-mail: {david.nelson,sue.stirk}@sunderland.ac.uk

Library of Congress Control Number: 2005928674

CR Subject Classification (1998): H.2, H.3, H.4

ISSN   0302-9743
ISBN-10   3-540-26973-8 Springer Berlin Heidelberg New York
ISBN-13   978-3-540-26973-1 Springer Berlin Heidelberg New York

Springer is a part of Springer Science+Business Media

springeronline.com

© Springer-Verlag Berlin Heidelberg 2005
Printed in Germany

Typesetting: Camera-ready by author, data conversion by Olgun Computergrafik
Printed on acid-free paper   SPIN: 11511854   06/3142   5 4 3 2 1 0

Preface

The British National Conference on Databases (BNCOD) was established in 1980 as a forum for research into the theory and practice of databases. The original conference in the series took place at the University of Aberdeen. To be precise, this conference was in fact entitled ICOD which stood for International Conference on Databases. It was the intention, when the series began, that an ICOD would take place every two years, whilst a BNCOD would run in the years in between. As the record shows ICOD was only held in 1980 and 1983. The more junior conference has managed to acquire a lifetime much longer than that of its senior relative!

If truth were known, however, BNCOD has, over the years, grown into ICOD and although the conference is still titled "British National," it is, in fact, an international conference that takes place on a yearly basis. Proof of this can be obtained simply by looking at the table of contents of these proceeding which clearly show that the majority of papers presented at this year's conference came from contributors whose affiliations are outside the UK.

Despite the range of papers on offer, BNCOD still retains its uniquely British flavor. The Programme Committee is drawn from UK academics and the conference is always held at a British university (or in earlier years a polytechnic!). BNCOD 2005 attracted a number of UK academics who can only be sure of meeting each other once a year at the annual BNCOD conference. For many UK database researchers an earlier BNCOD will have been their first experience of an academic conference and for many others BNCOD will be the arena in which they choose to showcase their early work.

Earlier BNCODs were a simple three-day affair. Arrive at lunchtime on the first day, conference dinner on the second evening and leave after lunch on the third day. Later BNCODs have grown in stature and are now linked with other events that take place in the same week as the conference. For some time a Doctorial Consortium has been associated with the conference and this has proved to be a valuable event that has helped to develop UK students attempting to gain a PhD by researching in the database topic area. Two years ago, when BNCOD was staged in Coventry, a workshop on Teaching, Learning and Assessment of Databases was run alongside the conference with the aim of encouraging the many academics in the UK who teach databases to engage with those academics who also conduct research in the area. This workshop has proved popular ran for the third time this year. Additionally, in recent years organizers of BNCOD have taken the opportunity of the presence of BNCOD delegates to run a workshop based on a topic of special interest to researchers in their department. This year's conference was partnered with a workshop on Data Mining and Knowledge Discovery in Databases.

One continuing tradition of BNCOD is that the conference should provide the UK database community with the opportunity of hearing speakers who have an academic track record of outstanding research. This year's BNCOD has maintained that tradition. The invited speakers are Rakesh Agrawal from IBM's Almaden Research Center and Paul Watson from the University of Newcastle upon Tyne.

Rakesh Agrawal's current research interests include privacy and security technologies for data systems, Web technologies, data mining and OLAP. He has pioneered fundamental concepts in data privacy, including the Hippocratic Database, Sovereign Information Sharing, and Privacy-Preserving Data Mining. He earlier developed key data mining concepts and technologies. IBM's commercial data mining product, Intelligent Miner, grew out of this work.

Rakesh has published more than 100 research papers and he has been granted more than 50 patents. He is the recipient of the ACM-SIGKDD First Innovation Award, ACM-SIGMOD Edgar F. Codd Innovations Award, as well as the ACM-SIGMOD Test of Time Award. He is also a Fellow of the IEEE and a Fellow of the ACM. Scientific American named him in the list of 50 top scientists and technologists in 2003. Unfortunately, Rakesh's busy schedule did not leave him sufficient spare time to prepare a paper for these proceedings and therefore his presentation has not been included in this volume.

Paul Watson is Professor of Computer Science and Director of the North East Regional e-Science Centre. In the 1980s, as a Lecturer at Manchester University, he was a designer of the Alvey Flagship and Esprit EDS systems. During 1990–1995 he worked for ICL as a system designer of the Goldrush MegaServer parallel database server, which was released as a product in 1994. In recent years his work has focused on "The Grid," specifically methods of accessing and integrating large amounts of data held in distributed databases.

Paul's paper, which is included in the proceedings, will be of interest to many database researchers looking for areas in which their work can be applied. The UK funding bodies seem to have long regarded the database arena as one that requires little further research work. This paper shows how database technology can be important in an area that has attracted considerable interest: Grid applications.

The full papers that were submitted to, and accepted by, the conference were grouped to form three sessions: Spatio-temporal Databases, Data Integration and Information Retrieval, and Data Processing and Provenance.

Elzbieta Malinowski and Esteban Zimányi's paper demonstrates that spatial techniques, previously associated with geographical information systems, can be usefully applied to data warehousing and OLAP. Taher Ahmed and Maryvonne Miquel complement this work by describing OLAP techniques for data that might arise from geographical analysis over time. Heidi Gregersen, in contrast, considers the conceptual aspects of database applications by seeking to extend the familiar Entity Relationship Model in order to be able to model temporal aspects of data.

Mohamed Basel Al-Mourad and Nick Fiddian present a rule based approach to combining data from heterogeneous databases, their work concentrates on object databases. Wenxin Liang and Haruo Yokota seek to solve a similar problem;

however their area of interest is XML documents. Carson Leung and Wookey Lee consider a different type of data integration that is found in data warehousing. Their paper demonstrates a method for improving the update of data warehouse views which relies on the constraints that apply to the source data. Jun Hong, Weiru Liu, David Bell and Qingyuan Bai demonstrate how the performance of queries that involve views can be improved when the constraints represented by the functional dependencies associated with those views are taken into consideration.

The final grouping of papers contains research that describes techniques for selecting data and for tracing where data selections have been derived. Keke Cai describes a method for choosing the data to be broadcast in a broadcast network. Rainer Gemulla, Henrike Berthold and Wolfgang Lehner demonstrate how to select samples of data in order to speedily obtain information from a data warehouse. Hao Fan and Alexandra Poulovassilis present a technique that traces the way in which integrated information has been derived from data sources.

Over recent years BNCOD has also included short papers. These papers are presented at the conference by their authors but they are allocated a shorter timeslot than that set aside for full papers. Typically, short papers describe interesting work in progress that has not yet generated the full volume of results expected in a full paper. The short papers in this year's BNCOD were separated into two groups: those that are concerned with data expressed in XML and those that describe application areas of information management.

Peter Pleshachkov, Petr Chardin and Sergey Kuznetsov set out a scheme that makes it possible for users to concurrently access an XML database. They propose a locking technique that is based on the Xpath language. Pensri Amornsinlaphachai, Akhtar Ali and Nick Rossiter are similarly concerned with XML databases and describe a methodology to update linked XML documents.

Dong Liang, Jie Yang, Jinjun Lu and Yuchou Chang discuss a technique that improves the accuracy of image retrieval. Patricio Mois, Marcos Sepúlveda and Humberto Pröschle demonstrate an algorithm which uses text processing to improve the accuracy of data entry in geographical information systems. Ben Sissons, Alex Gray, Anthony Bater and Dave Morrey describe an implementation of a patient information system designed to operate within an environment in which correctness and security are critical issues. Werner Nutt and Alisdair Gray propose a technique for integrating streams of data into a global schema that uses a publish/subscribe architecture.

The contributions summarized above are representative of the fact that BNCOD is fortunate in being able to attract a good number of high quality submissions. The papers accepted were selected from the 66 submitted. Many of the submissions that for reasons of time and space could not be included in the conference contained descriptions of high-class database research. The conference organizers thank everyone who submitted a paper and hope that they will continue to support BNCOD in the years to come.

Acknowledgements

The effort that is necessary for the operation of a successful conference necessarily involves a number of people who work together to make things happen. Thanks are due to the Programme Committee who turned round their reviews in a very short time and produced helpful and constructive comments for all the authors.

April 2005   Mike Jackson, David Nelson and Sue Stirk

Conference Committees

Organizing Committee

David Nelson	(Chair)	University of Sunderland
Sue Stirk	(Chair)	University of Sunderland

Programme Committee

Mike Jackson (Chair)	University of Central England
David Bell	Queen's University Belfast
Jagdev Bhogal	University of Central England
Albert Burger	Heriot-Watt University
Bernadette Byrne	University of Wolverhampton
Ernesto Compatangelo	University of Aberdeen
Richard Connor	University of Strathclyde
Richard Cooper	University of Glasgow
Barry Eaglestone	University of Sheffield
Suzanne Embury	University of Manchester
Wenfei Fan	Bell Labs/University of Edinburgh
Alvaro Fernandes	University of Manchester
Mary Garvey	University of Wolverhampton
Alex Gray	Cardiff University
Anne James	Coventry University
Keith Jeffery	CLRC Rutherford Appleton Laboratory
Graham Kemp	Chalmers University of Technology
Jessie Kennedy	Napier University
Brian Lings	University of Exeter
Nigel Martin	Birkbeck College
Lachlan MacKinnon	Heriot-Watt University
Ken Moody	University of Cambridge
David Nelson	University of Sunderland
Alex Poulovassilis	Birkbeck College
Sue Stirk	University of Sunderland
Stratis Viglas	University of Edinburgh
Howard Williams	Heriot-Watt University
Peter Wood	Birkbeck College

Steering Committee

Brian Lings (Chair)	University of Exeter
Barry Eaglestone	University of Sheffield
Alex Gray	Cardiff University
Anne James	Coventry University
Keith Jeffery	CLRC Rutherford Appleton Laboratory
Roger Johnson	Birkbeck College, University of London
Lachlan MacKinnon	Heriot-Watt University
Alex Poulovassilis	Birkbeck College, University of London

Table of Contents

XML

Applied Information Management

Author Index

Databases in Grid Applications: Locality and Distribution

Paul Watson

School of Computing Science, University of Newcastle, Newcastle-upon-Tyne, UK
Paul.Watson@newcastle.ac.uk

Abstract. This paper focuses on two areas that experience in building database-oriented e-science applications has shown to be important. Firstly, methods of promoting data locality are vital due to the high cost of moving data in service-based distributed systems. Databases provide an excellent basis for achieving this due to their potential for moving computation to data. The paper also describes a new infrastructure that further promotes locality by enabling service-based computations to migrate to data. Secondly, the ability to combine information from a set of distributed databases has proved invaluable in many applications. The paper describes the design of an adaptive distributed query processing system that is able to exploit facilities offered by an underlying grid infrastructure. In addressing these two areas, the paper gives an overview of some of the generic components that have been designed to simplify the integration of databases into e-science applications.

1 Introduction

The 2001 paper "Databases and the Grid" ([1]) argued that databases should play an important role in e-science applications. This was because they offered a way to manage and publish the deluge of structured data that the large numbers of new grid computing [2] projects were planning to generate. Four years on, it is clear that e-science has encouraged the publication of information on an unprecedented scale. The cost of data collection, and the potential value of data to large groups of scientists is so great that funding bodies are now insisting that projects make their data available for others to use. The days in which much scientific data was stored on the "C:" drive of a researcher's computer, unavailable to others and likely to disappear at the end of the project, are now thankfully coming to an end.

The 2001 paper argued that database servers provide a wide range of facilities that both publishers and consumers can exploit in order to meet their requirements, including the ability to manage very large quantities of information, security, querying, update, concurrency control, high availability, manageability, resource control, versioning, schema evolution and change notification. However, it went further and argued that simply encouraging the use of databases was not enough, and that it was necessary to provide technology to reduce the complexity of making databases available through a service-based interface (now that Web Services is becoming the most commonly used distributed systems technology for building grid applications), and to remove the need to write bespoke consumers for every database to be accessed by an application. Consequently, the paper argued that there were advantages in defining and making available implementations of a generic wrapper for exposing a database as a service.

M. Jackson et al. (Eds.): BNCOD 2005, LNCS 3567, pp. 1–16, 2005.
© Springer-Verlag Berlin Heidelberg 2005

It may be argued that databases should not be directly exposed at all to external clients. It is certainly the case that when databases are made available over the web, the database itself is almost always hidden behind an application that presents only a restricted set of functionalities. There are often good business reasons for this: organisations present those functionalities that are most likely to benefit them in their aims. So an on-line bookstore will present ways of keyword searching and viewing a customer's shopping basket. But, it will not allow arbitrary queries against its databases because they might negatively affect its business. e.g. by making it easy for another store to download information about the prices of all the books so they can then set their own prices accordingly.

This approach of offering only restricted functionality could be taken by e-science systems: the owners of data could decide on a particular set of functions and make only those available, rather than provide a general query interface. This approach is adopted by some e-science systems (especially those that provide a web interface), but it is clear that this can be restrictive as it requires the data owners to guess in advance how scientists may wish to use the data; e.g. what patterns they will search for, and how they will choose to combine data from multiple databases. For file-based scientific data, the predominant solution to the equivalent problem has been to make all the data available for copying (e.g. by FTP) to a client's local disk from where it can be processed in whatever way is required. However, this approach is generally not feasible for databases due to the costs of transferring large amounts of data (some scientific databases hold Terabytes of data), of installing and configuring a local database to hold the data, and, of keeping the local database synchronised with the remote database. Therefore, if data publishers do not wish to restrict the potential uses of their data, they will need to make it available by storing it in a database, and then exposing generic functionalities – in particular query processing – to external clients.

In this paper, we give an overview of some work that has had the aim of easing the construction of efficient, database-oriented, e-science applications. It focuses on two main areas that experience has shown to be important. Section 2 describes some approaches to promoting data locality given the high cost of moving data around in service-based distributed systems. It explains how the use of databases provides an excellent basis for achieving this, and introduces a new infrastructure that further promotes locality by enabling service-based computation to migrate to data. Section 3 then considers the integration of information from a set of distributed databases. This includes the design of an adaptive distributed query processing system that is able to exploit facilities offered by an underlying grid infrastructure. In addressing these areas, both sections give an overview some of the generic components that have been designed to make it easier to integrate databases into e-science applications. Finally, Section 4 draws conclusions and attempts to look-ahead to research and industry trends that are likely to have implications for future work on databases and e-science.

2   Promoting Locality

One of the main lessons that have been learnt from the experience to date of designing and deploying grid applications based around databases is that data movement is very expensive, and should be avoided where possible. While this is a general rule to be followed in the design of distributed systems in which there is the potential for large amounts of information to be moved over networks [3], the problem is accentuated in grids due to the fact that exchanging messages between Web Services is very expensive. Currently, the main expense is due to the fact that data held within a service (e.g. in a database) is converted to and from a character-based representation of XML so that it can be packaged in a SOAP message and sent between services. This imposes a CPU cost for converting to and from the XML. It also results in a large increase in size between an efficient representation within a service (e.g. within a database) and the tagged, character-based XML representation, incurring increased transfer costs as more bytes are shipped. A further overhead is imposed if messages are encrypted by the commonly used WS-Security protocol due to the cost of converting the XML into canonical form before encryption.

In fact, it is not actually necessary to represent data in character-encoded XML in order to send it between services. SOAP is defined as an Infoset [4], so allowing more efficient representations between services [5], though today it is very rare to find services that support them.

Given these overheads, it is very important to minimise both the number of messages exchanged between services, and the amount of data contained within them. In general, when designing service-based applications, to minimise the number of messages exchanged it is very important to design services that operate at as large a granularity as possible. Currently, there are two approaches to designing a Web Service, one of which has a tendency to lead to poor service design (ironically, this is the one best supported by tools). The approaches are:

1. Take an existing object-oriented program, select the methods that you wish to expose remotely and make those the operations of the Web Service. This is supported and encouraged by many Web Service tools, which will automatically generate Web Service interfaces (WSDL) from methods selected by the user. Similarly, client-side tools allow consumers to bind to operations offered by a remote service as if they were object methods, and perform "remote method calls" on them. This has the advantage that the programmer of the client and server do not need to know anything about web service interfaces (WSDL), or SOAP messages as those are automatically generated. However, the grave danger is that this approach leads to fine-grained operations that are suitable for efficient object-oriented programming within a service or possibly over a LAN, but are hopelessly inefficient for building internet-scale distributed systems, given the overheads of SOAP and the cost of transferring data between remote services.

2. First, design the messages that will be exchanged by the service. A key aim should be to design messages that encourage large-granularity, inter-service interactions. For example, it is better not to design messages that encourage a consumer to get results from a database one at a time if it is possible to batch data so as to reduce the total number of inter-service interactions. Once the messages have been designed then services can be written to generate and consume them. This approach requires more thought and implementation work for programmer than does (1) but it leads to more efficient services and distributed applications.

In data-oriented applications, the main way to minimise both the number of message exchanges and the amount of data exchanged is to try to avoid moving data as much as possible through moving the computation to the data, rather than vica versa. Data services built around databases have tremendous potential to apply this principle as they allow clients to send queries the database for processing. This is in contrast with file-based services in which, except for some exceptions [6], it is usually necessary for the client to copy the data locally (e.g. by FTP) for processing.

We now consider three components that exploit database technology, and have been designed on the principle of reducing data movement where possible. These are the OGSA-DAI database service, the SkyServer MyDB, and the Active Information Repository.

2.1 OGSA-DAI

The OGSA Data Access and Integration project (OGSA-DAI) is a collaboration between groups within EPCC, the UK National e-Science Centre, IBM, Oracle and the Universities of Newcastle and Manchester. Since 2002, it has provided a Web Service database wrapper that supports common operations such as querying [7].

Consumers interact with the service through *Perform* documents that encapsulate a set of activities. Supported activities include queries (e.g. SQL queries for relational databases and XPath queries for XML datastores) and a variety of methods for delivering the results (e.g. store locally for later access or return the result to a 3rd party). By allowing consumers to pack a set of activities into a single interaction with the service, OGSA-DAI encourages the large-grained interactions that are necessary for efficient, service-based distributed computing. The activity mechanism is extensible, so service providers may define their own new activities for particular tasks (e.g. a text database could offer specialist text-searching activities). Interactions between consumers and the database service can be secured, e.g. by GSI [8]) or WS-Security [9].

OGSA-DAI therefore simplifies the process of publishing data. It also assists consumers by providing a common interface to a database that is independent of the specific DBMS product that has been wrapped (the main exception to this is in the different forms of SQL supported by different vendors; however our experience is that the problems can be largely mitigated by sticking to SQL standards widely supported across the database vendors). As will be seen in Section 3, this also simplifies the task of integrating data from multiple databases. The DAIS [10] working group of the Global Grid Forum is attempting to set a standard for exposing data through a Web Service interface. Ideally, the database vendors would themselves agree on, and support, such a standard. This would remove the need for third parties to provide wrappers for each different DBMS, and would also open the way for internal performance optimisations, e.g. in generating XML result sets directly from the internal representation.

Building on the foundation offered by OGSA-DAI for sending a set of activities to a database server in a single message, there are other steps that can be taken to further minimise the amount of data that is transferred. Stored Functions and methods (in object and object-relational database servers) allow users to define computations that are executed in the database server when called from within queries. These can often be used to process or filter results in the database engine so as to reduce the amount of data returned to the client [11]. This is almost always more efficient than to have the database service return the result of a query to the consumer and then have it process the result. There are two exceptions: a) where the method/function call results in a result set that is significantly greater than the result set before the method is applied and b) if the database server is overloaded then the overall performance of an application may be slowed by the cost of executing the computation in the DBMS rather than on an external compute server.

Stored procedures can also be used to encapsulate a set of operations or queries at the database server so that they can be repeatedly called by a consumer specifying only the identifier and any parameters.

2.2 Storing Query Results in the Database

In many cases, the result of one query will later be the subject to further query processing (for example to further filter information), possibly by another client. Allowing query results to be stored back in the database service, rather than returned to the client, has the potential to reduce the number of times when data is transferred between the database service and the consumer. It can also reduce the load on the database server by preventing the need to re-execute queries to re-generate results. Finally, it also removes the need for the consumer to devote resources to storing the (potentially large) results of queries. A successful pioneer of this approach is the MyDB facility in the SkyServer [11] which gives users their own logical space in the database to store the results of queries.

2.3 Providing Computational Resources Close to the Database

Despite the opportunities to exploit stored procedures and methods in queries, it is not always possible to perform all computation within the database service itself. For example, it may be necessary for a complex piece of software to analyse the data produced by a query. In general, this usually means that the consumer sends the query to the database service and receives in return the results that are then sent to an analysis service. This incurs the expense of transferring potentially large amounts of data from the database service to a remote machine for analysis (in practice, it may well travel indirectly, via the consumer that sent the query to the database server, so incurring extra data transfers).

We have been investigating a way to address this problem by deploying database servers closely coupled to local compute resources. In practice, this usually means deploying the DBMS on one or more nodes of a cluster, while making the other nodes available to run services that can query the database and analyse the results. We call this combination of database server and local compute nodes an Active Information Repository (AIR) [12].

An example application is shown in Figure 1. A bioinformatics service analyses data from a database that is made available as a Web Service through an interface such as OGSA-DAI. The analysis service sends a query to the database and receives back from it a large quantity of data. It then processes this data and sends a small result set back to the consumer (the thickness of the arrows indicates the quantity of data transferred).

In order to avoid transferring large amounts of data over long distances, it is advantageous to deploy the analysis service close to the database on which it operates. Therefore, the database provider may deploy an AIR, with a cluster of compute serv-

Fig. 1. Interactions between an Analysis Service and a Database Service

ers close to the data. This raises the question of how the owner of the analysis service can deploy it on the AIR so that it is close to the database. If the service is created by the owner of the AIR then it may be straightforward for them to do so, but in e-science systems, remote scientists will invariably continually be devising new ways of analysing data, and it would be advantageous for there needs to be a way for general users of the database service to deploy services on it.

We have devised a general infrastructure (named Dynasoar) for the dynamic deployment of Web Services over a grid (or the Internet) [13]. We first describe the generic Dynasoar architecture before showing how it can be used to dynamically deploy services on an AIR, close to the database on which they operate.

Dynasoar provides a generic infrastructure for the dynamic deployment of Web Services in response to the arrival of messages for them to process. This is achieved by dividing the handling of the messages sent to a service between two components – a *Web Service Provider* and a *Host Provider* – with a well-defined interface through which they interact. The *Web Service Provider* receives the incoming SOAP message sent to the Web Service. It arranges for it to be processed by choosing a *Host Provider* and passing to it the SOAP message and any associated QoS information. The *Web Service Provider* holds a copy of the service code (in a "Service Store") ready for when dynamic service deployment is required. The *Host Provider* controls computational resources (e.g. a cluster or a grid) on which services can be deployed, and messages processed. Therefore, it accepts the SOAP message from the *Web Service Provider* (along with any associated information) and is responsible for processing it and returning a response to the consumer (if one is required). When the message reaches the *Host Provider*, there are two main cases, depending on whether or not the service is already deployed on the node on which the message is to be processed.

If the Web Service is already deployed on one or more of the nodes that it controls, and those deployments can meet any QoS requirements, then the SOAP message is simply passed to one of the deployed services for processing. This case is shown in Figure 2. A request for a Web Service (s2) is sent by the Consumer to the endpoint at the *Web Service Provider* which passes it on to a *Host Provider*. In this case, the *Host Provider* already has the service s2 deployed (on nodes 1 and n in the diagram) and so, based on current loading information it chooses one (node n) and routes the request to it for processing. A response is then routed back to the consumer. Note that the *Web Service Provider* is not aware of the internal structure of the *Host Provider*, e.g. the nodes on which the service is deployed nor the node to which the message is sent. It simply communicates with the *Host Provider*, which manages its own internal resources.

The other case is where the Web Service is **not** already deployed. This may be because the *Host Provider* has no deployments of the service, or it may be because existing deployments cannot meet the QoS requirements (the GridSHED project

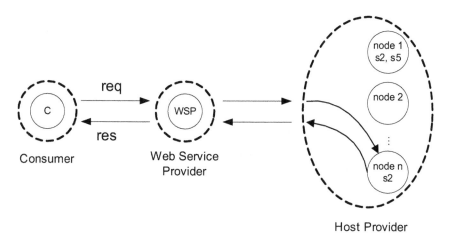

Fig. 2. A request is routed to an existing deployment of the service

[14],[15] has used mathematical models to generate heuristics that determine when it is desirable to install a service on another node, rather than use an existing deployment). Included in the information that the *Web Service Provider* sends to the *Host Provider* along with the SOAP message is an identifier for the service being called and the endpoint of the Service Store that contains the service code to be deployed. If the *Host Provider* must deploy a service in order to process the SOAP message then it sends a request to the Service Store to retrieve the service code. The *Host Provider* then installs the service on the selected node and routes the message to it. The message is then processed and the result (if any) returned to the consumer. An example of this case is shown in Figure 3. A request for a service (s4) is sent to by the consumer to the endpoint at the *Web Service Provider* which passes it on to a *Host Provider* (step 1 in the Figure). The *Host Provider* does not have the service s4 deployed on any of the nodes it controls and so, based on current loading information it chooses one (node 2), fetches the service code from the *Web Service Provider* and installs the service on that node (step 2). It then routes the request to it for processing (step 3). A response is then routed back to the consumer. Node 2 continues to host service s4, and so it is ready to process any other messages routed to it by the *Host Provider*.

It should be noted that the Consumer need not in any way be aware of the fact that a Web Service is dynamically deployed – its interaction with the service is through the standard mechanism of sending a message to the service endpoint offered by the *Web Service Provider*.

Once a service is installed on a node it remains in place ready to process future messages until it needs to be reclaimed. This has the potential to generate large efficiency gains when compared to job-based scheduling systems in which each job execution requires its own transport and installation of the code.

The Dynasoar infrastructure can support the dynamic deployment of services on the AIR (Figure 4). The AIR cluster runs the Host Provider component. The provider of the Analysis Service (which may be a lone researcher or a commercial company that specialises in writing analysis services) runs the Web Service Provider component, and makes the service available through this. Either the consumer (through pro-

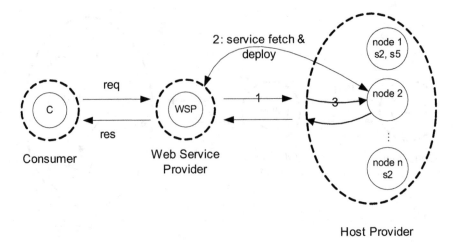

Fig. 3. A service is dynamically deployed to process a request

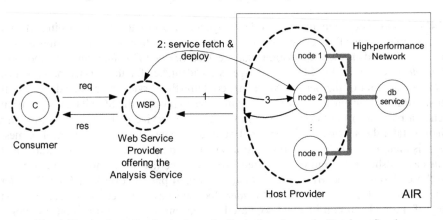

Fig. 4. The Analysis Service is dynamically deployed near the Database Service

viding the information in the request header) or the Analysis service provider can specify that the service should run on the AIR cluster close to the database service. Therefore when the Web Service Provider receives a message for the Analysis Service, it passes it to the cluster's Host Provider to ensure that it is processed close to the data (Figure 4 step 1). In the Figure, the Host Provider fetches and deploys the Analysis service from the Web Service Provider (Figure 4 step2) before the request is processed (on node 2).

By utilising the AIR and Dynasoar, services can be dynamically deployed close to the database service so as to avoid moving large amounts of data over long distances. To further reduce data movement, the SkyServer MyDB approach can be used to store results back in the database for further, later analysis and sharing. Therefore, the overall aim is to restrict analysis and movement of the data to within the AIR where possible. Only when absolutely necessary should data be moved outside the AIR. This may occur, for example, if data is to be combined with data from another database. In this case, a method is needed to efficiently query over data held in a set of distributed databases. This is the subject of the next section.

3 Querying Distributed Data

While Section 2 has promoted the localisation of computations on data so as to avoid the cost of moving it, it is actually rare that all the information that could usefully be harnessed by a scientist exists in a single location. Therefore, the ability to combine information from multiple sources is a common requirement in e-science applications. The normal way to combine information in service-based distributed computing is through the use of workflow systems [16]. These allow expert users to choreograph the interactions between a set of services in order to combine their functionality in some way. For example, a workflow used in bioinformatics may take as input data from an experiment, use one service to do some preliminary analysis, compare the results with existing data extracted from a database service, and then use a literature service to find relevant papers that may shed light on the results [17]. Workflows provide a way to capture expert knowledge on how to carry out such a process. Once captured, the analysis of data can be automatically enacted in a performant, consistent and reproducible manner. As a result, we have seen examples where the cost of analysing the data generated by an experiment has been reduced by a factor of ten when compared to manually controlled analysis using web sites and scripts.

However, where it is necessary to access and combine information from more than one database, then the workflow would have to incorporate services to implement standard operations on data such as joins, unions, filters etc. The danger is therefore that the workflow designer must design, implement and deploy services to perform a specialised form of Distributed Query Processing (DQP) on data accesses from a set of specific database services. Further, there is a real risk of poor performance, or failure due to data overload, as workflow enactment engines do not offer the sophisticated data buffering and flow control found in DQP systems.

Consequently, the OGSA-DQP project was created to design and build a distributed query processing system [18] that would: (i) provide a generic way of compiling, optimising and executing distributed queries over a set of OGSA-DAI database systems, and (ii) explore how to exploit the underlying grid infrastructure. It should be stressed that the aim was to complement and enhance, rather than replace, workflow systems; whilst a distributed query can be run in a "stand-alone" manner within an application, it can also be called from within a workflow.

The OGSA-DQP system works as follows. A distributed query processing service is deployed. This has the same interface as the OGSA-DAI database service (e.g. consumers can send queries to it in *perform* documents). However, a client wishing to use the DQP service must also identify the set of OGSA-DAI database systems that it wishes to run queries over. The DQP service then sends *perform* documents to those services to obtain logical and physical metadata. Logical metadata includes information on the tables that these services offer, while the physical metadata includes information that will be of use to a query compiler and optimiser, such as table sizes and the availability of indices.

The consumer can then submit queries to the DQP service which compiles and optimises them. One of the aims of grid infrastructure is to provide a way by which applications can discover and exploit computational resources that are available to them (for example by locating a suitable server on which a job can then be run [19],[20]). Therefore, the DQP service takes this approach and utilises a set of dynamically acquired computing resources for executing the query. The DQP optimiser uses grid information services to determine the computational resources that are available and then works out how best to map the query to them.

The result is a query plan which is distributed over query evaluator services that are deployed on the available hosts. Execution can then take place, with each evaluator executing some portion of the query plan. This may be one or more operators (e.g. join, select) or, in order to exploit parallelism to improve performance, part of an operator (e.g. one element of a parallel hash join). Consider an example query over two distributed databases: the Gene Ontology Database GO, and the genome database GIMS:

```
select  p.proteinId, Blast(p.sequence)
from    protein p, proteinTerm t
where   t.termId   = '8372'
and     p.proteinId = t.proteinId
```

This identifies proteins that are similar to human proteins with a GO term of 8372. It includes a call to a *Blast* sequence similarity service in order to return a set of protein ids and their associated similarity scores (OGSA-DQP allows computations encapsulated as Web Services to be incorporated into queries).

Figure 5a shows the query tree after logical and physical optimisation. The optimiser assesses the options for mapping the query plan onto the available nodes (as determined by the grid information service) and chooses a plan that attempts to reduce the response time by parallelising the hash join over a cluster of nodes such that the hash tables can fit entirely into main memory. This results in the execution plan of Figure 5b. The dashed boxes indicate how the plan is partitioned over a set of nodes. The exchange operators [21] manage the transfer of data between the partitions. In Figure 5b, these are shown at the intersection of partitions. In practise, an instance of the exchange operator is planted in each of the two overlapping partitions, one to send tuples and the other to receive. The iterator model [21] is used to control the flow of data around the execution plan (repeated requests for the next result tuple flow down from the top of the execution tree, and in response the tuples are generated and returned back up the tree), but rather than transfer data a tuple at a time between nodes in response to requests (calls to "next" in the iterator model), data is buffered by the exchange operators, and sent in blocks for efficiency [18].

The identifiers of the nodes over which the partition is to be distributed are shown within the partitions in Figure 5b. In this example, the hash join is to be distributed over nodes 5 to 12. The exchange operators on nodes 1 and 2 perform a hash on the join key of each outgoing tuple, and send the tuple to the appropriate node (5-12) where a local join can take place. In this way, parallelism can be utilised to speed-up queries by spreading operators over multiple nodes.

3.1 Exploiting Dynamic Adaptivity

The DQP optimiser makes a decision on how best to distribute the query plan, based on the availability of resources just before the query is executed. However, there are

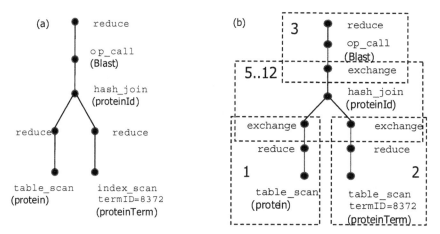

Fig. 5. (a) The Plan after Logical & Physical Optimisation; (b) the Execution Plan

obvious dangers in doing this in a dynamically changing environment. For example, what if during query execution a node becomes unable to deliver the expected performance as it is now also serving another, higher-priority service? What if one or more cheap, high-performance nodes become available just after a long query execution has begun? Or, what if the optimisers predictions about the required computing resources prove highly inaccurate (for example, because a join produces more rows than expected) and so the consumer will not get the query result within the time they require? Finally, what if a node is withdrawn by its owner from the pool of available resources, or simply fails during query execution? To address such problems and opportunities without killing and re-starting the query, with all the delays and wastage of resources that entails, requires the DQP infrastructure to be adaptive. It must monitor the progress of the execution and the availability of resources, and take dynamic decisions about whether or not to make dynamic changes. Work in the Polar* project has been investigating the opportunities for adaptivity in distributed query execution [22],[23]. It has focussed on two areas that are now discussed: recovering from node failure, and adapting to improve performance.

In order to allow a query to recover from the failure of one of the nodes being used by DQP, uniquely numbered checkpoint markers are inserted by the exchange operators into the streams of tuples flowing between nodes. Further, copies of tuples are retained by the exchange operators in a local recovery log after they have been transmitted. The basic scheme will be illustrated by reference to a simple linear chain of operators distributed over three nodes as shown in Figure 6. The *exchange a* operator regularly inserts a checkpoint marker into the stream of tuples that it sends from node 1 to node 2. It also buffers the tuples that it sends to node 2 in a local recovery log. When a tuple arrives at node 2, it is processed by Operator 2 and the result is passed to *exchange b* for transmission to node 3. When a checkpoint marker arrives at *exchange b* on node 3, this indicates that it is safe for all the tuples that preceded the sending of that marker by *exchange a* on node 1 to be deleted from its recovery log. To cause this to happen, *exchange b* on node 3 sends an acknowledgement to *exchange a* on node 1 containing the number of the checkpoint marker.

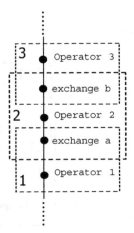

Fig. 6. A Linear Chain of Operators distributed over three nodes

This ensures that the failure of node 2 cannot cause the failure of the whole query. If node 2 fails, then a new node (2') is acquired and configured to act in its place. The *exchange a* operator on node 1 is informed that from now on it should send tuples to node 2', and requested to retransmit the tuples held in its recovery log to the new node.

The scheme can be used to recover from the failure of any node involved in the query processing. All the exchange operators buffer tuples in a local recovery log as they send them, until they receive an acknowledgement message from the node that is two places downstream in the query execution plan. In fact, by extending the span of the acknowledgements (e.g. retaining copies of tuples until the checkpoint marker has arrived *n* nodes downstream) an arbitrary number of node failures can be accommodated. The scheme also extends to more complex query graphs with arbitrary fan-in and fan-out by duplicating (fan-out) and aggregating (fan-in) checkpoint markers [22].

Work on DQP adaptivity has also encompassed making dynamic changes to the query plan to improve performance. For example in many DQP plans the work of an operator is shared across a set of nodes in order to exploit parallelism (e.g. the join operator in Figure 5). However, the data may not be evenly spread over the nodes, or some nodes may be more powerful than others. This can result in an imbalance of work that degrades the overall performance. Polar* has investigated the addition of a Monitoring-Assessment-Response framework [23] to detect and attempt to correct such imbalances. When the monitoring component detects an imbalance then the assessment component is called to decide whether a response is appropriate, and if so which of the possible range of responses is best. For example, if one node is underperforming relative to the others it may be better to redistribute work away from it, or, if a suitable new node is available, to configure and then utilise the new node to replace the underperformer.

In summary, the work on DQP has demonstrated its potential for combining information when compared to ad-hoc approaches such as bespoke workflow construction. Having the user express their intent through a declarative query language allows the compiler/optimiser to generate an execution plan that exploits parallelism, dynamic acquisition of grid resources, distribution and flow-control without any user intervention. There is also the added potential for exploiting adaptivity so as to allow dynamic re-configuration to improve performance and automatically recover from failure. The DQP design also shows that grid infrastructures have great potential as the basis for other forms of adaptive computation because they provide information on resource availability and offer ways to dynamically deploy computations on those resources.

4 Conclusions and Future Challenges

The past few years have seen a large investment in building e-science applications. Many of these exploit databases, though many more could but don't. We believe that in order to allow application builders to exploit the potential of databases then two approaches are needed. Firstly, we must advertise the potential benefits of using database technology, as they are often not obvious to those who do not come from a database background (to many scientists, files are the natural way to store data). In the above paper, we have attempted to do this by describing their potential for achieving high-performance through moving computation to data, and for combining distributed information. The success stories of e-science applications that are already successfully utilising databases should also be influential. These come from a wide range of domains including Astronomy [11],[24], Meteorology [25] and Bioinformatics [17].

Secondly, it is important to try to provide "off-the-shelf" building-blocks that simplify the task of integrating databases into e-science applications. OGSA-DAI and OGSA-DQP are two existing examples of this, but in order to identify opportunities for new, useful services that could have generic usage it is necessary to try to identify likely trends in the use of databases in e-science.

In the short term the growth in the use of databases may be driven by the increasing importance of managing and exploiting structured metadata [26],[27]. By providing semantic information about data, this will in turn increase the potential and importance of distributed query processing for data federation.

In the medium term, the main data-related trend that we expect to see is a huge growth in real-time data being generated by sensors, e.g. for environmental and traffic monitoring. Dealing effectively with this new deluge of information will pose great challenges. One approach would be to simply store the sensor information into a database as it is produced and then allow clients to query it retrospectively. However, this misses the opportunity to act in near real time as new data arrives. For example, data from river water level sensors could, when levels rise sufficiently high, trigger flood plane modelling (possibly on a dynamically acquired server) to predict whether flooding will occur, and if so take necessary action. A key to acting on sensor data is the ability to detect patterns in the low-level events (e.g. a sensor reading) that represent important high-level events on which action can be taken, e.g. "water levels becoming dangerously high". The results of existing research into continuous queries will clearly have a part to play here, and commercial database companies are making large investments in this area, largely due to the commercial importance of RFID tags [28]. Once a high-level event has been generated, then there is the need to take the appropriate action. This may include associating a workflow with an event (e.g. to run a flood plane model and plot the results on a map before sending an e-mail warning to those likely to be affected), or combining events (e.g. correlating a rise in pollution levels from a set of sensors in one area). Consequently, we expect that there will be an increase in the demand for middleware that can process events ([29],[30]). Section 3 described how the adoption of a common way of providing query access to databases allows the use of generic tools such as OGSA- DQP. In the same way, there would be an advantage in projects agreeing a common way to publish event-driven data. This would encourage the development of generic services to route, filter, log, replay and correlate events.

Over the coming years, we expect databases to become a basic component of all computer systems. Their footprint, in terms of disk, memory and CPU, is now relatively low compared even to a typical, cheap laptop PC. Consequently, there is no reason why their functionality and versatility should not be routinely exploited. This can be seen in moves by many operating systems designers to base their filesystems on a database (e.g. WinFS [31]). Where there exist compute resources that do not currently run a database, then dynamic service deployment systems such as Dynasoar, possibly exploiting Virtual Machine technologies, offer the opportunities to dynamically deploy a database on a node. This "databases everywhere" trend raises questions as to how these databases can be used to good effect. Clearly, there is the potential to utilise them for DQP query processing, but it would also be possible to use them to act as data caches, replicating all or some of the data from remote databases to reduce data transfer costs and query response times.

In conclusion, existing projects are now demonstrating the advantages of utilising databases in e-science projects. The functionality offered by database servers are proving highly useful for applications where sophisticated data querying and integration are required. However, they are also proving to be a good basis for building performant applications through their potential to minimise data movement. Consequently, as experience spreads through he community, we expect the use of databases in e-science to grow. In the short term this may be driven by the increasing importance of managing and exploiting structured metadata. In the medium term, the growth of event-driven processing for e-science will also increase the demand for database-oriented solutions, though much further work is needed to provide middleware to enable scientists to routinely write applications to extract full value from this dynamic data.

Acknowledgements

I would like to thank all of my collaborators at Newcastle and elsewhere for their contributions to the work described in this paper including: the longstanding Polar teams at Newcastle (Jim Smith) and Manchester (Norman Paton, Alvaro Fernandes, Rizos Sakellariou, Nedim Alpdemir, Sandra Sampaio, Tasos Gounaris); the Dynasoar and GridShed project teams (Chris Fowler, Charles Kubicek, John Colquhoun, Arijit Mukherjee, Mark Hewitt, Jennie Palmer, Isi Mitrani, Mike Fisher (BT), Paul McKee (BT)); the OGSA-DAI teams at Newcastle (Arijit Mukherjee), Edinburgh (Malcolm Atkinson), EPCC (Neil Chue Hong, Mario Antonioletti), IBM (Simon Laws, Brian Collins) and Oracle (Dave Pearson); the GAF team (Savas Parastatidis & Jim Webber); [my]Grid (Carole Goble and her team) and Rob Smith. The work described in this paper has undertaken in projects funded by the EPSRC, BBSRC, DTI and the UK e-Science core programme.

References

1. P. Watson, "Databases and the Grid," in *Grid Computing: Making the Global Infrastructure a Reality*, F. Berman, G. Fox, and A. J. G. Hey, Eds.: Wiley, 2002, pp. 1060.
2. I. Foster, C. Kesselman, and S. Tuecke, "The Anatomy of the Grid: Enabling Scalable Virtual Organizations," *International Journal of Supercomputer Applications*, vol. 15, 2001.
3. J. Gray, "Distributed Computing Economics," presented at "A Tribute to Roger Needham", Springer Monographs in Computing Science, 2004.
4. W3C, "SOAP 1.1." http://www.w3.org/TR/2000/NOTE-SOAP-20000508/
5. P. Sandoz, A. Triglia, and S. Pericas-Geertsen, "Fast Infoset," Sun Microsystems, 2004, http://java.sun.com/developer/technicalArticles/xml/fastinfoset
6. T. M. Kuric, U. V. Catalyurek, C. Chang, and J. H. Saltz, "DataCutter and A Client Interface for the Storage Resource Broker with DataCuttter Services," University of Maryland, CS-TR-4133, 2000 2000.
7. OGSA-DAI, "OGSA-DAI." http://www.ogsadai.org.uk/
8. V. Welch, I. Foster, C. Kesselman, O. Mulmo, L. Pearlman, S. Tuecke, J. Gawor, S. Meder, and F. Siebenlist, "Security for Grid Services," presented at High-Performance Distributed Computing, Seattle, 2003.
9. OASIS, "Web Services Security (WS-Security)." http://www.oasis-open.org/committees/wss
10. Global Grid Forum, "GGF, Database Access and Integration Services (DAIS-WG)," 2005.
11. M. A. Nieto-Santisteban, A. S. Szalay, A. R. Thakar, W. J. O'Mullane, J. Gray, and J. Annis, "When Database Systems Meet the Grid," Microsoft Research, MSR-TR-2004-81, December 2004.
12. P. Watson and P. Lee, "The NU-Grid Persistent Object Computation Server.," presented at 1st European Grid Workshop, Poznan, Poland, 2000.
13. P. Watson and C. Fowler, "An Architecture for the Dynamic Deployment of Web Services on a Grid or the Internet," School of Computing Science, University of Newcastle CS-TR-890, February 2005.
14. J. Palmer and I. Mitrani, "Optimal Server Allocation in Reconfigurable Clusters with Multiple Job Types," presented at Computational Science and its Applications (ICCSA 2004), Assisi, Italy, 2004.
15. C. Kubicek, M. Fisher, P. McKee, and R. Smith, "Dynamic Allocation of Servers to Jobs in a Grid Hosting Environment," *BT Technology Journal*, vol. 22, pp. 251-260, 2004.
16. OASIS, "OASIS Web Services Business Process Execution Language." http://www.oasis-open.org/committees/wsbpel
17. R. Stevens, R. McEntire, C. A. Goble, M. Greenwood, J. Zhao, A. Wipat, and P. Li, "myGrid and the Drug Discovery Process," *BIOSILICO*, vol. 2, pp. 140-148, 2004.
18. M. N. Alpdemir, A. Mukherjee, N. W. Paton, P. Watson, A. A. A. Fernandes, A. Gounaris, and J. Smith, "Service Based Distributed Querying on the Grid," presented at First International Conference on Service Oriented Computing, Trento, Italy, 2003.
19. T. Tannenbaum, D. Wright, K. Miller, and M. Livny, "Condor – A Distributed Job Scheduler," in *Beowulf Cluster Computing with Linux*, T. Sterling, Ed.: The MIT Press, 2002.
20. I. Foster, C. Kesselman, "Globus: A Metacomputing Infrastructure Toolkit," *International Journal of Supercomputing*, vol. 11, pp. 115-128, 1997.
21. G. Graefe, "Encapsulation of Parallelism in the Volcano Query Processing System," presented at SIGMOD Conference, Atlantic City, NJ, USA, 1990.
22. J. Smith and P. Watson, "Fault-Tolerance in Distributed Query Processing," School of Computing Science, University of Newcastle CS-TR-893, Feb 2005.
23. A. Gounaris, N. W. Paton, A. A. A. Fernandes, and R. Sakellariou, "Self-monitoring Query Execution for Adaptive Query Processing," *Data and Knowledge Engineering*, vol. 51, pp. 325-348, 2004.

24. N. A. Walton, A. Lawrence, and T. Linde, "AstroGrid: Initial Deployment of the UK's Virtual Observatory," presented at Astronomical Data Analysis Software and Systems XIII, Strasbourg, 2003.

25. B. Plale, J. Alameda, B. Wilhelmson, D. Gannon, S. Hampton, A. Rossi, and K. Droegemeier, "User-oriented Active Management of Scientific Data with myLEAD," *IEEE Internet Computing*, vol. 9, pp. 27-34, 2005.

26. T. Berners-Lee, J. Hendler, and O. Lassila, "The Semantic Web," *Scientific American*, 2001.

27. D. D. Roure, N. R. Jennings, and N. R. Shadbolt, "The Semantic Grid: Past, Present and Future," *Proceedings of the IEEE*, vol. 93, pp. 669-681, 2005.

28. ORACLE, "RFID and Sensor-Based Services," www.oracle.com/technologies/rfid, 2005.

29. G. Fox and S. Pallickara, "The Narada Event Brokering System: Overview and Extensions," presented at International Conference on Parallel and Distributed Processing Techniques and Applications, 2002.

30. J. Bacon, J. Bates, R. Hayton, and K. Moody, "Using Events to Build Distributed Applications," presented at 2nd International Workshop on Services in Distributed and Networked Environments, 1995.

31. Microsoft, "WinFS,", msdn.microsoft.com/data/winfs/, 2005.

Spatial Hierarchies
and Topological Relationships
in the Spatial MultiDimER Model*

Elzbieta Malinowski** and Esteban Zimányi

Department of Informatics & Networks
Université Libre de Bruxelles
{emalinow,ezimanyi}@ulb.ac.be

Abstract. In Data Warehouses and On-Line Analytical Processing systems hierarchies are used to analyze high volumes of historical data. On the other hand, the advantage of using spatial data in the analysis process is widely recognized. Therefore, in order to satisfy the growing requirements of decision-making users it is necessary to extend hierarchies for representing spatial data. Based on an analysis of real-world spatial applications, this paper defines different kinds of spatial hierarchies and gives a conceptual representation of them. Further, we study the summarizability problem and classify the topological relationships between hierarchy levels according to the procedures required for ensuring correct measure aggregation.

1 Introduction

Data Warehouses (DWs) and On-Line Analytical Processing (OLAP) systems are used to store and analyze high volumes of historical data. These systems rely on a multidimensional view of data, which is usually represented as a star/snowflake structure consisting of fact tables, dimension tables, and hierarchies. A fact table represents the focus of analysis and contains attributes called measures, e.g., quantity sold. A dimension table includes attributes allowing the user to explore the measures from different analysis perspectives. These attributes may either form a hierarchy, e.g., City – State – Region or be descriptive, e.g., Store number. Hierarchies allow both a detailed view and a general view of data using the roll-up and drill-down operations. The former transforms detailed measures into aggregated data (e.g., daily into monthly or yearly sales) while the latter does the contrary.

Although the location dimension has been widely integrated in DWs and OLAP systems, it is usually represented in an alphanumeric, non-spatial manner. Taking into account the growing demand of including spatial data in the decision-making process, in this work we extend traditional hierarchies for including spatial data. We realize such extension using a conceptual model approach. Furthermore, we consider the issue of measure aggregation and analyze

---

* The work of E. Malinowski was funded by a scholarship of the Cooperation Department of the Université Libre de Bruxelles
** Currently on leave from the Universidad de Costa Rica

M. Jackson et al. (Eds.): BNCOD 2005, LNCS 3567, pp. 17–28, 2005.

the topological relationships existing between hierarchy levels in order to establish whether the summarizability problem arises.

Presenting the different kinds of spatial hierarchies using a conceptual approach will help decision-making users to better express their requirements without being bothered with implementation considerations. Additionally, the classification of topological relationships between hierarchy levels according to the required procedure for measure aggregation helps implementers of spatial OLAP tools to develop correct and efficient solutions for spatial data manipulations relying on common specifications.

This paper is organized as follows. Section 2 defines spatial hierarchies and the associated notation. Section 3 presents different kinds of spatial hierarchies including their graphical representation. Section 4 analyzes the summarizability problem in the light of the different topological relationships existing between spatial hierarchy levels. Section 5 surveys works related to representing spatial hierarchies and Section 6 gives conclusions and future perspectives.

2   The Spatial MultiDimER Model

The Spatial MultiDimER model [7, 8] is a spatial conceptual model for multidimensional data. A schema is defined as a finite set of dimensions and fact relationships. A dimension includes either a level, or one or more hierarchies. Levels are represented as entity types (Figure 1 a). An instance of a level is called a member.

A hierarchy has several related levels (Figure 1 b). Given two consecutive levels of a hierarchy, the higher level is called parent and the lower level is called child. Cardinalities (Figure 1 c) indicate the minimum and the maximum number of members in one level that can be related to a member in another

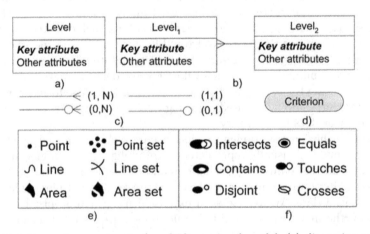

Fig. 1. Notations of our conceptual multidimensional model: (a) dimension with one level, (b) hierarchy with several levels, (c) cardinalities, (d) analysis criterion, (e) pictograms for spatial data types, and (f) pictograms for topological relationships

level. A level of a hierarchy that does not have a child level is called leaf and the one that does not have a parent level is called root and represents the most general view of data. Hierarchies express different structures according to the analysis criteria, e.g., geographical location (Figure 1 d).

Levels have one or several key attributes (represented in bold and italic in Figure 1) and may also have other descriptive attributes. Key attributes of a parent level show how child members are grouped. Key attributes in a leaf level indicate the granularity of measures in the associated fact relationship.

We define a spatial level as a level for which the application needs to keep its spatial characteristics. This is captured by its geometry, which is represented using spatial data types such as point, line, area, or a collection of these data types. We use the pictograms of MADS [10] for representing the geometry of spatial levels and the topological relationships between these levels. We adopt an orthogonal approach where a level may have geometry independently of the fact that it has spatial attributes. This achieves maximal expressive power where, e.g., a level such as State may be spatial or not depending on application requirements, and may have (descriptive) spatial attributes such as Capital.

A hierarchy (resp. dimension) is spatial if it has at least one spatial level (resp. hierarchy). Usual non-spatial dimensions, hierarchies, and levels are called thematic. Our definition of spatial dimension extends that in [13] where spatial dimensions are based on spatial references of hierarchy members. Spatial hierarchies can combine thematic and spatial levels. Figure 2 a) shows a hierarchy where all levels are spatial. As shown in the figure, each level is associated with a spatial data type determining its geometry: Point for Store, Simple Area for County, and Area Set for State. We call a hierarchy fully spatial when all its levels are spatial, it is called partly spatial when it contains both spatial and thematic levels. Notice that in our model it is easy to distinguish between thematic, partly-spatial, and spatial hierarchies depending on whether a spatial pictogram is present in the hierarchy levels.

As shown in Figure 2 a), our model also allows to represent the topological relationship between a spatial child and a spatial parent levels. The pictogram in the figure corresponds to the within/contains topological relationship meaning, e.g., that the spatial extent of a county is contained into the spatial extent of its related state. If no topological relationship is specified by the user, it is assumed by default that the link between spatial hierarchy levels represents a within/contains topological relationship.

3   Different Kinds of Spatial Hierarchies

In this section we briefly present the classification of hierarchies given in [7] using examples from the spatial domain. This allows to show that this categorization can be applied for non-spatial as well as for spatial hierarchies.

3.1   Simple Spatial Hierarchies

Simple spatial hierarchies are those hierarchies where the relationship between their members can be represented as a tree. Further, these hierarchies use only one criterion for analysis. Simple spatial hierarchies can be further categorized into symmetric, asymmetric, and generalized spatial hierarchies.

Symmetric spatial hierarchies have at the schema level only one path where all levels are mandatory. An example is given in Figure 2. At the instance level the members form a tree where all the branches have the same length. As implied by the cardinalities, all parent members must have at least one child member and a child member cannot belong to more than one parent member.

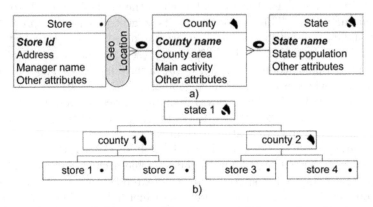

Fig. 2. A symmetric hierarchy: (a) schema and (b) examples of instances

Asymmetric spatial hierarchies have only one path at the schema level (Figure 3) but, as implied by the cardinalities, some lower levels of the hierarchy are not mandatory. Thus, at the instance level the members represent a non-balanced tree, i.e., the branches of the tree have different lengths. The example

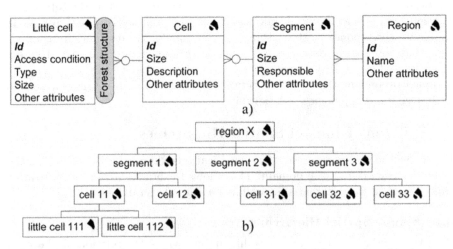

Fig. 3. An asymmetric spatial hierarchy: (a) schema and (b) examples of instances

of Figure 3 represents an asymmetric spatial hierarchy for a forest division consisting of little cell, cell, segment, and region. Since some parts of the forest are located in the mountain and are difficult to access, detailed representations of all areas are not available for analysis purposes and some hierarchy members are leaves at the segment or at the cell levels.

Generalized hierarchies contain multiple exclusive paths sharing some levels (Figure 4). All these paths represent one hierarchy and account for the same analysis criterion. At the instance level each member of the hierarchy belongs to only one path. The symbol $\otimes$ indicates that for every member the paths are exclusive. In the example, it is supposed that road segments can belong to either city roads or to highways, where the management of city roads is the responsibility of districts while that of highways is privatized. Notice that the geometry associated to the Company level (a simple area) represents the spatial extent that a company is responsible for maintenance.

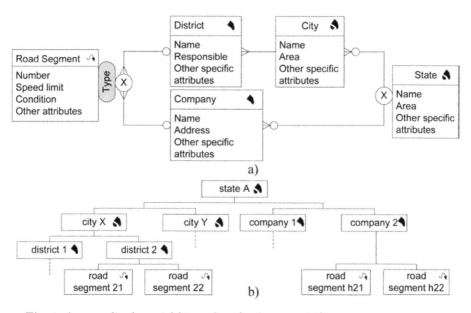

Fig. 4. A generalized spatial hierarchy: a) schema and b) examples of instances

As another example, the data model of the U.S. Census-Administrative Boundaries [15] includes several generalized hierarchies. One of them represents a spatial hierarchy containing a county level. However, in Maryland, Missouri, Nevada, and Virginia the county level is replaced by independent cities or places, whereas in American Samoa, county is replaced by district and islands.

Generalized spatial hierarchies include a special case commonly referred to as non-covering hierarchies. In these hierarchies, some paths skip one or several levels having in common at least the leaf and root levels.

3.2   Non-strict Spatial Hierarchies

Until now we have assumed that the parent-child links have one-to-many cardinalities, i.e., a child member is related to at most one parent member and a parent member may be related to several child members. However, many-to-many cardinalities are very common in real-life applications: e.g., a mobile phone network cell may belong to several ZIP areas [4], several tribal subdivisions in the U.S. Census hierarchy belong both to the American Indian reservation and to the Alaska Native areas [15].

We call a spatial hierarchy non-strict if it has at least one many-to-many cardinality; it is called strict if all cardinalities are one-to-many. The members of a non-strict hierarchy form a graph. The fact that a hierarchy is strict or not is orthogonal to its type. Thus, the different kinds of hierarchies already presented can be either strict or non-strict.

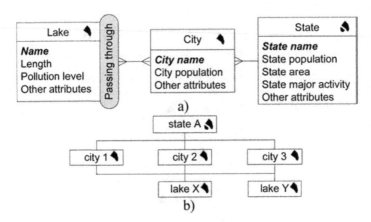

Fig. 5. A symmetric non-strict hierarchy: (a) model and (b) example of instances

Figure 5 shows a symmetric non-strict spatial hierarchy. The many-to-many cardinality represents the fact that a lake may belong to more than one city. This hierarchy may be used, e.g., for controlling the lake contamination level caused by neighbour cities.

Most non-strict hierarchies arise when a partial containment relationship takes place [4], e.g., when only part of a highway belongs to a state. In real situations it is difficult to find non-strict hierarchies with a full containment relationship, i.e., when a spatial member of a lower level wholly belongs to more than one spatial member of a higher level.

3.3   Multiple Alternative Spatial Hierarchies

Multiple alternative spatial hierarchies have several non-exclusive simple spatial hierarchies sharing some levels. However, all these hierarchies account for the same analysis criterion. At the instance level such hierarchies form a graph since a child member can be associated with more than one parent member belonging to different levels. In multiple alternative spatial hierarchies, it is not semantically correct to simultaneously traverse the different composing hierarchies: The user must choose one of the alternative hierarchies for analysis.

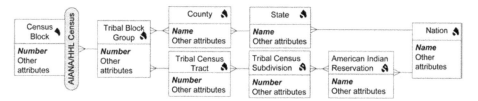

Fig. 6. Multiple alternative hierarchies formed by two non-strict symmetric hierarchies

The example given in Figure 6 represents part of the hierarchies used in the U.S. Census Bureau [15]. The hierarchy for American Indian and Alaska Native Areas, and Hawaii Home Land (AIANA/HHL) uses a particular subdivision of the territory (lower path of the figure). However, the usual hierarchy composed, among others, of County and State levels[1] (upper path of the figure) provides another subdivision of the same territory. This path can be used for obtaining statistics of American Indian by counties and states. It is obvious that both hierarchies cannot be simultaneously used during analysis.

Notice the difference between generalized and multiple hierarchies (Figures 4 and 6). Although both hierarchies share some levels and use only one analysis criterion, they represent different situations. In a generalized hierarchy a child member is related to one of the paths, whereas in multiple hierarchies a child member is related to all paths, and the user must choose one of them for analysis.

3.4   Parallel Spatial Hierarchies

Parallel spatial hierarchies arise when a dimension has associated several spatial hierarchies accounting for different analysis criteria. Such hierarchies can be independent or dependent. In a parallel independent spatial hierarchy, the different hierarchies do not share levels, i.e., they represent non-overlapping sets of hierarchies. An example is given in Figure 7.

In contrast, parallel dependent spatial hierarchies, have different hierarchies sharing some levels. The example in Figure 8 represents an insurance company that includes hospitalization services for clients. The Client dimension contains two hierarchies: a symmetric hierarchy representing the hospitalization structure and a non-covering one representing the geographic division of the client's address. Both hierarchies share the common levels of City and State. Notice that the difference between multiple alternative and parallel dependent hierarchies (Figures 6 and 8) consists in allowing one or several analysis criteria.

---

[1] To simplify the example, we ignore that some states are not divided in counties

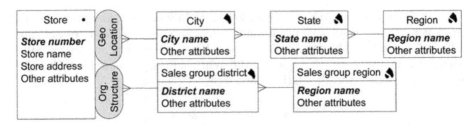

Fig. 7. Parallel independent spatial hierarchies associated to one dimension

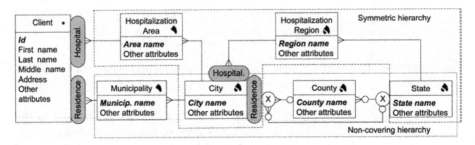

Fig. 8. Parallel dependent spatial hierarchies

4   Topological Relationships Between Spatial Levels

As already said, the levels related by a child-parent relationship may be spatial or non-spatial. This leads to 4 possible combinations: non-spatial-to-non-spatial (the child and parent levels are thematic), spatial-to-non-spatial (a spatial level rolls-up to a non-spatial level), non-spatial-to-spatial (a non-spatial level rolls-up to a spatial level), and spatial-to-spatial (both levels are spatial). To each one of these combinations corresponds a different relationship type: (1) a containment function for non-spatial-to-non-spatial relationships, (2) a mapping from a spatial to a non-spatial domain for spatial-to-non-spatial relationships, (3) a mapping from a non-spatial to a spatial domain for non-spatial-to-spatial relationships, and (4) a topological relationship for spatial-to-spatial relationships.

The first kind of relationship has been widely investigated. Mappings from spatial to non-spatial domains (or vice versa) can be easily implemented. The question that remains is which kinds of topological relationships should be allowed between spatial levels considering that these hierarchies are used for aggregating measure values when traversing levels.

For non-spatial hierarchies, summarizability conditions [6] must hold for ensuring the correct aggregation of measures in higher levels taking into account existing aggregations in lower levels. These conditions include, among others, a simple-value mapping between hierarchy levels and completeness (i.e., no missing values and existence of a parent member for every child member). Since asymmetric, generalized, and non-strict hierarchies do not satisfy summarizability conditions, it is required to apply either special aggregation procedures (e.g., implemented in Microsoft Analysis Services [9] for asymmetric and non-covering hierarchies), or transformations (e.g., described in [4] for asymmetric, non-covering, and non-strict hierarchies).

Although the summarizability conditions have been established for non-spatial hierarchies they must also hold for spatial hierarchies. However, summarizability problems may also arise depending on the topological relationship existing between spatial levels. Several solutions may be applied: an extreme one is to disallow the topological relationships that cause problems whereas another solution is to define customized procedures for ensuring correct measure aggregation.

We give next a classification of topological relationships[2] according to the required procedures for establishing measure aggregation. Our classification, shown in Figure 9, is based on the intersection between the geometric union of the spatial extents of child members (denoted by $GU(C_{ext})$) and the spatial extent of their associated parent member (denoted by P_{ext}). To simplify the discussion, we only consider spatial hierarchies with distributive numeric measures, e.g., sum[3].

The disjoint topological relationship is not allowed between spatial hierarchy levels since during a roll-up operation the next hierarchy level cannot be reached. Thus, a non-empty intersection between $GU(C_{ext})$ and P_{ext} is required.

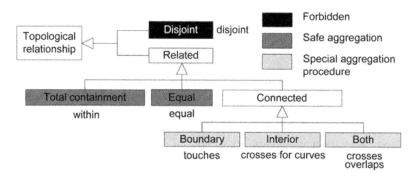

Fig. 9. Classification of topological relationship for aggregation procedures

Different topological relationship may exist if the intersection of P_{ext} and $GU(C_{ext})$ is not empty. If $GU(C_{ext})$ within P_{ext}, then the geometric union of the child member extents (as well as the extent of each child member) is included in their parent member extent. In this case, the aggregation of measures from a child to a parent level can be done safely using a traditional approach. Similar situation occurs if $GU(C_{ext})$ equals P_{ext} with the additional constraint that both spatial extents are equal and have common boundaries.

The situation is different if the extents of child and parent members are related by a topological relationship distinct from within or equal. As can be seen in Figure 9 different topological relationships belong to this category, e.g., touches,

---

[2] We consider the topological relations from the SQL/MM standard [3]

[3] We do not consider spatial measures obtained by applying spatial operators or functions to spatial objects [8] as proposed by [11]

crosses. As in [12], we distinguish three possibilities depending on whether a topological relationship exists between the boundaries, the interiors, or both the boundaries and the interiors of the spatial extents of child and parent members. For example, this distinction is important in Figure 8 for determining how to realize aggregations if a lake touches a city and overlaps another.

When developing aggregation procedures, if $GU(C_{ext})$ intersects P_{ext} and this intersection is different from equal or within, the spatial extent of some (or all) child members is not completely included in the spatial extent of a parent member. The topological relationship existing between the spatial extents of individual child members and a parent member determines which measure values can be considered in its entirety for aggregation and which must be partitioned. For example, if in the hierarchy in Figure 2 the geographic union of the points representing stores is not within the spatial extent of their county, every individual store must be analyzed for determining how the measure (for example, required taxes) should be distributed between two or more counties. Therefore, an appropriate procedure for measure aggregation according to application particularities must be developed, such as that proposed by [4] for partial containment topological relationship. As already said, another solution is to disallow these topological relationships in spatial hierarchies.

5   Related Work

Many works focus on conceptual modelling for Spatial Databases (e.g., [10]) or for DWs (e.g., [14]) based on either the ER model or the UML. However, a multidimensional model is seldom used for spatial data modelling. Moreover, even though organizations such as ESRI recognize the necessity of conceptual modelling by introducing templates of spatial data models in different areas of human activities [1], these models often refer to particular aspects of the logical-level design and are too complex to be understood by decision-making users.

Ferri et al. [2] refer to common key elements between spatial and multidimensional databases: time and space. They formally define a geographic data model including contains and full-contains relationships between hierarchy levels. Based on these relationships, the integration between GIS and DW/OLAP environments can be achieved by a mapping between the hierarchical structures of both environments. The concept of mapping between hierarchies is also exploited by Kouba et al. [5]. To ensure the consistent navigation in a hierarchy between OLAP systems and GISs, they propose a dynamic correspondence through classes, instances, and action levels.

Stefanovic et al. [13] distinguish three types of spatial dimensions based on the spatial references of the hierarchy members: non-spatial (a traditional non-spatial hierarchy), spatial-to-non-spatial (a spatial level rolls-up to a non-spatial level), and fully spatial (all hierarchy levels are spatial).

Jensen et al. [4] present a general scenario for location-based services (LBSs) including a data warehouse as central storage platform. Their model includes several dimensions, one of which is a spatial dimension. They proposed a model with hierarchies including a new partial containment relationship where only part of the spatial extent of a member belongs to a higher hierarchy level.

Although the works mentioned above refer to spatial hierarchies in DW and/or OLAP, only [4] classify spatial hierarchies. However, they neither include generalized hierarchies nor distinguish partly and fully spatial hierarchies. Further, since they do not focus on the graphical representation of the different kinds of hierarchies, some of them are difficult to distinguish, e.g., non-covering and multiple hierarchies.

The work of Pedersen and Tryfona [11] refers to pre-aggregation in spatial DWs. However, we consider that the analysis they present and the solution they proposed are adequate for managing spatial measure represented by geometry [8] and it goes out of the scope of this article.

6   Conclusions

DW and OLAP systems use a multidimensional model for representing user requirements for decision making. In this model hierarchies allow to view data at different levels of detail using roll-up and drill-down operations. On the other hand, Geographic Information Systems (GISs) have been successfully used for many years in a great number of applications areas. Since it is estimated that 80% of the data stored in databases has a spatial component, the merging of both technologies, DWs and GISs, provides an opportunity to enhance the decision-making process. However, the lack of a conceptual approach for multidimensional modelling, joined with the absence of a commonly-accepted conceptual model for spatial applications, makes that representing real-world hierarchies including spatial levels is a challenging task.

We extended the different kinds of hierarchies proposed in [7] by the inclusion of spatial levels. Hierarchies may be fully or partly spatial depending on whether all their levels are spatial. Combining spatial and non-spatial levels leads to different relationships between hierarchy levels. Finally, we addressed the summarizability problem that arises for some types of hierarchies. We emphasized that the summarizability problem may also occur due to the different topological relationships existing between hierarchy levels. We classify these relationships according to the complexity required for developing procedures for measure aggregation.

The present work belongs to a larger project aiming at developing a conceptual model for spatio-temporal data warehouses. We are currently working on the inclusion of temporal features in our model.

References

1. ESRI, Inc. ArcGIS data models.
   http://www.esri.com/software/arcgisdatamodels/index.html, 2004.
2. F. Ferri, E. Pourabbas, M. Rafanelli, and F. Ricci. Extending geographic databases for a query language to support queries involving statistical data. In *Proc. of the 12th Int. Conf. on Scientific and Statistical Database Management*, pages 220–230, 2000.

3. ISO. SQL multimedia and application packages - part 3: Spatial. Technical report, ISO/IEC FCD 13249-3:2003, 2002.
4. C. Jensen, A. Klygis, T. Pedersen, and I. Timko. Multidimensional data modeling for location-based services. *VLDB Journal*, 13(1):1–21, 2004.
5. Z. Kouba, K. Matoušek, and P. Mikšovský. Novel knowledge discovery tools in industrial applications. In *Proc. of the Workshop on Intelligent Methods for Quality Improvement in Industrial Practice*, pages 72–83, 2002.
6. H. Lenz and A. Shoshani. Summarizability in OLAP and statistical databases. In *Proc. of the 9th Int. Conf. on Scientific and Statistical Database Management*, pages 132–143, 1997.
7. E. Malinowski and E. Zimányi. OLAP hierarchies: A conceptual perspective. In *Proc. of the 16th Int. Conf. on Advanced Information Systems Engineering*, pages 477–491, 2004.
8. E. Malinowski and E. Zimányi. Representing spatiality in a conceptual multidimensional model. In *Proc. of the 12th ACM Symposium on Advances in Geographic Information Systems*, pages 12–21, 2004.
9. Microsoft Corporation. SQL Server 2000. Books Online. http://www.microsoft.com/sql/techinfo/productdoc/2000/books.asp, 2003.
10. C. Parent, S. Spaccapietra, and E. Zimányi. Spatio-temporal conceptual models: Data structures + Space + Time. In *Proc. of the 7th ACM Symposium on Advances in Geographic Information Systems*, pages 26–33, 1999.
11. T. Pedersen and N. Tryfona. Pre-aggregation in spatial data warehouses. In *Proc. of the 7th Int. Symposium on Advances in Spatial and Temporal Databases*, pages 460–478, 2001.
12. R. Price, N. Tryfona, and C. Jensen. Modeling topological constraints in spatial part-whole relationships. In *Proc. of the 20th Int. Conference on Conceptual Modeling*, pages 27–40, 2001.
13. N. Stefanovic, J. Han, and K. Koperski. Object-based selective materialization for efficient implementation of spatial data cubes. *IEEE Trans. on Knowledge and Data Engineering*, 12(6):938–958, 2000.
14. N. Tryfona, F. Busborg, and J. Borch. StarER: A conceptual model for data warehouse design. In *Proc. of the 2nd ACM Int. Workshop on Data Warehousing and OLAP*, pages 3–8, 1999.
15. U.S. Census Bureau. Standard Hierarchy of Census Geographic Entities and Hierarchy of American Indian, Alaska Native, and Hawaiian Entities. http://www.census.gov/geo/www/geodiagram.pdf, 2004.

Multidimensional Structures Dedicated to Continuous Spatiotemporal Phenomena

Taher Omran Ahmed and Maryvonne Miquel

LIRIS – INSA de Lyon, Bât. Blaise Pascal 501.302
7 Ave. Jean Capelle, 69621 Villeurbanne, France
{taher.ahmed,maryvonne.miquel}@insa-lyon.fr

Abstract. Multidimensional structures or hypercubes are commonly used in OLAP to store and organize data to optimize query response time. The multidimensional approach is based on the concept of facts analyzed with respect to various dimensions. Dimensions are seen as axes of analysis forming a vector space in which each cell is located by a set of coordinates. In conventional multidimensional structures, dimensions have discrete values and are organized in different levels of hierarchies. However, when analysing natural phenomena like meteorology or pollution the discrete structures are not adequate. We will introduce mechanisms, based on interpolation, to spatial and temporal dimensions which will give the user the impression of navigating in a continuous hypercube. In this paper we go over the research issues associated with continuous multidimensional structures, we give some of their potentials and we propose a multidimensional model and some operations used for an OLAP of field-based data.

1 Introduction

The volume of data generated by the daily operations of the different kinds of businesses has experienced an explosive growth. Data warehouses play an important role in helping decision makers obtain the maximum benefits of these large amounts of data. Data are extracted from several sources, cleansed, customized and inserted into the data warehouse. A data warehouse is defined as a "subject oriented, integrated, time-variant and non-volatile collection of data in support of management's decision-making process" [10]. The most popular analysis mean is the *On-Line Analytical Processing (OLAP)* which enables users to examine, retrieve and summarize data within a multidimensional model.

Multidimensional structures are based on the concept of facts or measures (e.g business facts to be analyzed like *sales*) and dimensions representing the context in which these measures are analyzed. Usually dimensions are discrete and organized in hierarchies composed of numerous levels, each representing a level of detail as required by the desired analysis. Conventional data warehousing deals with alphanumeric data. In the real world, spatial data makes a large part of data stored in databases. It has been estimated that about 80% of such data has a spatial component to it, like an address or a postal code [7]. In most data warehouses, spatial components are represented as a dimension table in the star schema. Time, is also an important dimension of every data warehouse, and it is usually represented as discrete points of time with appropriate hierarchy. In applications that deal with natural phenomena, it

M. Jackson et al. (Eds.): BNCOD 2005, LNCS 3567, pp. 29–40, 2005.

is not possible to measure the continuous phenomena everywhere and at every instant of time. Therefore only sample points are used to capture the phenomena, which leads to a discrete representation and results in discrete dimensions. Discrete dimensions may hide important data that can be used for data analysis and exploration. Therefore, there is a need to incorporate spatiotemporal continuity within the multidimensional structures to rightfully represent and analyze continuous phenomena. One of the motivations for this work is that continuous representation may provide an estimate of the information that was lost due to the use of discrete dimensions. The second motivation is the need, that arises in several cases, for analysis at a very low level of temporal and/or spatial granularities like in catastrophe analysis. A third motivation is the need to observe natural phenomena in a continuous manner. It would be more realistic for environmentalists to analyze natural phenomena *naturally* as they occur in real life, not as a collection of discrete pieces.

In this paper we present the concepts, research issues and potentials of continuous multidimensional structures. In this respect, we propose a multidimensional model for continuous field data. The rest of the paper is organized as follows: in section 2 we give some of the related work on spatial data warehousing and we give a short survey of multidimensional models. In section 3 we present the concepts of continuous data warehousing, go over some of the research issues and give some of the potential uses. In section 4 we present our model for continuous multidimensional structures using a running example. We define continuous fields in section 5 and give some of the operations to manipulate them in multidimensional structures and conclude the paper in section 6.

2   Related Work

2.1   Spatial and Spatiotemporal Data Warehousing

A lot of work has been done on spatial and spatiotemporal data warehousing. A spatial data warehouse is a data warehouse of both spatial and non-spatial data [16]. There are both spatial and non-spatial measures and dimensions. The spatial cube contains any of three types of spatial dimensions: (1) Non spatial, (2) Spatial-to-non spatial and (3) Spatial-to-spatial [14,16]. The work of [13] describes a framework for supporting OLAP operations over spatiotemporal data. The main differences pointed out between traditional OLAP and spatiotemporal OLAP is the lack of predefined hierarchies. Hence the positions and ranges of spatiotemporal query window do not conform to pre-defined hierarchies and are not known in advance. Several indexing solutions are proposed. A study of data integration in spatiotemporal data warehouse is presented in [12]. The work concerns modelling heterogeneous data in multidimensional structures. Heterogeneity can be temporal, spatial and semantic. Two approaches were proposed to model such data: by using a unique temporally integrated hypercube for all time periods, or by using a hypercube for each time period (or view) that users want to analyze. [2] defines a spatial OLAP (*SOLAP*) as a visual platform built to support rapid and easy spatiotemporal analysis and exploration of data in a multidimensional approach, comprised of aggregation levels available in cartographic displays as well as in tabular and diagram displays. The work of [4] deals with the temporal aspect of multidimensional structures and the slowly changing dimensions A temporal model for supporting evolutions in multidimensional structures is defined and implemented.

To the best of our knowledge, no work has been done on continuous spatiotemporal data warehousing. However, [15] propose a representation of data cube that deals with continuous dimensions in the sense of not needing a predefined discrete hierarchy. The main focus of this work is on using the known density of data to calculate aggregate queries without accessing the data. The representation reduces the storage requirements, but does not present the continuity in the same way we do since we estimate non-existing measures based on sample data values. In our model the number of members of the continuous dimensions is not known in advance whereas in [15] the domain of dimension levels is predefined.

2.2 Multidimensional Models

Despite the multitude of multidimensional models that have been proposed during the past years, there is still no agreement on a formalism for modeling multidimensional databases. In this section we present brief description of the essential points of some of these models. For detailed and profound comparisons we refer the reader to [3][18].

The model of [1] treats measures and dimensions symmetrically. A set of algebraic operations is also presented. Data is organized in one or more k-dimensional hypercubes. A cube is defined as a triple $(D, E(C), N)$ where D is a set of k dimension names. Each dimension has a domain dom_i. $E(C)$ is a mapping function that defines the elements of the cells of the cube. N is a n-tuple describing the elements of the cube. In [5,6] the authors propose a formal multidimensional model and a descriptive query language. The model is based on the notions of dimensions and f-tables. A dimension is defined as a triple $(L, \leq, R\text{-}UP)$ where L is the set of finite levels, $\leq$ is a partial order among levels of dimensions and $R\text{-}UP$ is a collection of roll-up functions that define mappings of lower level elements to higher level elements. The work of [9] describes a conceptual multidimensional model. An n-dimensional table schema is a triple $<D, R, par>$ where $D = \{d_1, ..., d_n\}$ is a set of dimension names, $R = \{A_1, .., A_m\}$ is a set of attributes and par is a mapping function. In [17] a model which contains the natural OLAP operations is presented. Dimensions are defined as in [4]. A dimension is a lattice $(H, \leq)$ where $H=\{DL_1, DL_2, ...DL_n\}$ is a set of levels with a domain of values $dom(DL_i)$ attached to each level DL_i and $\leq$ denotes that each dimension path is a totally ordered list of levels. The model is based on the notion of basic cubes C_b, which is a cube with the most detailed data and it is formally defined as a triple $<D_b, L_b, R_b>$. D_b is a list of the dimensions $<D_1, D_2, ..., D_n, M>$ characterizing the cube and also contains a special measure dimension M. L_b is the list of atomic dimension levels. R_b is a set of cell data containing the tuples of the data cube. Cubes are built from the basic cube using a set of operations. A formal definition of the cube is a 4-tuple $<D, L, C_b, R>$ where C_b is the basic cube used to compute the *higher* cubes. The work of [11] is one of the rare models for multidimensional exploratory spatiotemporal analysis. This work focuses more on the hierarchy theory and it can be seen as a framework rather than a model. Moreover, there is no formalism of the common operators. The multidimensional data cube is seen as the logical model for spatiotemporal analysis. A dimension hierarchy is a 4-tuple $H=(V, F, G, \leq)$ where $V=\{v_1, v_2, \ldots\}$ denotes the node or the vertex of a hierarchy. Each v is associated with a domain of elements. $G = \{g_1, g_2, \ldots\}$ is the dimension path which is a totally ordered list of nodes. The symbol $\leq$ denotes that a dimension path is a linear totally ordered list of nodes. Every adjacent vertex pair in a path is associated with a partition mapping function called, *categorization function*.

3   Research Issues and Potential Uses

There are several challenges that arise from defining and implementing continuous hypercubes. Some of the research issues that need to be addressed are:

- **Modeling continuous structures.** The structures we propose will be used solely for field-based data. Existing multidimensional models are not adequate for this type of data. Therefore a new model that takes in consideration the spatiotemporal continuity has to be proposed.
- **Storage cost versus response time.** There will always be cells of the hypercube whose data must be calculated which poses the need of a compromise between the storage cost and response time. There is a choice between storing only sample values hence reducing storage cost, or storing all sample points and some approximated values so that response time will be faster at a higher storage cost.
- **Estimating none measured values.** To obtain estimated values at all points of space and time of the study area, spatial and temporal interpolation methods will be used. These methods differ in their assumptions and complexity and should be applied based on the modeled phenomena. We are considering two approaches: (1) predetermined methods or (2) the user is given a choice between several methods and (s)he can choose what is suitable for the application.
- **Navigation in the continuous hypercube.** Introducing continuity could change the results of some operators. In addition to the continuous dimensions there will always be discrete dimensions. The classic OLAP operators are suitable to navigate along the discrete dimensions, however in the continuous dimensions these operators have to be extended and redefined. There is also a need to add and formally describe new operators to facilitate the continuous navigation.
- **Data visualization.** It is easier to observe complex spatial relationships when they are viewed as a map instead of a table. The interface will be composed of two main parts as in [14]: a navigation panel and a visualization window. The navigation panel permits selections of measures to be viewed with respect to all possible members of dimensions. The visualization space shows information in different format: graphical or non graphical. There will also be quality indicators to indicate the accuracy of displayed results since the precision of estimated values varies depending on several factor (like number of sample points, method used, ... etc.)

Continuous data warehouses will not be suitable for every type of application. There is no sense of having continuous spatial or temporal dimensions for a data warehouse intended for applications of discrete nature (like sales). These structures are most advantageous for applications that deal with spatiotemporal data that represent the behavior of natural phenomena like meteorology, pollution or oceanography.

One of the domains of use is the analysis of catastrophes. The first example is the spread of forest fires. Historical forest fire data can be modeled in a continuous hypercube. Data can be analyzed at the lowest level of spatial and temporal detail with respect to the different dimensions that affect the behavior of fire like localization, wind speed and rainfall. Another application could be the analysis of oil spills. The dispersion of the spills depends on different factors: type of spill, location, wind speed. Based on these factors historical disaster data can be analyzed at the lowest level of spatial and temporal hierarchies to gain new edges on how to limit the damages when future accidents occur.

4 Continuous Multidimensional Model

4.1 Motivating Example

To illustrate our model, we will use the following motivating example of an application for the analysis of air pollution in the Parisian region. The dimensions of analysis are *Pollutant*, *Station*, *Localization* and *Time*. *Pollution* is the measure to be analyzed as in Fig. 1.

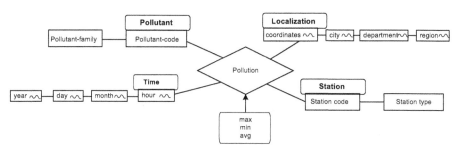

Fig. 1. A hypercube for the analysis of air pollution

From this schema we distinguish two classes of dimensions: discrete and continuous. Dimensions *Pollutant* and *Stations* are discrete since at all levels of their respective hierarchies there is a defined number of members. In the second class we find the dimensions *Time* and *Localization* where at every level of each dimension there is a temporal and a spatial continuity respectively. In the dimension *Time*, the lowest level represents the interval at which stations measure pollution, i.e. at every hour. The temporal continuity assumes that there is a value that could be measured or estimated at every instant in time. Similarly, in the *Localization* dimension, the lowest level is the station coordinates that indicate its location. Spatial continuity implies that a value of pollution exists at every single point in the space of the study. Some levels can be denied from being continuous if reasons exist (like inability to estimate or store data at this level).The continuous levels are designated by the symbol ∿. Continuity at the detailed levels is based on actual measured values whereas in the general levels it is based on aggregated values. The data used throughout this paper are real data collected by AIRPARIF (http://www.airparif.asso.fr/) which is an organization charged of monitoring air quality in the Parisian region known administratively as "Ile de France".

The continuous hypercube is built as follows: data are collected by several sensors distributed over the study area. Sensors read data at different points in time and at different intervals depending on the phenomena being measured. The readings are stored in a relational database. From this database, a discrete hypercube is built that will enable multidimensional analysis. To build the continuous hypercube, spatial and temporal interpolation methods are applied to the discrete hypercube. The results can be represented in different formats (graphic, tabular or as a curve) consisting from both the actual and estimated values (Fig. 2).

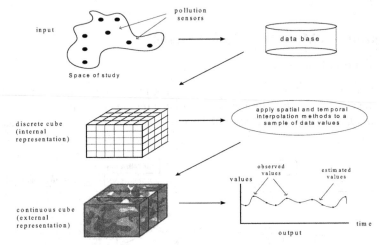

Fig. 2. Steps of building a continuous cube

Introducing continuity in spatial and temporal dimensions enables the continuous navigation in the hypercube and the analysis at all levels of continuous dimensions. Starting from a conventional hypercube we aim at giving the user the illusion that (s)he is navigating through a continuous hypercube where there will be data values at every point in space and in time. There will be two levels of representation: the first is a discrete representation of the data at the implementation level and the second is the continuous representation as seen by the user. The continuous representation is achieved by using interpolation techniques to estimate values where no actual values exist. In addition to the continuous vision, the use of interpolation function will help solving the problems of missing or erroneous data, which is a frequent problem, since sensors can get blocked, malfunction or even break down.

4.2 Basic Definitions

In the field of analysis and exploration of natural continuous phenomena there is a need to perform the analysis in a continuous manner analogous to the natural behavior of the phenomena being analyzed. The continuous data warehouse will be built, as a second layer, on top of a discrete data warehouse. From the studied multidimensional models, [17] presents the richest model with respect to multidimensional semantics. The model includes all formal definitions of most of the necessary operations and those that are not defined can be derived in terms of the defined ones. The model is based on the notion of basic cubes. The idea of basic cube is very important since it allows for the serial performing of operations which is typical in OLAP applications. It will also be the base for interpolating results to have a continuous vision of values or for estimating missing cell values. Thus based on this model we present the essential extensions to support continuous multidimensional structures.

In this model, we keep most of the basic definitions of the original model and we add to them the necessary elements. We refer the reader to [17] for the detailed original definitions. As stated above there are 2 classes of dimensions: discrete and continuous. Some of the following definitions concern only the continuous class of dimensions, while for the discrete class the definitions of the original model hold.

Let n be the number of dimensions, and let r be the rank of dimension levels starting from the most detailed level (*level 1*) going all the way up to the most general level (*level r*) and let k be the cardinality (number of members) of a given dimension level DL_i. The domain of values $dom(DL_i)$ for the dimension level DL_i may contain two types of members: predefined members and any possible value between any two given members to give a continuous representation of the dimension level. From [17] a value x belonging to a specific dimension level DL_i can have *ancestors* and *descendants* which are specific instances related to x at higher and lower dimension levels respectively. They are defined as:

$ancestor(x, DL_j) = y$ where $y \in dom(DL_j)$ and $DL_i < DL_j$
$descendants(x, DL_j) = \{x_1, x_2,...,x_k\}$ where $x_1, x_2,...,x_k \in dom(DL_j)$ and $DL_i > DL_j$

The same definition for *ancestor* holds as in the original model however we extend the definition of *descendants* as follows:

$descendants(x, DL_j) = \{x_1, x_2,..., x_k\} \cup \{y_1, y_2,...\}$ where $\{x_1, x_2,...,x_k\} \in dom(DL_j)$ and $\{y_1, y_2,...\}$ are all the possible domain values in a continuous representation.

e.g.: $descendants(5\ mars\ 2004, hour) = \{1:00\ 5\ mars\ 2004, 1:09\ 5\ mars\ 2004, ..., 1:15\ 5\ mars\ 2004, ..., 1:59:59.45\ 5\ mars\ 2004, ...\}$

The basic cubes are cubes at the lowest level of detail. The *discrete basic cube* **discC**$_b$ is a 3-tuple $<D_b, L_b, R_b>$ where D_b is a list of dimensions including a dimension measure M. L_b is the list of the lowest levels of each dimension and R_b is a set of cell data represented as a set of tuples containing level members and measures in the form of $x = [x_1, x_2,...x_n, m]$ where m is the dimension that represents the measure. Table 1 shows an extraction of a **discC**$_b$.

Table 1. An extraction of **discC**$_b$ (D$_b$: time, station, pollutant, localization), (L$_b$: hour, station-code, pollutant-code, coordinates), M: Pollution

Time	Station	Pollutant	Localization	Pollution
15-16/05/2002	EVRY	NO	2.43056, 48.63778	81
23-25/04/2002	MONTG	O3	2,45556, 48,70778	19
17-01/07/2002	MONTG	NO2	2,45556, 48,70778	20
12-01/9/2002	ELYS	CO	2,30944, 48,86889	200

In order to achieve a continuous representation of the basic cube, estimated measures related to the infinite members of a given spatial and temporal dimensions' levels are calculated using actual cell values from $discC_b$. This of course necessitates applying interpolation functions to a sample of $discC_b$ values to calculate the measures corresponding to the new dimension members which will give the *continuous basic cube* $contC_b$.

The number of tuples in $contC_b$ is theoretically infinite since a dimension level in the class of continuous dimensions contains theoretically an infinite number of members. We define $contC_b$, as 4-tuple $<D_b, (D'_b,F), L_b, R'_b>$. Where D_b, D'_b are the discrete and continuous dimensions respectively. In the example D_b is {*station, pollutant*} and D'_b is {*time, localization*}. F is a set of interpolation functions associated with the continuous dimensions and has the same cardinality as D'_b. So for our example since card(D'_b) is 2 then Card(F) = 2. So $F = \{f_1, f_2\}$ where f_1 is a spatial interpolation function and f_2 is a temporal interpolation function used to calculate the measures to achieve the continuous representation of the cube. L_b is the list of the lowest levels of each dimension as defined above. The continuous representation is defined over a spatial and/or temporal interval. Therefore we define R'_b as a set of tuples of the form $x = [x_1, x_2, \dots x_n, m]$ where $x_i \in [minDom(L_{bi}) - \Delta, maxDom(L_{bi}) + \Delta]$ with Δ being a small predefined value used to (1) allow for continuous representation using greater and smaller values than the domain of the dimension levels, and (2) predict values outside the specified interval. The measure m $\subseteq$ M is defined as:

- **Using interpolation functions**
  Interpolation functions can be applied in two different ways. Either by defining a number of observed values to be used for estimation or using all observed values lying within a predefined diameter. So based on the way of applying interpolation methods, the measure m is defined as:
    - $m= f(m_1, m_2, \dots m_k)$ where f is a spatial or temporal interpolation function using $(1 \leq n \leq k)$ cells for value estimation and $m_j \in M$,
    - $m= f(m_1, m_2, \dots m_k)$ using values lying within a predefined spatial or temporal distance d, or
    - $m = f_1 \circ f_2 (m_1, m_2, \dots m_k)$ or $m = f_2 \circ f_1 (m_1, m_2, \dots m_k)$. The order of applying the interpolating functions depends on the phenomena being modeled.
- **Without interpolation functions**
    - m is an actual cell value without a need for interpolation.
  It can be clearly seen that $discC_b \subseteq contC_b$.

4.3 Cubes

Cubes are built from basic cubes by applying a set of operations. A cube C is defined as 4-tuple $<D, L, contC_b, R>$ where, D is a list of dimensions including M as defined above, L is the respective dimension level, R is cell data and **$contC_b$** is the basic cube from which C is built. Because of the nature of the continuous field data, different aggregation function are used to build the cube at higher dimension hierarchies. For example, the sum of measures for a specific region or a specific period of time will be represented as an integral. Other aggregation functions like *min, max* or *average* will be performed on **$contC_b$** and their results will be assigned to the higher levels of the hierarchy. We will illustrate how the cubes are built using some examples.

Example 1 C1: A cube showing the maximum pollution values by department for pollutants NO2, NO, CO for a given day.

The first step in building this cube is applying a temporal interpolation function to the continuous basic cube to estimate pollution values for a whole day. Then apply the aggregation function, *max*, and roll the results up to the department level. An example of the results is in table 2.

Table 2. Cube C1 (D: Time, Station, Localization, Pollutant), (L: day, station-code, department, pollutant-code,), M: max(pollution)

Time	Station	Localization	Pollutant	Max(Pollution)
16/05/2002	CELES	Paris	NO	216
28/06/2002	CELES	Paris	NO2	55
07/01/2002	BONAP	Paris	CO	500

Example 2 C2: A cube showing the average pollution values by pollutant family by department for the period between 1/07/2002 and 31/12/2002.

As in example 1, we apply the necessary interpolation functions from the continuous basic cube on the values measured within the period specified, then we apply the *sum* and *count* aggregation functions and roll-up the results to the *department* level (*Localization* dimension) and to the *pollutant-family* (*Pollutant* dimension) we then calculate the average. Table 3 shows an extraction of this cube.

Table 3. An extraction of Cube C2 (D: Localization, Pollutant), (L: department, pollutant-family), (M: average (pollution))

Localization	Pollutant	AVG(Pollution)
Paris	PRIMARY	364,8339
	SECONDARY	55,8253
Seine-et-Marne	PRIMARY	16,8268
	SECONDARY	44,1650
Val-de-Marne	PRIMARY	20,1957
	SECONDARY	39,7254

5 Continuous Vision of the User

The vision of the user is different from that of the computer. Data is stored discretely in the hypercube. Even what we called a *continuous basic cube* is in fact only a discrete representation containing both measured data and interpolation functions. There is a step between this representation and the user. From the continuous basic cube we will apply the aggregation functions to cell values and to some defined operations. Aggregation results will be treated as measures in the continuous representation.

The aggregation functions are similar to those used in conventional data warehousing, however they are calculated differently due to the nature of the data used. To illustrate these functions let us first define the continuous field. Based on [8] a continuous field **F** is defined as follows:

F= (D, T, S, V, f**)** where,

D geographic domain of the field, i.e. the region where the phenomenon takes place,

T temporal domain of the field, i.e. the temporal space during which the phenomenon takes place,

S $\subseteq$ **D** × **T** set of $s_i = (p_i, t_i)$ with $p_i \in$ **D**, $t_i \in$ **T** such that the phenomenon is known at the position p_i and time t_i. $s_i \in$ **S** is called a sample point,

V is the domain of the set of values of the field,

f: **D** × **T** $\rightarrow$ **V** such that for $s_i \in$ S, $f(s_i) = v_i$. f is the function describing the phenomena.

On this continuous field we define 2 types of operations. The first concerns the discrete operations and the second groups the continuous operations:

Discrete operations. Only the sample points are used.

DiscMax = v_i such that $v_i \geq f(s_k)$ $\forall$ $s_k \in$ S

DiscMin = v_i such that $v_i \leq f(s_k)$ $\forall$ $s_k \in$ S

Disc Sum = $\displaystyle\sum_{e_k \in E} f(s_k)$

DiscCount = Card(S)

DiscAvg = SumDisc/CountDisc

Continuous operations. All values of the field are used.

ContMax = v_i such that $v_i \geq f(s_k)$ $\forall$ $s_k \in$ D × T

Cont Min = v_i such that $v_i \leq f(s_k)$ $\forall$ $s_k \in$ D × T

ContSpatSum = $\int f(s)dp$

ContTempSum = $\int f(s)$ dt

ContSpatAvg = $\int f(s)dp/$(area of region)

ContTempAvg = $\int f(s)dt /(t_2-t_1)$ where $[t_1: t_2]$ is a time interval

SpatSpeed = $f'(x)$= df/dx speed of the spread of pollution in space

TempSpeed = $f'(t)$= df/dt speed of the spread of pollution in time

Gradient: the change of the value of the field per unit of space or time

Continuity is considered on either an interval of time or on a specified region at all levels of hierarchy. If interpolation functions vary, for example depending on the type of pollutant, the user must specify the members of the discrete dimensions that will be used for the exploration and then (s)he will deal with only the class of continuous dimensions (Fig. 3).

6 Conclusions and Future Work

Data warehousing and OLAP are the corner stone of the decision support systems. We aim at extending these structures so that decision support systems will be appli-

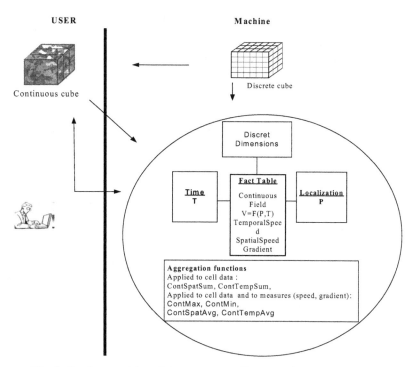

Fig. 3. Continuous vision of the user versus discrete vision of the computer

cable to more domains and in new different ways. Continuous hypercube are structures that can be used for multidimensional analysis and exploration of data in a continuous manner. By the means of interpolation functions we will provide a continuous vision of the discrete hypercube and we will deal with the problems of missing and erroneous data. In this paper we presented the concepts, challenges and potentials of continuous data warehousing, and proposed a continuous multidimensional data model suitable for the analysis and exploration of continuous phenomena. The model uses discrete and continuous basic cubes and from the basic cube a hypercube can be built by applying special aggregation functions. We also defined continuous fields, discrete and continuous operations that deal with multidimensional structures for field-based data. New aggregation functions to deal with continuous field data have been defined. In future work we will concentrate on the formal definitions and methods of calculating aggregating functions within the continuous hypercube.

References

1. Agrawal, R., Gupta, A. and Sarawagi S. Modeling multidimensional databases. 13th Int. Conf. on Data Engineering, (ICDE'97), Birmingham, U. K., (1997) 232-243.
2. Bedard Y. 1997: Spatial OLAP. Vidéo-conférence. 2ème Forum annuel sur la R-D, Géomatique VI: Un monde accessible, Montréal.
   http://sirs.scg.ulval.ca/yvanbedard/public-ation/pub_97.htm consulted on 3/01/2005

3. Blaschka, M. Sapia, C. Höfling, Dinter, G. B. Finding your way through multidimensional data models, Proc. of the Int. Workshop on Data Warehouse Design and OLAP Technology (DWDOT, in connection with DEXA), Vienna, Austria, (1998)
4. Body, M., Miquel, M., Bedard, Y. and Tchounikine, A. Handling evolutions in multidimensional structures. Proc. of IEEE 19th Int. Conf. on Data Engineering (ICDE), India. (2003) 581- 591
5. Cabibbo, L., Torlone, R. Querying Multidimensional Databases. Proc. of the 6th Int. Workshop on Database Programming Languages (DBPL), Estes Park, Colorado, USA (1997)
6. Cabibbo, L., Torlone, R. A Logical Approach to Multidimensional Databases. Proc. of the 6th Int. Conf. on Extending Database Technology (EDBT), Valencia, Spain (1998)
7. Franklin, C. An Introduction to geographic Information Systems: Linking Maps to databases. Database, (1992) 13-21.
8. Gordillo, S. Modelling and manipulation of spatiotemporal phenomena. PhD. Thesis, Claude Bernard University Lyon I, France (2001) In French.
9. Gyssens, M., Lakshmanan, L.V.S. A Foundation for Multi-Dimensional Databases. Proc. of 23rd Int. Conf. on Very Large Data Bases, Athens, Greece, (1997)
10. Inmon, W. H.: Building the data warehouse. John Wiley and sons. (1992)
11. Kemp, Z. and Lee, H.: A Multidimensional Model for Exploratory Spatiotemporal Analysis. Proc. of the 5th Int. Conf. on GeoComputation, University of Greenwich, UK. (2000)
12. Miquel, M., Bedard, Y., Brisebois, A., Pouliot, J., Marchand, P., Brodeur, J. Modeling multidimensional spatiotemporal data warehouse in a context of evolving specifications. Symposium on Geospatial Theory, Processing and Applications, Ottawa (2002)
13. Paradias, D., Tao, Y., Zhang, J., Mamoulis, N., Shen, Q., Sun, J. Indexing and retrieval of historical aggregate information about moving objects. Bulletin of the IEEE Computer Society Technical Committee on Data Engineering, Vol. 25, No. 2. (2002) 10-17
14. Rivest, S., Bedard, Y., Proulx, M.J. and Nadeau, M. SOLAP: A new type of user interface to support spatiotemporal multidimensional data exploration and analysis. In Proc. of ISPRS workshop on Spatial, Temporal and Multidimensional Data Modeling and Analysis, Québec City, Canada. (2003)
15. Shanmugasundaram, J., Fayyad, U. M. and Bradely, P. S. Compressed data cubes for OLAP aggregate query approximation on continuous dimensions. Proc. of the 5th ACM conf. (KDD99) ACM Press New York (1999) 223-232
16. Stefanovic, N., Han, J. and Koperski, K. Object-based selective materialization for efficient implementation of spatial data cubes. IEEE Transaction on Knowledge and Data Engineering, Vol. 12 No. 6 (2000) 938 – 957
17. Vassiliadis, P. Modeling Multidimensional Databases, Cubes and Cube Operations. *Proc.* of the 10th Int. Conf. on Sci. and Stat. Database Management (SSDBM), Italy, 1998.
18. Vassiliadis, P. and Sellis, T. A Survey of Logical Models for OLAP Databases. SIGMOD Record, Vol. 28 No. 4 (1999)

TimeER*plus*:
A Temporal EER Model Supporting Schema Changes

Heidi Gregersen

Department of Marketing, Informatics and Statistics,
Aarhus School of Business, Fuglesangs Allé 4, DK-8210 Aarhus V

Abstract. A wide range of database applications manage information that varies over time. Many of the underlying database schemas of these were designed using one of the several versions, with varying syntax and semantics, of the Entity-Relationship (ER) model. In the research community as well as in industry, it is common knowledge that the temporal aspects of the mini-world are important, but are also difficult to capture using the ER model. Not surprisingly, enhancements to the ER model have been proposed in an attempt to more naturally support the modeling of temporal aspects of information. Common to the existing temporally extended ER models, few or no specific requirements to the models were given by their designers.

With the existing proposals, an ontological foundation, and novel requirements as its basis, this paper defines a novel temporally extended ER model satisfying an array of properties not satisfied by any single previously proposed model.

1 Introduction

A wide range of existing database applications manage time-varying information. Frequently, existing temporal-database applications employ the Entity-Relationship (ER) model [2], in one of its different incarnations, for database design. The model is easy to understand and use, and an ER diagram provides a good overview of a database design. The focus of the model is on the structural aspects of the mini-world, as opposed to the behavioral aspects.

It has been recognized that although temporal aspects of mini-worlds are important for most applications, they are also difficult to capture using the ER model. The temporal aspects have to be modeled explicitly in the ER diagrams, resulting in ER diagrams with entities and attributes that model the temporal aspects, which make the diagrams difficult to understand. As a result, some industrial users simply ignore all temporal aspects in their ER diagrams and supplement the diagrams with textual phrases such as "full temporal support," indicating that the temporal aspects of data should somehow be captured. The result is that the mapping of ER diagrams to the relational tables of the underlying DBMS must be performed by hand; and the ER diagrams do not document well the temporally extended relational database schemas used by the application programmers. An example, Fig. 1 illustrates how temporal aspects may clutter an otherwise simple ER diagram.

Example 1. Figure 1 presents an ER diagram for a company divided into different departments. Each department has a number, a name, some locations, and is responsible

M. Jackson et al. (Eds.): BNCOD 2005, LNCS 3567, pp. 41–59, 2005.

for a number of projects. The company keeps track of when a department is inserted and deleted. It also keep track of the various locations of a department. A department keeps track of the profits it makes on its projects. Because the company would like to be able to make statistics on its profits, each department must record the history of its profits over periods of time.

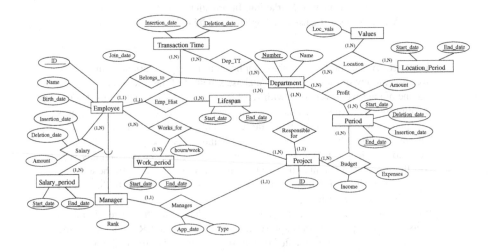

Fig. 1. ER Diagram Modeling Temporal Aspects

Each project has a manager who manages the project and some employees who work for the project. Each project has an ID and a budget. The company registers the history of the budget of a project. Each project is associated with a department that is responsible for the project. Each employee belongs to a single department throughout his or her employment. For each employee, the company registers the ID, the name, the date of birth, and the salary. The company also records the history of employments. The departments would like to keep records of the different employees' salary histories. For reasons of accountability, it is important to be able to trace previous records of both profits and salaries.

Employees work on one project at a time, but employees may be reassigned to other projects, e.g., due to the fact that a project may require employees with special skills. Therefore, it is important to keep track of who works for which project at any given point in time and when they are suppose to be finished working on their current project. Some of the employees are project managers. Once a manager is assigned to a project, the manager will manage the project until it is completed or otherwise terminated.

The research community's response to the shortcomings of the ER model for the modeling of temporal aspects, such as valid and transaction time, has been to develop temporally enhanced ER models, and a number of models have been reported in the research literature [1, 12, 18, 20].

The approaches taken to add built-in temporal support into the ER model are quite different. One approach is to devise new notational shorthands that replace some of the patterns that occur frequently in ER diagrams when temporal aspects are being modeled. Another approach is to change the semantics of the existing ER model constructs, making them temporal.

While the existing temporal ER models represent a rich body of insight into the modeling of temporal data, an evaluation [13] of the models according to a dozen evaluation criteria indicate that no model is entirely satisfactory. For example, only two models supports the transaction-time aspect of data [18, 19]. A common characteristic of the existing temporal ER models is that few or no specific requirements to the models were given by their designers. Rather than being systematically founded on an analysis of general concepts and temporal aspects, their designs are often ad hoc. For example, the design of one model is the result of the need for the modeling of temporal aspects in a specific application [10]. These conditions make it difficult to identify the ideas behind the designs of the models and to understand their semantics. Section 4 compares the proposed model to the existing models in more detail.

It is our contention that there is a need for a temporally extended ER model with an ontological foundation that analyzes and explicitly describes concepts fundamental to temporally enhanced data modeling. It is also essential that this model has explicitly formulated design goals and a comprehensive and precise definition.

We define a graphical, temporally extended ER model, called TIMEER*plus*, that extends the EER model as defined by Elmasri and Navathe [8] to provide built-in support for capturing temporal aspects of entities, relationships, superclasses and subclasses, and attributes. The design of the model is based on an ontology, which defines database objects, fundamental aspects of time, and indicates which aspects of time may be associated meaningfully with which database objects. Finally, the model is designed to satisfy additional, explicitly formulated design goals for temporally extended ER models.

The paper is structured as follows. Section 2 first gives the ontological foundation of the TIMEER*plus* model, then formulates the design goals for the model. Section 3 proceeds to define the TIMEER*plus* model. Section 4 compares TIMEER*plus* with the previously proposed temporal ER models, pointing out the obtained improvements. Finally, Sect. 5 provides a short summary.

2   Ontological Foundations and Requirements

This section first relates the aspects of reality that may be captured by an ER model to the fundamental modeling constructs in ER modeling. Then follows an introduction of generic temporal aspects of information that are candidates for being given built-in support in an ER model. We proceed to introduce two fundamental distinctions; different decisions for these distinctions lead to fundamentally different ER models. Finally, we present a set of requirements to a temporal ER model. We first relate the modeling constructs and temporal aspects, thus identifying exactly which combinations are meaningful. Next, we present design guidelines derived from a set of criteria for evaluating temporally extended ER models that we have previously developed [13].

Database Objects. Anything that exists in the mini-world and can be separated from other things in the mini-world is an *entity*; hence, a data model used for capturing a database representation of an entity should provide means of conveniently modeling the existence and unique identification of entities. The time during which an entity exists in the mini-world, that is, the time during which it is of interest to the mini-world we call the *existence time* of the entity. Other models has another view of existence time [7, 9].

Beyond having an independent existence, an entity is characterized by its properties, modeled by attributes. At any given point in time, an entity has a value for each of its attributes. The values of some attributes remain unchanged over time while others vary over time. We assume that it is meaningful for entities to have properties exactly when they exist.

A relationship type among some entity types defines a set of relations among entities of these types. Each relationship relates exactly one entity from each of the entity types that the relationship type is defined over.

Another type of relationships exists, namely the superclass/subclass relationships that classifies entities of a superclass into different subclasses, e.g., employees may be divided into secretaries, engineers, and technicians. It is the same entities that occur in the subclasses and in the superclass; superclass/subclass relationships represent inheritance hierarchies rather than relate entities. The entities of the subclasses inherit all the properties of entities of the superclass. It is not possible in subclasses to delete or modify the inherited properties, but it is possible to add new properties.

Aspects of Time. In the database community, several types of temporal aspects of information have been discussed over the years. In this paper, we focus on four distinct types of temporal aspects that are candidates for being given built-in support in an ER model, namely *valid time*, *lifespan*, *transaction time*, and *user-defined time* [14].

We use the term "fact" to denote any statement that can be assigned a truth value, i.e., true or false. The notion of *valid time* applies to facts: the valid time of a fact is the time when that fact is true in the mini-world. Thus, any fact in the database may be associated with a valid time. However, the valid time may or may not be captured explicitly in the database.

In ER models, unlike in the relational model, a database is not structured as a collection of facts, but rather as a set of entities and relationships with attributes, with the database facts being implicit. Thus, the valid times are associated only indirectly with facts. As an example consider an Employee entity $e1$ with a Department attribute. A valid time of June 2003 associated with the value "Shipping" does not say that "Shipping" is valid during June 2003, but rather that the fact *"e1 is in Shipping"* is valid during June 2003. Thus, when valid time is captured for an attribute such as Department, the database will record the varying Department values for the Employee entities. If it is not captured, the database will (at any time) record only one department value for each Employee entity.

The *lifespan* of an entity captures the existence time of the entity [14]. If the concept of lifespan of entities is supported, this means that the model has built-in support for capturing the times when entities exist in the mini-world. The lifespan of an entity e may be seen as the valid time of the related fact, "*e exists.*" However, we choose to consider lifespans as separate aspects since the recording of lifespans of entities is important for many applications.

The *transaction time* of a database fact is the time when the fact is current in the database and may be retrieved. As is the case for lifespans, the transaction time of a fact f may be seen as the valid time of a related fact, namely the fact, "*f is current in the database*," but we have also chosen to record transaction time as a separate aspect. Unlike valid time, transaction time may be associated with any element stored in a database, not only with facts. Thus, all database elements have a transaction-time aspect.

User-defined time is supported when time-valued attributes are available in the data model [24]. These are then employed for giving temporal semantics – not captured in the data model, but only externally, in the application code and by the database designer – to the ER diagrams. For employee entities, such attributes could record birth dates, hiring dates, etc.

2.1   Fundamental Design Decisions

Two questions must be answered initially – the answers to these fundamentally affect the nature and properties of a temporally extended ER model.

Temporal Support, How?   The first question is whether temporal support should be achieved by giving new temporal semantics to the existing constructs, or by introducing completely new temporal constructs.

The approach where all existing ER model constructs are given temporal semantics has been used in several of the existing temporal models [7, 9, 19] and has its strong points. Database designers are likely to be familiar with the existing ER constructs. So, after understanding the principle of making these constructs temporal, the designers are ready to work with, and benefit from using, the temporal ER model. However, this approach is not without problems. In its extreme, this approach rules out the possibility of designing non-temporal databases, i.e., databases that do not capture the temporal aspects of data. It is also not possible to design databases with non-temporal parts. Another problem is that old diagrams are no longer correct, i.e., while their syntax is legal, their semantics have changed, and they therefore no longer describe the underlying relational database schemas.

It is possible to retain the existing ER constructs with their usual semantics while achieving temporal support. This is accomplished by adding new temporal constructs to the model that provide the support, and this approach is widely used [10, 17, 18, 21, 22, 27, 28, 30]. The extent of the changes made to the ER model may range from minor changes to a total redefinition of the model.

Two types of new temporal constructs may be distinguished. With *implicit* temporal support, the timestamp attributes used for capturing a temporal aspect are "hidden" in the new modeling constructs – explicit timestamps for capturing the temporal aspects are absent. In contrast, with *explicit* temporal support, timestamp attributes are explicit, and the semantics of the existing ER constructs are retained. Any new modeling constructs are notational shorthands for elements of regular ER diagrams, introduced to make the modeling of temporal aspects more convenient[10].

The models that retain the existing constructs with their old semantics and introduce new temporal constructs also have problems. If their extensions are comprehensive, they are likely to be more difficult for the database designers to learn and understand. On the other hand, this approach avoid the problem of legacy diagrams not describing the underlying database, since the semantics of the existing ER constructs are retained.

Design Model or Implementation Model? The second question is whether the temporal ER model should have a query language, or whether algorithms that map ER diagrams to implementation platforms should be provided.

An algorithm may map temporal ER diagrams directly to relational database schemas [10, 17, 19, 21, 22, 28], or a two-phase approach may be adopted where temporal ER diagrams are first mapped to conventional ER diagrams and then mapped to relational database schemas, reusing mappings from the conventional ER model to the relational model [10, 27, 30]. For minor extensions of the ER model, the reuse in the two-phase approach may be attractive. However, the two-phase translation yields less control over what relational schemas result from the combined mapping.

As an alternative to mapping ER diagrams to the schema of a separate implementation platform, another approach is to assume a system that implements the ER model directly [7, 9, 19–21, 28]. With this approach, a mapping to an implementation platform is not required. Instead, a query language should be available for querying ER databases.

2.2   Requirements for Capturing Temporal Aspects

Valid and transaction time are general – rather than application specific – aspects of all database facts [24]. Lifespan and transaction time are general aspect of entities. As such, these aspects are prime candidates for being built into a temporal ER model.

We distinguish between two uses of a conceptual model, namely the use of a model for *analysis* and the use for *design*. When a model is used for analysis, it is used for modeling a small part of reality and should therefore provide constructs for modeling valid time and lifespans. When used for design, the aim is to model the underlying implementation, which is usually the relational database model and should therefore provide constructs that enables the users to capture transactions time in addition to valid time and lifespan. Since we cannot anticipate if the users will use the model for analysis and/or design the model must provide constructs such that valid time, lifespans, and transaction time can be captured.

Lifespan. Lifespans are used for capturing existence time in the database, so a temporal ER model should offer built-in support for the registration of lifespans of entity types. Lifespans may or may not, at the designer's discretion, be captured in the database.

Built-in support for capturing lifespans of entities is important because lifespans are important in many applications and because entities may exist beyond the times when their attributes have (non-null) values – it is thus not possible to infer lifespans of entities from the valid times of the attribute values associated with the entities.

Valid Time. Because facts have valid time and attributes are the modeling constructs used to capture facts at the conceptual level, a temporal ER model should support the possibility to register valid time for attributes. Built-in support for valid time is important because it is fundamentally important in a large class of applications to know at what times the facts recorded in the database are true.

Three different cases arise in connection with the recording (or non-recording) of the valid time of an attribute. First, if we record the valid time, this implies that we obtain the ability to capture all the values that have ever been valid for the attribute. Second, if we do not register the valid time of the attribute, this may be because the value of the attribute either never changes or because we are only interested in the current value of the attribute. Third, it could be that we do not know the valid time of the attribute – we know the valid value, but not the time when it is valid.

An inherent constraint applies to valid time and lifespans. Specifically, at any time during the database's evolution, the valid time of any attribute value of any entity must be a subset of the lifespan of the entity. Since we perceive a relationship as an attribute of the participating entities, the data model should also provide built-in support for capturing the valid times of relationships. Superclass/subclass relationships are excluded because these are not considered attributes of the involved entities.

Transaction Time. Transaction time is similar to valid time, but there are also some differences. Anything, not just facts, that may be stored in a database has a transaction time. With transaction time captured, past states of a database are retained, which is essential in applications with accountability or trace-ability requirements, of which there are many. The need for recording transaction time is thus widespread. Since transaction time is orthogonal to both existence time and valid time this implies that entities and attribute values can be captured in the database proactively and retroactively.

User-Defined Time. User-defined time attributes, i.e., time-valued attributes with no special support, are already available in the ER model and should also be available in a temporally extended ER model. Figure 2 summarizes the temporal support we believe a temporal ER model must offer.

	Entity types	Relationship types	Superclass/subclass Relationships	Attributes
Lifespan	Yes	No	No	No
Valid time	No	Yes	No	Yes
Transaction time	Yes	Yes	No	Yes

Fig. 2. Modeling Constructs and Their Supported Aspects of Time

Maximally Meaningful and Flexible Support. So far, we have argued that the different temporal aspects should be supported for exactly the modeling constructs where the aspects make sense. This provides maximum meaningful temporal support.

The different temporal aspects may or may not, depending on the application requirements, be captured in the database. Therefore, the support for these aspects should be user-specifiable and maximally flexible. This is achieved if the temporal ER model permits the database designer to decide which temporal aspects to capture of the different database elements. It must be possible to make these decisions independently for independent database elements. Following this principle, the granules of temporal support in an ER model are the following: Entity types, relationship types, and attributes.

This means that the ER model should allow the designer to, e.g., specify the temporal support of an attribute and the attribute's entity independently. For example, the designer may capture lifespans for the Employee entity type while capturing both transaction time and valid time for some of the attributes of Employee.

Time Data Type Support. Different time data types may be used for capturing the temporal aspects of database objects, including instants, time intervals, and temporal elements [11].

A temporal ER model may provide the database designer with a choice of data types, thereby increasing the utility of the model. Instants, time intervals, and temporal elements may all be used for encoding durations. When instants are used for this purpose, they have associated interpolation functions. The instant data type may also encode the occurrence of instantaneous events.

Support for Interpolation. Temporal interpolation functions derive information about times for which no data is explicitly stored in the database (see, [15, 17]). For example, it is possible to record times when new salaries of employees take effect and then define an interpolation function that gives the salaries of employees at any time during their employment. In the scientific domain, interpolation is particularly important, e.g., when variables are sampled.

Support for Granularities and Temporal (Im-) Precision. It may be that the temporal variability of different objects in the mini-world is captured using times of different granularities [4, 29]. It should then also be possible to capture the variability of the different objects in the database using these different granularities. To exemplify, the granularity of a minute may be used when recording the actual working hours of employees, while the granularity of a day may be used when recording the assignment of employees to projects.

The temporal variability of different objects in the mini-world may be known with different precisions [3, 5, 6, 17], and although some imprecision may be captured using multiple granularities, granularities do not provide a general solution.

For example, the variability of an attribute may be recorded using timestamps with the granularity of a second, but the varying values may only be known to the precision of ± 5 seconds of the recorded time. This phenomenon may be prevalent and important to capture in scientific and monitoring applications that store measurements made by instruments. Thus the usability of a temporal ER model would be increased if support for temporal precision is provided.

Upward Compatibility. To increase the usability of a new ER model, it is very important that legacy ER diagrams remain correct in the new model. This property, briefly mentioned earlier, is called *upward compatibility*. A temporal ER model is upward compatible with respect to a conventional ER model if any legal conventional ER diagram is also a legal ER diagram in the temporal model and if the semantics of the diagrams in the two models are the same. Upward compatibility protects investments in legacy systems and provides the basis for a smooth transition from a conventional ER model to a temporally enhanced ER model [26]. We thus require that a temporal ER model be upward compatible with respect to the conventional ER model it extends.

Snapshot Reducible Temporal Support. The next property of a temporal extension is that of snapshot reducibility [25], which may be explained as follows. A temporal ER model that adds temporal support implicitly may provide temporal counterparts of, e.g., the ordinary attribute types, meaning that it provides temporal single-valued, temporal multi-valued, temporal composite, and temporal derived attribute types.

These temporal attribute types may be snapshot reducible with respect to their corresponding snapshot attribute types. In general, this occurs if snapshots of the databases described by a temporal ER diagram are the same as the databases described by the corresponding snapshot ER diagram where all temporal constructs are replaced by their snapshot counterparts.

Beyond attributes, snapshot reducibility also applies to the various constraints that may be defined on relationship types, including specialized relationship types such as superclass/subclass (ISA) and PART-OF (composite/component) relationships.

Time Sequence Attributes. Some attributes are expected to change over time within specific patterns of time. Such attributes are called time sequence attributes [14], but are also known as time-series data [20] or periodic attributes [22]. An example of an attribute in our company database that could store time sequence data is the profit attribute of the Department entity type.

Update Patterns. The update pattern of an attribute is the times the value of the attribute is updated in the database [16], e.g., update patterns relate to transaction time. Given that two or more attributes should be updated simultaneously in the database, e.g, they follow the same update pattern, that is the update of one attribute triggers an update of the other attributes, then we will say that such attributes participate in an update pattern relationship.

Observation Patterns. The observation pattern for an attribute is the times it is given a particular value [16] in the mini-world, e.g., observation patterns relate to valid time. The assignment of the value can be caused by an observation, a prediction or an estimation. We could have a situation where we actually know that if one attribute of an entity type change its value in the mini-world this implies that another attribute also must change its value and vice versa.

Schema Changes. Given that we know, at the design time of the database, that the schema of the database will change at a given point in time this would be useful information to model in the TimeER*plus* diagram.

Changes to a database schema can be divided into three different concepts: schema modification, schema evolution, and schema versioning. The three concepts are defined as follows in Roddick, et al. [23].

1. **Schema Modification** is accommodated when a database system allows for changes to the schema definition of a populated database
2. **Schema Evolution** is accommodated when a database system permits the modification of the database schema without loss of the semantic content of existing data
3. **Schema Versioning** is accommodated when the database system allows the viewing of all data, both retrospectively and prospectively, through user definable interfaces

3   The Time Extended EER Model (TIMEER*plus*)

In this sect. the Time-Extended-EER model, TIMEER*plus*, is presented. First, the model on which to base the new model and positions regarding the fundamental design decisions from Sect. 2.1 are chosen. Second, the constructs of the new model are described.

The Basic Model of TIMEER*plus*.   Since its publication, the ER model [2] has had various notations and semantics. It has been extended in order to capture superclass/subclass relationships and complex entity types, to name but a few extensions, and is then known as the EER model. Because no EER model has become a standard, the EER model presented by Elmasri and Navathe [8] is chosen as the basic model of TIMEER*plus*. The reader is assumed to be familiar with this model.

With respect to the fundamental design decisions presented in Sect. 2, the following choices are made. We have chosen to introduce new temporal constructs and provide *implicit* temporal support for the TIMEER*plus* model. This choice makes it possible to achieve a temporal ER model that is upward compatible with the ER model it extends. We have chosen to provide mapping algorithms for the TIMEER*plus* model. The algorithm is under development. This decision is consistent with most temporal ER models being considered design models and with current practice in industry. A description of the mapping algorithms is beyond the context of this paper.

TIMEER*plus* supports the time data types "instant" and "temporal element."

3.1   TIMEER*plus* Modeling Constructs

We proceed to present the modeling constructs of TIMEER*plus* model. The TIMEER *plus* extends the EER model to include, where indicated, built-in temporal support for entities, relationships, superclasses/subclasses, and attributes.

Regular Entity Types.   A regular entity type is represented by a rectangle. Since all entities represented by an entity type have existence time, modeled by lifespans in the database, and a transaction time aspect, the TIMEER*plus* model offers support for lifespans and transaction time for entity types.

If the lifespan or the transaction time of an entity type is to be captured, this is indicated by placing an LS (LifeSpan) or a TT (Transaction Time) in the upper right corner of the rectangle, respectively. If both lifespan and the transaction time are captured, an LT (Lifespan and Transaction time) is placed as before. Entity types that capture at least one temporal aspect are termed temporal entity types; otherwise, they are termed non-temporal.

In Fig. 1 in Example 1, we model that we want to capture both the lifespan and the transaction time of the entity type Employee, by associating it with two different time period entity types, Lifespan and Transaction Time. In the TIMEER*plus* this is modeled as shown in Fig. 4, see page 55.

Weak Entity Types.   Weak entity types are represented by double rectangles and are used to represent entities that are existence dependent on specific entities of another entity type and that cannot by themselves be lexically uniquely identified. A weak entity type must therefore be related via an (or a chain of) identifying relationship type (represented by a double diamond) to at least one regular entity type that is then the owner of the weak entity type. Weak entity types can be specified to capture the same temporal aspects as regular entity types, and this specification is independent of the temporal support specified for the owner(s) of the weak entity type. It is an inherent constraint that the existence time of a weak entity must be included in the existence time of the owner entity, due to the existence dependency.

Attributes. Entities are characterized by their attributes. A single-valued attribute is represented by an oval, a multi-valued attribute is represented by a double oval, and a composite attribute is represented by an oval connected directly to other ovals representing the component attributes of the composite attribute.

All facts, modeled by attributes, have a valid time and a transaction time aspect, and the TIMEER*plus* model offers support for valid time and transaction time for all attribute types. If the valid time of an attribute is be captured, a VT is placed to the right in the oval; if transaction time is captured, a TT is placed as before. If both the valid time and the transaction time is captured, a BT (BiTemporal) is used. The components of a temporal composite attribute inherit the temporal specification for the composite attribute because we assume that all the components change synchronously. If no temporal aspects of an attribute are captured, we call the attribute non-temporal; otherwise, it is temporal.

It is meaningful for both temporal and non-temporal entity types to have temporal and non-temporal attributes. Temporal entity types may have non-temporal attributes; for example, it could be that the application at hand does not require the capture of any temporal aspects of the attributes of a temporal entity type; it could also be that some attributes are temporal. Similarly, for non-temporal entity types, it is possible that temporal aspects of some attributes are to be captured.

In Fig. 1 in Example 1, we model that we want to capture the valid time and the transaction time of the Salary of an Employee. To be able to capture the valid time, we convert the attribute Salary into a relationship type, Salary, between Employee and Salary_period, with an single-valued attribute Amount to actually record the salary. The transaction time is captured by associating the attributes Insertion_date and Deletion_date with the relationship. In TIMEER*plus* this may be modeled as shown in Fig. 4.

Key Attributes. To indicate that a set of attributes represent the key of an entity type, the attribute names of the involved attributes are underlined. Key attributes of an entity type can be specified as temporal or non-temporal. Simple and composite attributes may be specified as key attributes.

We allow key attributes to be specified as temporal and define these in terms of conventional keys and snapshot reducibility. Snapshot reducibility ensures, for example, that a single-valued attribute capturing valid time, at any point in the valid-time domain, is single-valued. Thus, combining snapshot reducibility of attribute types with the application of the conventional key constraint, we have that any key attribute at any point in time uniquely identifies an entity.

Relationship Types. A relationship type is represented by a diamond. The model offers support for valid and transaction time for relationship types and the indication is placed in the lower corner of the diamond. If some temporal aspect is captured for a relationship type, we call it temporal; otherwise, it is non-temporal.

In Fig.1 in Example 1, we model that we want to capture the valid time of the relationship Works_for between Employee and Project. We therefore have to make the relationship type ternary by associating an entity type Work_period with the attributes Start_date and End_date to model this. A corresponding TIMEER*plus* diagram is shown in Fig. 4.

The temporal support of a relationship type can be specified independently of the temporal support for the participating entity types.

Snapshot Participation Constraints. The snapshot participation constraint of an entity type E with respect to a relationship type R is represented by placing min and max values in parentheses by the line connecting entity type E with relationship type R. If $min = 0$ then the participation of the entities of E is optional; if $min \geq 1$ then the participation is total (mandatory). If $max = 1$, this means that the entities of E cannot participate in more than one relationship at a time, whereas a $max = n$, with $n > 1$ means that E entities can participate in n relationships at a time.

3.2   Advanced Features

The previous sect. described the fundamental design of the TIMEER*plus* model. This sect. proceeds to present additional features of the model.

Lifespan Participation Constraints. The snapshot participation constraints already described constrain the participation of the entities at each isolated point in time. It is also useful to be able to describe the participation of an entity in a relationship over the entire existence time of the entity. This is useful if, for example, we want to state that an employee only can be assigned to at most one project at a time, but can be assigned to any number of projects and must be on at least one during the entire employment.

The snapshot participation constraint ensures that an employee participates in exactly one relationship at any point in time, but it says nothing about the entire employment period. If we change the participation constraint from $(1, 1)$ to $(1, N)$, this means that an employee at any single point in time is now allowed to appear in Works_for N times, which is not intended. Another type of participation constraint, called the lifespan participation constraint, must instead be added to the model, making it possible to express participation constraints throughout the existence times of the entities.

The lifespan participation constraint of entity type E with respect to relationship type R is represented by placing min and max values in square brackets by the line connecting entity type E with relationship type R. The lifespan participation constraint specified for the participation of an entity type with respect to a non-temporal relation-

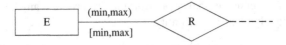

Fig. 3. Representation of Lifespan Participation Constraint in TIMEER*plus*

ship type must be the same as the specified snapshot participation constraint, for which reason they can be omitted from the diagrams.

There are combinations of snapshot and lifespan participation constraints that are contradictory. For constraints (a, b) and $[c, d]$, this occurs when $a > d$, which is the case for the combination of (M, N) and $[1, 1]$.

Other cases exist where lifespan participation constraints do not add to preexisting snapshot participation constraints. For example, a lifespan participation constraint $[1, N]$ does not add to the snapshot participation constraint $(1, 1)$.

Generally, we expect the *min* of the lifespan participation constraint to be equal to or larger than the *min* of the snapshot participation constraint; and the *max* of the lifespan participation constraint is expected to be equal to or larger than the *max* of the snapshot participation constraint.

Using both participation constraints, we can state that any employee must be assigned to at most one project at a time, but must be assigned to at least one project during the employment period. This is shown in Fig. 4.

Superclasses and Subclasses. We offer support for specifying superclass/subclass relationships. The syntax is as in the EER model.

All subclasses inherit the attributes of the their superclasses, and just as inherited attributes cannot be given new data types, it is not possible to change the temporal support given in the superclasses to the inherited attributes. But it is possible to add temporal and non-temporal attributes in the subclasses.

We have chosen that subclasses inherit the temporal aspects of their superclasses and that the inherited time specification is expandable, e.g., if we decide to capture lifespans for Employee entities and let Secretary be a subclass of entity type Employee, we can decide to capture both lifespans and transaction time for Secretary entities. It is not possible to delete the inherited temporal support. This choice is consistent with the fact that subclasses inherit all properties, and thereby also the temporal support, of their superclasses and that it is not possible to delete or modify inherited properties, but only to add properties.

Temporal Interpolation Functions. As described earlier, temporal interpolation functions derive information about times for which no data is explicitly stored in the database. Support for interpolation is perhaps particularly important in applications where processes are monitored and variables are sampled.

We provide the designer with the possibility to define not only temporal interpolation, but also derivation functions for derived attributes, and we extend the model with temporal (and non-temporal) derived attributes. These are represented by dotted ovals with the same possibilities for specifying temporal support as for the stored attributes. The interpolation functions must be specified in the query language of the intended target platform, since we do not provide a query language with the TIMEER*plus* model. The tool implementing the model must provide means for linking the derived attribute with its defining query-language statement.

Time Sequence Attributes. As mentioned earlier, an example of an attribute in our company database that could store time sequence data is the profit attribute of the Department entity type. The company want to record the profit of each department on a monthly basis. This is indicated in the diagram by extending the temporal annotation of the attribute *BT* with a M inclosed by parentheses *(M)*, see Fig. 4. The meaning of this is that we each month record the profit of each Department in the database. The letter inclosed by parentheses indicates the calendar (time pattern) which determines how often the attribute is to be recorded in the database. The specified calendar apply only to the valid time aspect of a temporal attribute. The calendars we provide for time sequence data is year (Y), month (M), week (W), day (D), hour (H), minute (Mi), and second (S). All types of attributes can be specified as time sequenced given that the valid time aspect of the attribute is captured.

Attribute Update Pattern Relationship. An example of attributes from our running example that participates in an update pattern relationship is the attribute *Level* of the *Trainee* entity type and the attribute *Salary* of the *Employee* entity type, since the level of the trainee determines the salary of the trainee. The notation for the update pattern relationship is a small circle annotated with *up* inside and lines connecting the circle and the participating attributes, see Fig. 4.

Even though update patterns relate to transaction time [16] it is not required that the attributes involved in the update pattern relationship capture their transaction time aspect. The semantics of the update is as usual for the participating attributes, e.g., for a non-temporal attribute this means that the new value is stored instead of the old value and for transaction time attributes the old value is terminated and the new value is inserted.

Attribute Observation Pattern Relationship. An example of attributes from our running example that participates in an update pattern relationship is the attribute *Title* of the *Scientist* entity type and the attribute *Salary* of the *Employee* entity type, since the title of an scientist determines the salary of the scientist. The notation for the observation pattern relationship is a small circle annotated with *ob* inside and lines connecting the circle and the participating attributes, see Fig. 4.

As it is the case with attributes participating in an update pattern relationships we do not require the attributes participating in an observation pattern relationship capture their valid time aspect. The semantics of the assignment of new values to the attribute remain as usual for both non-temporal and valid time attributes.

Schema Changes. Consider the running example of the paper, and let us assume that we know that the company will start a new department called Research and Development at November 1, 2004 . Therefore, we need to add another subclass of the employee entity type to the database called *Scientist*. At the same date the registration of employees will extended with information about their address. This leads to a change in the database schema on November 1, 2004. The notation for documenting this change is very simple, just add {*startdate, enddate*} after the name of the construct, see Fig. 4. A dash (-) is used to indicate if either the the start- or the enddate is unknown. It will be useless to have both the startdate and the enddate specified as unknown, since this would semanticly be the same as not using the construct. The startdate indicate when the new construct become valid in the database, meaning that from that date it should be possible to query the new part of the database. If the startdate is unknown we must assume that is is valid currently and will be until the enddate. And if the enddate is unknown this means that it will be valid from the startdate and until "forever". The notation can also be used for documenting changes in the database schema not known at design time.

Example 2. Figure 4 gives a TIMEER*plus* diagram that corresponds to the the EER diagram given in Fig. 1.

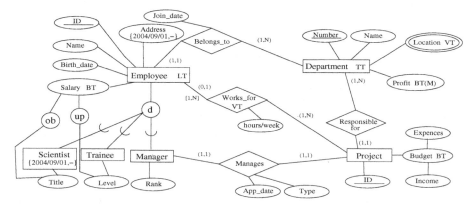

Fig. 4. TIMEER*plus* Diagram of the Example

3.3   Properties of the TIMEER*plus* Model

In Sect. 2 we listed a set of design goals. Having introduced TIMEER*plus*, we now examine its design with respect to the goals.

Temporal Aspects Supported. We provide built-in support for capturing lifespans and transaction time for entities. Similarly, built-in support for capturing valid time and transaction time for attributes and relationships is provided. The model also provides notation for specification of time sequence attributes, observation- and update pattern relationship. Finally, user-defined time attributes are available.

Maximally Meaningful and Flexible Support. TIMEER*plus* provides maximally meaningful and flexible temporal support, since the database designer is able for each modeling construct to specify whether or not to capture each meaningful temporal aspect of the construct. The model has optional use of the temporal constructs, providing the database designer with the possibility of mixing temporal and non-temporal constructs in the same diagram.

Time Data Type Support. TIMEER*plus* supports time data types for the modeling of both instantaneous events and phenomena that persist in time, namely the "instant" and "temporal element" types.

Support for Interpolation. The model provides support for defining temporal interpolation functions and derivation functions for derived attributes. The interpolation functions must be specified in the query language of the intended target platform – a separate language for this is not provided.

Support for Granularities and Temporal (Im-) Precision. The time granularities supported by TIMEER*plus* are second, minute, hour, day, week, month, and year. The model does not, at present, support temporal imprecision.

Upward Compatibility. The designed model is upward compatible with respect to the EER model [8] because we *extend* this model with new temporal constructs while retaining all original EER constructs, with their original syntax and semantics.

Snapshot Reducible Temporal Support. TIMEER*plus* has implicit temporal support and includes snapshot reducible temporal counterparts of the ordinary attribute types, i.e., provides temporal single valued, temporal multi-valued, temporal composite, and temporal derived attribute types.

Next, the snapshot participation constraints are also snapshot reducible, while lifespan participation constraints have no non-temporal counterparts. Finally, the constraints associated with superclass/subclass relationships are snapshot reducible. For example, the temporal participation constraint (*disjoint, total*) for a superclass/subclass relationship is snapshot reducible, so that for any snapshot of the underlying database, any entity of the superclass is present in exactly one subclass.

Schema Changes. The TIMEER*plus* model provides notation for specifying changes to the database schema explicitly in TIMEER*plus* diagrams. The notation can be used for specifying schema modification, schema evolution, and schema versioning depending on the database system support for these concepts.

4   Related Research

A comprehensive survey [12] of all previously proposed temporally extended ER models, and models published after late 1998 [1, 18, 20] have been studied. The study of these models pointed to varying limitations in the existing models, motivating the development of a new temporal ER model that attempted to build maximally on the insights accumulated in the existing models.

More specifically, the existing temporal ER models represent quite diverse approaches to capturing temporal aspects of data at the conceptual level, and it is our contention that the models, to varying degrees, have succeeded in more elegantly capturing the temporal aspects of data than does the ER model. However, evaluating the existing models against a list of desirable properties [13] reveals that no single model satisfies all properties, but that the models collectively cover the design space well.

As mentioned in the introduction, a common characteristic for the existing temporally extended ER models is that few or no specific requirements to the models are given by their designers. In contrast, we have based the design of the TIMEER*plus* model on the design goals presented in Sect. 2, some of which are based on ontological considerations, and some of which are derived from previously presented properties [13].

One approach to developing a temporal extension is to give the existing ER constructs new temporal semantics. This approach has been followed in several models [7, 9, 19], and it has its strong points. But there are also weaknesses. The main weakness is the lack of upward compatibility, and for this reason we have not chosen this approach for TIMEER*plus*.

Another approach is to retain the existing ER constructs with their usual semantics and introduce new temporal constructs that provide temporal support. This can be done by offering new modeling constructs with either implicit temporal support [1, 17, 18, 20–22, 27, 28, 30] or explicit temporal support [10]. Since the latter type of support still leads to cluttered diagrams, although to a lesser degree than in the ER model, we have chosen to add new temporal constructs with implicit temporal support.

The ideal temporal ER model is easy to understand in terms of the ER model; does not invalidate legacy diagrams and database applications; and does not restrict databases to be temporal, but rather permits the designer to mix temporal and non-temporal parts. We believe that the TIMEER*plus* model has these properties.

The concept of snapshot reducibility applies to attributes as well as the various constraints that may be defined on relationship types, including those on superclass/subclass hierarchies. Satisfying reducibility is very important because this provides a uniform and natural generalization of standard, snapshot ER modeling constructs to temporal counterparts.

Although we have seen that this requirement never previously has been applied explicitly to an ER model, aspects of existing temporal ER models turn out to be snapshot reducible. Only three temporal ER models have snapshot reducible relationship constraints [18, 27, 30], while most models have snapshot reducible attributes [7, 9, 10, 17–20, 22, 30], This latter property of the various models follows implicitly from how the temporal attributes are defined as shorthands for patterns made up of conventional constructs, from the properties of the models' mapping algorithms, from explicitly formulated semantics for the attributes, or from the attributes being defined in terms of snapshot reducible temporal relationships types.

The TIMEER*plus* model provides snapshot reducible attribute types as well as relationship constraints. Lifespan participation constraints do not have non-temporal counterparts to reduce to.

All but two of the existing temporal ER models support valid time only. We believe that the support for transaction time is just as important, and TIMEER*plus* supports both time aspects. Support for lifespans is also included, which is only provided by a subset of the existing temporal ER models [7, 9, 17, 19, 28, 30]. Only two models support time sequence attributes [20, 22]. The TIMEER*plus* model is the only model that supports observation- and update pattern relationships and schema changes.

5 Summary

Temporal aspects are prevalent in most real-world database applications, but they are also difficult to capture elegantly using the ER model. In an attempt to alleviate this problem, this paper presents a temporally extended ER model capable of more elegantly and naturally capturing temporal aspects of data.

The TIMEER*plus* model systematically extends the EER model [8] with new, enhanced modeling constructs with implicit temporal support. The new constructs provide built-in support for capturing lifespans of entities and relationships and provides built-in support for capturing valid times for attributes and relationships. And the model provides built-in support for capturing the transaction times for all modeling constructs.

The temporal aspects of the modeling constructs are captured using either instants or temporal elements, and support for multiple granularities is included. The database designer may, or may not, use the new temporal constructs, and the resulting model is upward compatible with respect to the EER model. Furthermore, the TIMEER*plus* model offers enhanced modeling construct for modeling time sequenced attributes, update pattern relationships, observation pattern relationships, and notation for describing changes to the database schema.

References

1. S. Bergamaschi and C. Sartori. Chrono: A Conceptual Design Framework for Temporal Entities. In T. W. Ling, S. Ram, and M-L. Lee, editors, *Conceptual Modeling - ER '98, 17th International Conference on Conceptual Modeling, Singapore, November 16-19, 1998, Proceedings*, volume 1507 of *Lecture Notes in Computer Science*, pages 35–50. Springer, 1998.
2. P. P-S. Chen. The Entity-Relationship Model – Toward a Unified View of Data. *Transaction on Database Systems*, 1(1):9–36, March 1976.
3. C. E. Dyreson and R. T. Snodgrass. Temporal Granularity and Indeterminacy: Two Sides of the Same Coin. Technical Report TR 94-06, University of Arizona, Department of Computer Science, February 1994.
4. C. E. Dyreson and R. T. Snodgrass. Temporal Granularity. In *The TSQL2 Temporal Query Language*, chapter 19, pages 347–383. Kluwer Academic Press, 1995.
5. C. E. Dyreson and R. T. Snodgrass. Temporal Indeterminacy. In R. T. Snodgrass, editor, *The TSQL2 Temporal Query Language*, chapter 18, pages 327–346. Kluwer Academic Publishers, 1995.
6. C. E. Dyreson and R. T. Snodgrass. Supporting Valid-time Indeterminancy. *ACM Transaction on Database Systems*, 23(1):1–57, March 1998.
7. R. Elmasri, I. El-Assal, and V. Kouramajian. Semantics of Temporal Data in an Extended ER Model. In *9th International Conference on the Entity-Relationship Approach*, pages 239–254, Lausanne, Switzerland, October 1990.
8. R. Elmasri and S. B. Navathe. *Fundamentals of Database Systems*. The Benjamin/Cummings Publishing Company, INC, 2. edition, 1994. ISBN 0-8053-1753-8.
9. R. Elmasri and G. T. J. Wuu. A Temporal Model and Query Language for ER Databases. In *Proceedings of the Sixth International Conference on Data Engineering*, pages 76–83, 1990.
10. S. Ferg. Modeling the Time Dimension in an Entity-Relationship Diagram. In *4th International Conference on the Entity-Relationship Approach*, pages 280–286, Silver Spring, MD, 1985. Computer Society Press.
11. S. K. Gadia. A Homogeneous Relational Model and Query Languages for Temporal Databases. *Transactions on Database Systems*, 13(4):418–448, December 1988.
12. H. Gregersen and C. S. Jensen. Temporal Entity-Relationship Models – a Survey. *IEEE Transactions on Knowledge an Data Engineering*, 11(3):464–497, May 1999.
13. H. Gregersen, C. S. Jensen, and L. Mark. Evaluating Temporally Extended ER Models. In K. Siau, Y. Wand, and J. Parsons, editors, *Proceedings of the Second CAiSE/IFIP8.1 International Workshop on Evaluation of Modeling Methods in Systems Analysis and Design*, page 12, June 1997.
14. C. S. Jensen and C. E. Dyreson[editors]. The Consensus Glossary of Temporal Database Concepts - February 1998 Version. In O. Etzion, S. Jajodia, and S. Sripada, editors, *Temporal Databases: Research and Practice*, volume 1399 of *Lecture Notes in Computer Science*, pages 367–405. Springer-Verlag, 1998.

15. C. S. Jensen and R. T. Snodgrass. Semantics of Time-Varying Information. *Information Systems*, 21(4):311–352, March 1996.

16. C. S. Jensen and R. T. Snodgrass. Temporally Enhanced Database Design. In M. P. Papazoglou, S. Spaccapietra, and Z. Tari, editors, *Advances in Object-Oriented Data Modeling*, chapter 7, pages 163–193. MIT Press, 2000.

17. M. R. Klopprogge. TERM: An Approach to Include the Time Dimension in the Entity-Relationship Model. In *Proceedings of the Second International Conference on the Entity Relationship Approach*, pages 477–512, Washington, DC, October 1981.

18. P. Kraft and J. O. Sørensen. Translation of a High-Level Temporal Model into Lower Level Models. In H. S.Kunii, S. Jajodia, and A. Sølvberg, editors, *Conceptual Modeling - ER 2001*, volume 2224 of *Lecture Notes in Computer Science*, pages 383–396. Springer, 2001.

19. V. S. Lai, J-P. Kuilboer, and J. L. Guynes. Temporal Databases: Model Design and Commercialization Prospects. *DATA BASE*, 25(3):6–18, 1994.

20. J. Y. Lee and R. Elmasri. An EER-Based Conceptual Model and Query Language for Time-Series Data. In T. W. Ling, S. Ram, and M-L. Lee, editors, *Conceptual Modeling - ER '98, 17th International Conference on Conceptual Modeling, Singapore, November 16-19, 1998, Proceedings*, volume 1507 of *Lecture Notes in Computer Science*, pages 21–34. Springer, 1998.

21. P. McBrien, A. H. Seltveit, and B. Wangler. An Entity-Relationship Model Extended to describe Historical information. In *International Conference on Information Systems and Management of Data*, pages 244–260, Bangalore, India, July 1992.

22. A. Narasimhalu. A Data Model for Object-Oriented Databases with Temporal Attributes and Relationships. Technical report, National University of Singapore, 1988.

23. J. F. Roddick, N. G. Craske, and T. J. Richards. A Taxonomy for Schema Versioning Based on the Relational and Entity Relationship Models. In R. Elmasri, V. Kouramajian, and B. Thalheim, editors, *Entity-Relationship Approach - ER'93, 12th International Conference on the Entity-Relationship Approach, Arlington, Texas, USA, December 15-17, 1993, Proceedings*, volume 823 of *Lecture Notes in Computer Science*, pages 137–148. Springer, 1993.

24. R. Snodgrass and I. Ahn. A Taxonomy of Time in Databases. In S. Navathe, editor, *Proceedings of ACM-SIGMOD 1985 International Conference on Management of Data*, pages 236–246, Austin, TX, May 1985.

25. R. T. Snodgrass. The Temporal Query Language TQuel. *ACM Transaction on Database Systems*, 12(2):247–298, June 1987.

26. R. T. Snodgrass, Böhlen M., C. S. Jensen, and A. Steiner. Change Proposal to SQL/Temporal: Adding Valid Time – Part A. *International Organization for Standardization*, page 40, December 1995. ANSI Expert's Contribution.

27. B. Tauzovich. Toward Temporal Extensions to the Entity-Relationship Model. In *The 10th International Conference on the Entity Relationship Approach*, pages 163–179, San Mateo, California, October 1991.

28. C. I. Theodoulidis, P. Loucopoulos, and B. Wangler. A Conceptual Modelling Formalism for Temporal Database Applications. *Information Systems*, 16(4):401–416, 1991.

29. G. Wiederhold, S. Jajodia, and W. Litwin. Dealing with Granularity of Time in Temporal Databases. In R. et al. Anderson, editor, *Proceedings of the 3rd International Conference on Advanced Information Systems Engineering*, volume 498 of *Lecture Notes in Computer Science*, pages 124–140, Trondheim, Norway, May 1991. Springer Verlag.

30. E. Zimanyi, C. Parent, S. Spaccapietra, and A. Pirotte. TERC+: A Temporal Conceptual Model. In *Proc. Int. Symp. on Digital Media Information Base*, November 1997.

Semantically Rich Materialisation Rules
for Integrating Heterogeneous Databases

M. Basel Al-Mourad[1], W. Alex Gray[2], and Nick J. Fiddian[2]

[1] Aston University, Computer Science Dept., B4 7ET, UK
m.b.al-mourad@aston.ac.uk
[2] Cardiff University, School of Computer Science, CF24 3AA, UK
{w.a.gray,n.j.fiddian}@cs.cf.ac.uk

Abstract. The need for accessing independently developed database systems using a unified or multiple global view(s) has been well recognised. This paper addresses the problem of redundancy of object retrieval in a multidatabase setting. We present the materialisation rules we have used for supporting data integration in a heterogeneous database environment. The materialisation rules are capable of directing the global query processor to combine data from different databases. Also, these rules are able to reconcile database heterogeneity that may be found due to independent database design.

1   Introduction

Database integration frequently involves combining information about the same object from different sources. This information could be replicated a number of times in these sources. Correlating data from different databases about the same object is redundant and time expensive; therefore a technique to eliminate redundancy and to reduce retrieval time is needed. Moreover, objects from different local databases are likely to be heterogeneous and this heterogeneity must be reconciled when data is aggregated and represented to the global users. In our research [1–3] we propose that interoperability between a set of heterogeneous databases is best achieved by building several tailored global views to fully meet user requirements and this allows local conflicts to be resolved in various ways (Fig. 1). Local database schemas are first translated into corresponding component schemas presented in a canonical data model [4, 5] which is compliant with the ODMG standard. Multiple views can support multiple semantics via customisability, in that users can define several views over the same local databases reflecting different needs. The views are defined in terms of virtual classes and materialisation rules [2, 6]. Virtual classes define the conceptual schema of each global view. A virtual class is created by integrating a number of related local classes in the local databases. This is achieved by applying one or more operators (union, merge, intersection) from our operator integration language [3]. The materialisation rules act as a proxy [7, 8] and they are semantically rich as they are responsible for: first, reconciling schema differences between entities which are the components of virtual classes; second, mapping the global queries into

M. Jackson et al. (Eds.): BNCOD 2005, LNCS 3567, pp. 60–69, 2005.

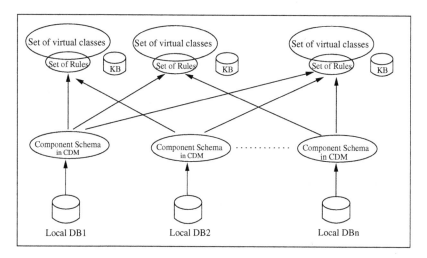

Fig. 1. Multiple Views for interoperability between a set of heterogeneous databases

local queries that are able to retrieve relevant data from the corresponding local classes in component databases. In other words the materialisation rules provide 1: N mapping of global objects to objects in local databases [9].

A fundamental issue here concerns the problem of retrieving the instances of the generated virtual classes (derived instances) from their corresponding local ones. Derived instances of a virtual class typically represent a combination of one or more real instances (actual stored values in local databases). In particular, the value of an attribute of a derived instance may be obtained as a result of combining values from attributes of several real instances. A derived instance (global object) differs from a real instance (local object) because a derived instance may represent an assortment of values that do not actually appear together as an instance in any local database.

In this paper, we present the materialisation rules we use to support the retrieval of global objects in global views. These rules are capable of combining information about the same object without redundancy. They are also able to reconcile any semantic heterogeneity that may be found due to independent local database design. In section 2, we present the general syntax of our materialisation rules. In section 3, we discuss our observations on the problem of matching objects in different local databases. Section 4 provides a sample case for integrating two local classes and represents the materialisation rules for this sample case. Section 5 presents our conclusion and future work.

2   The Materialisation Rules Syntax

The rules we are using have a familiar production rule syntax [10] of the form:

Rule <name> on retrieve to <virtual class properties>,
    do instead: retrieve <local corresponding properties>
where <condition> // the condition under which the rule is executed.

Each rule is given a unique rule-name, which is used by the global query processor and also to remove the rule by name when it is no longer needed. The keyword instead indicates that the rule directs the global query processor to retrieve data that corresponds to local corresponding properties. At the time of accessing a global object, the do instead part of the corresponding materialisation rule specifies the corresponding global object properties in local objects. If a certain global object property doesn't have a corresponding local property in a certain object, a NOT APPLICABLE value should be assigned to the corresponding do instead rule element. The < condition > reflects different global object extensions which are recognised based on a user defined function which in turn is able to recognise different local object extensions based on the Object Identifier (OID).

3   Observations on Global Object Identification

A fundamental issue in integrating information from heterogeneous distributed databases is the problem of object matching, that is, determining when object representations in different databases refer to the same real world object [11]. Most previous approaches to creating virtual integrated views have assumed that for each type of object (in the real world) there is some form of possible derived universal virtual key [12–14] that can be used to identify different representations of the same real world object (i.e. one approach is to use common attributes in each class and those attributes virtually represent Object IDentifiers (OIDs)). We define a 'g=' function[1] that compares two objects by using their virtual OIDs and determines whether two local objects are equivalent. This function is essential for materialisation rules, as different rules are generated for different types of local objects. The definition of this function is left to the user as it is difficult if not impossible to automate. For example, the user could assume that the combination of (first_name, surname, date_of_birth) represent the OID of graduate students in db1_GradStudent and the the combination of (f_name, family_name, birthdate) represent the OID of employees in in db2_Employee (see the example next). In this case the 'g=' function is a simple equivalent function that compares the values of corresponding attributes (i.e. first_name and f_name, surname and family_name, date_of_birth and birthdate). If the result of the comparison is true this means the two comparable OIDs and ultimately both objects represents the same real world object.

4   Case Example

We describe the materialisation rules by using a sample integration for schemas presented in Fig. 2. The first schema (DB1) defines information for a graduate student database, while the second schema (DB2) defines information for an employee database. For simplicity, we limit the information to one class per

---

[1] Note how the 'g=' function in the case example affects the retrieving of instances and how the rules are directed to the local properties

schema but the materialisation rule syntax can be applied to any number of classes as the integration process is done using the binary integration strategy [5, 15]. Also, we include various types of heterogeneity [16, 17] in both databases to explain how the materialisation rules are capable of reconciling this heterogeneity at the global level. For example, we consider the following conflicts:

- Naming conflict (first_name in DB1 versus f_name in DB2).
- Domain conflict (the domain of first_name in DB1 is a set of strings reflecting multiple first names versus a string for the domain of f_name in DB2).
- Domain conflict (the domain of live in DB1 is a set of addresses reflecting the fact that the student could have more than one address (term address and vacation address) while the domain of live in DB2 is address).
- Present - Absent conflict (course in DB1 and position in DB2).
- Semantic conflict (salary in DB1 is represented in Euros while salary in DB2 is represented in Sterling).

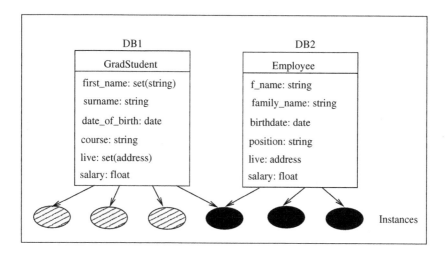

Fig. 2. Two local classes to be integrated by using the Union operator

The extensions (instances) of local classes are represented as ovals in Fig. 2. Grey ovals represent extensions that may belong to GradStudent and Employee classes. The integrator can use one of the integration operators (union, merge, intersection, etc) to integrate the classes in the local databases [3]. For example, if a global user is interested in information about all part time workers in both databases (assuming that some students work part-time while they are studying), the integrator should use the Union operator. This operator integrates two equivalent local classes c1, c2 by generating a common superclass Gc with two subclasses Gc1, Gc2. The Gc class's properties are the set of properties that belong to the intersection of the local classes's properties. The extension of the Gc class is the combination of the extents of the two local classes. The set of properties that belong to both classes is upward-inherited by the generated global superclass Gc [18, 19].

The result of applying Union on Employee and GradStudent (Fig. 3) is three global classes: G_PartTime_Emp, G_Employee and G_GradStudent, where G_PartTime_Emp is the common superclass for both Employee and GradStudent. The properties of G_PartTime_Emp are the intersection of the local class properties, namely {first_name, surname, date_of_birth, live, salary}[2]. The properties of subclass G_GradStudent are (course and all inherited properties from G_PartTime_Emp). The properties of subclass G_Employee are (position and all inherited properties from G_PartTime_Emp). We can differentiate three types of extensions (all ovals in Fig. 3) which reflect the real world objects at the global level. Therefore each global class needs at most three types of materialisation rules. We describe the materialisation rules generated for each global class as follows:

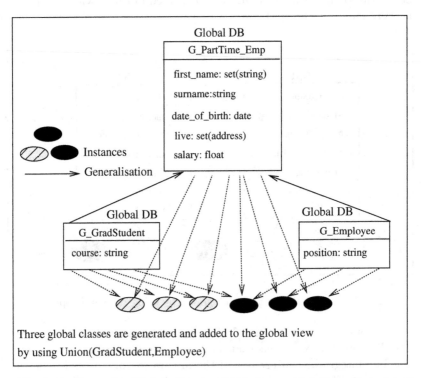

Fig. 3. An Example of integrating two local classes using Union operator

4.1   Materialisation Rules for G_PartTime_Emp

The extension of G_PartTime_Emp is the union of the local class extents (all ovals in Fig. 3), thus G_PartTime_Emp needs three materialisation rules:

---

[2] We assume that semantic heterogeneity has been detected and solved and the integrator prefers the representation of DB1 at the global level (e.g. first_name vs f_name, salary is represented in Euros)

- The first rule is responsible for retrieving data for instances that belong to GradStudent and do not belong to Employee (hashed ovals in Fig. 3). The rule retrieves these instances from GradStudent instances:

```
Define rule1 view_G_PartTime_Emp_rule1 on retrieve to
view_G_PartTime_Emp.first_name, view_G_PartTime_Emp.surname,
view_G_PartTime_Emp.date_of_birth, view_G_PartTime_Emp.live,
view_G_PartTime_Emp.salary
do instead retrieve
db1_GradStudent.first_name, db1_GradStudent.surname,
db1_GradStudent.date_of_birth, db1_GradStudent.live,
db1_GradStudent.salary
where current.OID = db1_GradStudent.OID &
not(db1_GradStudent.OID =g db2_Employee.OID)
```

- The second rule is responsible for retrieving data for instances that belong to Employee but do not belong to GradStudent (black ovals in Fig. 3). It retrieves these instances from Employee instances:

```
Define rule2 view_G_PartTime_Emp_rule2 on retrieve to
view_G_PartTime_Emp.first_name, view_G_PartTime_Emp.surname,
view_G_PartTime_Emp.date_of_birth, view_G_PartTime_Emp.live,
view_G_PartTime_Emp.salary
do instead retrieve
db2_Employee.f_name, db2_Employee.family_name,
db2_Employee.birthdate, db2_Employee.live,
SterlingToEuro(db2_Employee.salary)
where current.OID = db2_Employee.OID &
not(db1_GradStudent.OID =g db2_Employee.OID)
```

As this rule retrieves instances that belong to Employee the do instead part of the rule replaces the global attribute names with the ones that correspond to the Employee attribute names (f_name, family_name, birthdate). This will solve the naming conflict mentioned earlier. The rule also replaces the global attribute live with the attribute live of Employee. This is to make sure that the domain of live is set(address) when global instances correspond to the Employee instances. SterlingToEuro is a function that converts the salary from Sterling to Euros and its code is normally defined by the integrator. This function shows how the materialisation rules are capable of reconciling semantic heterogeneity that may be found during the integration process.

- The third rule is responsible for retrieving data for the intersecting extents (grey ovals in Fig. 3). It basically retrieves the data from GradStudent or Employee or both of them. Note that this is a special case where instances belong to both local classes. This occurs when a person is registered as a GradStudent in DB1 and an Employee in DB2. Thus when the G_Employee object and G_GradStudent object represent the same real world object (i.e. if they have the same name), our materialisation rule attached to G_PartTime_Emp retrieves the data of this type of instance from either one or both local classes:

```
Define rule3 view_G_PartTime_Emp_rule3 on retrieve to
view_G_PartTime_Emp.first_name, view_G_PartTime_Emp.surname,
view_G_PartTime_Emp.date_of_birth, view_G_PartTime_Emp.live,
view_G_ PartTime_Emp.salary
do instead retrieve
db1_GradStudent.first_name, db1_GradStudent.surname,
db1_GradStudent.date_of_birth, db1_GradStudent.live,
Function(db1_GradStudent.salary,db2_Employee.salary)
where db1_GradStudent.OID =g db2_Employee.OID
```

This third rule is defined to retrieve the information of intersection objects from DB1 as the definition of GradStudent structure is semantically richer than Employee (first_name attribute has a set of string domain and live attribute has a set of address domain). The salary is retrieved by applying a function on both local salaries (db1_GradStudent.salary, db2_Employee. salary). This function could be defined to: either combine both salaries if a person works part-time in two different places so the global salary of this person must be accumulated and represented to the global user as one salary; or preferably to retrieve one of them (in this case it is better to retrieve salary from DB1 as this saves the global query processor time). The function may also convert salaries to Euro representation.

4.2   Materialisation Rules for G_GradStudent

G_GradStudent is defined as a subclass of G_PartTime_Emp, therefore it inherits all its attributes. To retrieve course information for G_GradStudent three materialisation rules are needed:

- The first rule is responsible for retrieving data (course information) for instances that belong to GradStudent and do not belong to Employee (hashed ovals in Fig. 3). The rule retrieves these instances from GradStudent instances:

```
Define rule1 view_G_GradStudent on retrieve to
view_G_GradStudent.course
do instead retrieve
db1_GradStudent.course
where current.OID = db1_GradStudent.OID &
not(db1_GradStudent.OID =g db2_Employee.OID)
```

- The second rule is responsible for retrieving data (course information) for instances that belong to Employee but do not belong to GradStudent (black ovals in Fig. 3). As Employee doesn't provide course information a not applicable value is assigned to inform the query processor that it is not possible to retrieve course information from the Employee class. The rule has the following syntax:

```
Define rule2 view_G_GradStudent on retrieve to
view_G_GradStudent.course
do instead retrieve
not_applicable
where current.OID = db2_Employee.OID &
not(db1_GradStudent.OID =g db2_Employee.OID)
```

- The third rule is responsible for retrieving data (course information) for intersecting extents (grey ovals in Fig. 3). It basically retrieves this data from GradStudent as Employee doesn't provide course information:

```
Define rule3 view_G_GradStudent on retrieve to
view_G_GradStudent.course
do instead retrieve
db1_GradStudent.course
where db1_GradStudent.OID =g db2_Employee.OID
```

4.3 Materialisation Rules for G_Employee

G_Employee is defined as a subclass of G_PartTime_Emp therefore it inherits all its attributes. To retrieve position information for G_Employee three materialisation rules are needed:

- The first rule is responsible for retrieving data (position information) for instances that belong to Employee and do not belong to GradStudent (black ovals in Fig. 3). The rule retrieves these instances from Employee instances:

```
Define rule1 view_G_Employee on retrieve to
view_G_Employee.position
do instead retrieve
db1_Employee.position
where current.OID = db2_Employee.OID &
not(db2_Employee.OID =g db1_GradStudent.OID)
```

- The second rule is responsible for retrieving data (position information) for instances that belong to GradStudent but do not belong to Employee (hashed ovals in Fig. 3). As GradStudent doesn't provide position information a not applicable value is assigned to inform the query processor that it is not possible to retrieve position information from the GradStudent class. The rule has the following syntax:

```
Define rule2 view_G_Employee on retrieve to
view_G_Employee.position
do instead retrieve
not_applicable
where current.OID = db1_GradStudent.OID &
not(db1_GradStudent.OID =g db2_Employee.OID)
```

– The third rule is responsible for retrieving data (position information) for intersecting extents (grey ovals in Fig. 3). It basically retrieves this data from Employee as GradStudent doesn't provide position information:

```
Define rule3 view_G_Employee on retrieve to
view_G_Employee.position
do instead retrieve
db2_Employee.position
where db1_GradStudent.OID =g db2_Employee.OID
```

5   Conclusion and Future Work

This paper is concerned with correlating data from different databases. We described the materialisation rules we use to support global views that are used to achieve interoperability between a set of heterogeneous databases. These rules are able to map queries against global concepts into queries against local ones. The rules eliminate redundancy when different databases contain data about the same object. Also, we showed how the materialisation rules are capable of solving local semantic heterogeneities when data is retrieved and represented at the global level. The example presented in this paper shows the materialisation rules for integrating two equivalent classes. The same concept apply when we integrate two classes that have different types of relationship (overlap, inclusion, or semantically not related). The current materialisation rules support data retrieval only. We are now investigating the possibility of enhancing the materialisation rules to support update and delete at the global level.

References

1. Al-Mourad, M.B., Gray, W.A., Fiddian, N.J.: Detecting object semantic similarity by using structural and behavioural semantics. In: Proc. 5th World Multiconference on Systemics, Cybernetics and Informatics, Orlando, USA (2001)
2. Al-Mourad, M.B., Gray, W.A., Fiddian, N.J.: Mvmbs: A multiple views supporting multiple behaviours system for interoperable object-oriented database systems. In: New Horizons in Information Management, 20th British National Conference on Databases, BNCOD 20, Coventry, UK. (2003) 198–206
3. Al-Mourad, M.B., Gray, W.A., Fiddian, N.J.: Multiple views with multiple behaviours for interoperable object-oriented database systems. In: Database and Expert Systems Applications, 14th International Conference, DEXA 2003, Prague, Czech Republic. (2003)
4. Sheth, A.P., Gala, S.K., Navathe, S.B.: On automatic reasoning for schema integration. International Journal of Intelligent and Cooperative Information Systems **2** (1993) 23–50
5. Ozsu, M.T., Valduriez, P.: Principles of Distributed Database Systems. Prentice Hall (1999)
6. Sheth, A.P., Larson, J.A.: Federated database systems for managing distributed, heterogeneous and autonomous databases. ACM Computing Surveys (1990) 183–236

7. Kim, W.: The unisql/m system. Personal Communication (1992)
8. Lim, E.P., Chiang, R.H.L.: Accommodating instance heterogeneities in database integration. Decision Support Systems **38** (2004) 213–231
9. Giannadakis, N., Rowe, A., Ghanem, M., ke Guo, Y.: Infogrid: providing information integration for knowledge discovery. In: Information Sciences. Volume 155. (2003) 199–226
10. Stonebraker, M., Rowe, L.A., Hirohama, M.: The implementation of POSTGRES. IEEE Transactions on Knowledge and Data Engineering **2** (1990) 125–142
11. Tejada, S., Knoblock, C.A., Minton, S.: Learning object identification rules for information integration. In: Information Systems. Number 8 (2001) 607–633
12. Dayal, U., Hwang, H.: View definition and generalization for database integration in a multidatabase system. IEEE Transactions on Software Engineering **SE-10** (1984) 628–645
13. Zhao, K., King, R., Bouguettaya, A.: Incremental specification of views across databases. Proc. 1st International Workshop on Interoperability in Multidatabase Systems, Kyoto, Japan (1991) 187–190
14. Arens, Y., Chee, C.Y., Hsu, C., Knoblock, C.A.: Retrieving and integrating data from multiple information sources. International Journal of Intelligent and Cooperative Information Systems **2** (1993) 127–158
15. Batini, C., Lenzerini, M., Navathe, S.B.: A comparative analysis of methodologies for database schema integration. ACM Computing Surveys **18** (1986) 323–364
16. Kim, W., Choi, I., Gala, S., Scheevel, M.: On resolving schematic heterogeneity in multidatabase systems. Distributed and Parallel Databases **1** (1993) 251–279
17. Garcia-Solaco, M., Saltor, F., Castellanos, M.: Semantic heterogeneity in multidatabase systems. In Bukhres, O.A., Elmagarmid, A.K., eds.: Object-Oriented Multidatabase Systems, A Solution for Advanced Applications. Prentice-Hall (1996)
18. Schrefl, M., Neuhold, E.: Object class definition by generalization using upward inheritance. Proc. 4th International Conference on Data Engineering (1988)
19. Kaul, M., Drosten, K., Neuhold, E.: Viewsystem: Integrating heterogeneous information bases by object-oriented views. Proc. 6th International Conference on Data Engineering (1990)

Answering Queries Using Views
in the Presence of Functional Dependencies

Jun Hong[1], Weiru Liu[1], David Bell[1], and Qingyuan Bai[2]

[1] School of Computer Science, Queen's University Belfast, Belfast BT7 1NN, UK
[2] School of Computing and Mathematics, University of Ulster, Newtownabbey,
Co. Antrim BT37 0QB, UK

Abstract. This paper is concerned with the problem of answering queries using views in the presence of functional dependencies. Previous algorithms for answering queries using views, such as the MiniCon algorithm, have not taken into account the presence of functional dependencies. As a consequence, these algorithms may miss query rewritings in the presence of such dependencies. In this paper, we present an extension of the MiniCon algorithm to handle the presence of functional dependencies while still retaining the main properties of the algorithm and its computational advantage over the other algorithms.

1 Introduction

Data integration from multiple disparate data sources over the Internet has recently attracted a lot of attention in both the database and AI communities [1–4]. Data integration deals with pre-existing and autonomous data sources that have been created independently. It aims to provide a uniform interface to the underlying data sources, which allows users to make queries using the interface in terms of a mediated schema rather than interacting directly with the relevant sources using their individual schemas and combining the data from them. One main stage of data integration is query reformulation in which a user query over the mediated schema is reformulated into queries over the data-source schemas. A typical approach to query reformulation is called *local as view*, in which data sources are described by views over the mediated schema. The objective of query reformulation in this approach is to reformulate the user query using the given views (data source descriptions). The problem of query reformulation using the local-as-view approach is closely related to the broader problem of answering queries using views.

In this paper, we consider the problem of answering conjunctive queries using a large set of conjunctive views in the presence of functional dependencies. In the context of data integration, a number of algorithms, such as the MiniCon algorithm [5], have been developed for query reformulation. However, the presence of functional dependencies in the mediated schema has not been taken into account in these algorithms. As a consequence, these algorithms may miss query rewritings in the presence of such dependencies.

Example 1. Consider the following mediated schema that is used throughout this paper: $student(S, P, Y)$, $taught(P, D)$, and $program(P, C)$. The $student$ relation describes

M. Jackson et al. (Eds.): BNCOD 2005, LNCS 3567, pp. 70–81, 2005.
© Springer-Verlag Berlin Heidelberg 2005

the degree program P a student S takes and the year Y the student is in. The *taught* relation shows the department D in which a degree program P is taught. The *program* relation states the program code C of a degree program P. In the mediated schema, we also assume that a student takes only one degree program and is in a specific year, a degree program is taught in only one department, and a degree program has a unique program code. We therefore have the following functional dependencies in the mediated schema: $student : S \rightarrow P, S \rightarrow Y; taught : P \rightarrow D; program : P \rightarrow C$.

Suppose we have three data sources described by three views:

$v_1(S', Y', D')$:- $student(S', P', Y'), taught(P', D')$.
$v_2(S', P')$:- $student(S', P', Y')$.
$v_3(P', C')$:- $program(P', C')$.

v_1, v_2 and v_3 provide data showing the year and department a student is in, the degree program a student takes, and the program code of a degree program, respectively.

Assume that a user asks which degree program a student takes and in which year the student is: $q(S, P, Y)$:- $student(S, P, Y)$. The following is a correct rewriting of the query: $q'(S', P', Y')$:- $v_1(S', Y', D'), v_2(S', P')$. The rewriting is correct only because the functional dependencies $S \rightarrow P$ and $S \rightarrow Y$ hold in the mediated schema.

Example 2. Suppose that a user asks in which department the degree program $cs401$ is taught: $q(D)$:- $taught(P, D), program(P, C), C = cs401$. The following is a correct rewriting of the query:

$\quad q'(D')$:- $v_1(S', Y', D'), v_2(S', P'), v_3(P', C'), C' = cs401$.

The rewriting is correct only because the functional dependencies, $S \rightarrow P$ and $P \rightarrow D$, hold in the mediated schema. In particular, we have the transitive functional dependency, $S \rightarrow D$.

The previous algorithms for answering queries using views, such as the MiniCon algorithm, however fail to generate the above two rewritings since they do not take into account the presence of functional dependencies in the mediated schema. In this paper, we present an extension of the MiniCon algorithm for answering queries using views in the presence of functional dependencies. The extended MiniCon algorithm retains the main properties of the MiniCon algorithm and its computational advantage over the other algorithms. The paper is organised as follows. Section 2 describes the notation used in the paper and formally defines the problem. Section 3 gives a brief review of the MiniCon algorithm. Section 4 describes our extension of the MiniCon algorithm. Section 5 briefly discusses related work. We finally conclude in Section 6.

2 Preliminaries

Definition 1. (Mediated Schema, Query and View) *A mediated schema consists of a set of database relations over which user queries can be made and views describing data sources can be defined. A query is a conjunctive query of the form:*

$\quad q(\overline{X})$:- $r_1(\overline{X}_1),..., r_n(\overline{X}_n)$

over the mediated schema, where $\overline{X}, \overline{X}_1,...,\overline{X}_n$ are tuples containing either variables or constants and $\overline{X} \subseteq \overline{X}_1 \cup ... \cup \overline{X}_n$. The variables in $\overline{X}$ are the distinguished variables of the query and all the other variables are existential variables. A view is a named query describing a data source.

Definition 2. (Query Containment and Equivalence) *A query Q_1 is contained in a query Q_2, denoted by $Q_1 \sqsubseteq Q_2$, if for any database instance D, the answer of evaluating Q_1 over D, $Q_1(D)$, is a subset of the answer of evaluating Q_2 over D, $Q_2(D)$, that is $Q_1(D) \subseteq Q_2(D)$. Q_1 is equivalent to Q_2, denoted by $Q_1 \equiv Q_2$, if $Q_1 \sqsubseteq Q_2$ and $Q_2 \sqsubseteq Q_1$.*

Definition 3. (Contained Rewriting and Equivalent Rewriting) *Let Q be a query over a mediated schema, $\mathcal{V} = V_1, ..., V_n$ be a set of views over the same mediated schema, and $\mathcal{L}$ be a query language. The query Q' in $\mathcal{L}$ using $\mathcal{V}$ is a contained rewriting of Q if $Q'(\mathcal{V}) \sqsubseteq Q$, and an equivalent rewriting of Q if $Q'(\mathcal{V}) \equiv Q$.*

In the context of data integration, since data sources are often pre-existing and autonomous and have been created independently, it is often not possible for us to generate an equivalent rewriting of a user query. Instead we want to be able to generate the maximally-contained rewriting that provides all the possible answers from a given set of data sources.

Definition 4 (Maximally-Contained Rewriting). *Let Q be a query over a mediated schema, $\mathcal{V} = V_1, ..., V_n$ be a set of views over the same mediated schema, and $\mathcal{L}$ be a query language. The query Q' in $\mathcal{L}$ using $\mathcal{V}$ is a maximally-contained rewriting of Q if (1) $Q'(\mathcal{V}) \sqsubseteq Q$, and (2) there is no query Q'' in $\mathcal{L}$ using $\mathcal{V}$ that is not equivalent to Q', such that $Q'(\mathcal{V}) \sqsubseteq Q''(\mathcal{V}) \sqsubseteq Q$.*

Definition 5 (Functional Dependencies). *A functional dependency $r : a_1, ..., a_n \rightarrow b$ in the mediated schema, where $a_1, ..., a_n$ and b refer to attributes in the relation r, states that for every two tuples t and u in r if $t.a_i = u.a_i$ for $i = 1, ..., n$, then $t.b = u.b$.*

In the presence of functional dependencies in the mediated schema, query containment, query equivalence, contained rewritings, equivalent rewritings, and maximally-contained rewritings can be defined accordingly, taking into account the presence of such dependencies. For simplicity of the paper, we do not introduce any new notation to denote these. But whenever we talk about contained rewritings and maximally-contained rewritings, we always make it clear whether the presence of functional dependencies in the mediated schema has been taken into account.

The Problem: Given a conjunctive query Q over the mediated schema with a set of functional dependencies $\mathcal{F}$, and a set of conjunctive views $\mathcal{V} = V_1, ..., V_n$ also over the mediated schema describing a set of data sources $\mathcal{S} = S_1, ..., S_n$, the problem of answering conjunctive queries using conjunctive views in the presence of functional dependencies is to generate every conjunctive query Q' over $\mathcal{V}$, which is a contained rewriting of Q in the presence of $\mathcal{F}$ such that the union of all the contained rewritings of Q is a maximally-contained rewriting of Q using $\mathcal{V}$ in the presence of $\mathcal{F}$.

3   The MiniCon Algorithm

The MiniCon algorithm [5] is one of the algorithms for answering queries using views developed in the context of data integration. It generates all the contained rewritings of a given query, Q, whose union forms a maximally-contained rewriting of Q. In order to do this, it first finds every view that covers a minimal set of subgoals in Q as required and then combines every set of selected views that covers pair-wise disjoint subsets of subgoals in Q to generate a conjunctive rewriting that is contained in Q. Given a mapping τ from $Vars(Q)$ to $Vars(V)$, where $Vars(Q)$ and $Vars(V)$ denote the sets of variables in a query Q and a view V respectively, a view subgoal g' is said to cover a query subgoal g if $\tau(g) = g'$.

To find a view that covers a minimal set of subgoals in Q as required, the MiniCon algorithm first finds a view V containing a subgoal g' that a subgoal g in Q can be mapped to by a partial mapping from g to g'. A partial mapping from g to g' can be found by finding a unifier θ from g to g', i.e., θ is a variable mapping from g to g' such that $\theta(g) = \theta(g')$. In the meanwhile, the unifier θ also needs to meet the requirement that the distinguished query variables in the query subgoal g are mapped to the distinguished view variables in the view subgoal g'. Once it finds the partial mapping, it then considers the joins between the view V and some of the other subgoals in Q and finds out whether any of the other subgoals in Q need to be mapped to subgoals in V, given that g will be mapped to g'. If so the minimal set of such subgoals is obtained. The requirement for including any of the other query subgoals in the minimal set of subgoals in Q that need to be mapped to subgoals in V is that if any existential query variable in the query subgoal g is part of a join predicate between g and the other query subgoal, and it has not been mapped to a distinguished view variable.

The minimal set of subgoals in Q and the corresponding mapping information are contained in a so called *MiniCon Description* (MCD). If it turns out that a view V does not cover the minimal set of subgoals in Q as required, no MCD will be generated for Q over V. The MCD for Q over V ensures that V covers the minimal set of subgoals in Q that need to be mapped to subgoals in V so that V can be used in a non-redundant rewriting of the corresponding subgoals in Q. Therefore, the MiniCon algorithm deals with combinations of relevant views, each covering a set of subgoals in Q, as candidate rewritings. In the second phase, the MCDs that cover pair-wise disjoint sets of subgoals in Q are combined to generate the rewritings.

The MiniCon algorithm, in particular, considers a mapping from a query to a specialization of a view if no mapping from the query to the view itself exists, where some of the distinguished variables in the view may have been equated. Every MCD has an associated *head homomorphism*. A head homomorphism h on a view V is a mapping from $Vars(V)$ to $Vars(V)$ that is identity on the existential variables, but may equate distinguished variables. A head homomorphism on a view maps it to one of its specialisations.

Definition 6 (MiniCon Descriptions). *A MCD C for a query Q over a view V is a tuple of the form*

$$(h_C, V(Y)_C, \varphi_C, G_C)$$

where:

- h_C *is a head homomorphism on V,*
- $V(Y)_C$ *is the result of applying h_C to the head of V, i.e., $Y = h_C(A)$, where A are the head variables of V,*

- φ_C is a partial mapping from $Vars(Q)$ to $h_C(Vars(V))$,
- G_C is a subset of the subgoals in Q which are covered by some subgoals in $V(Y)_C$ using the mapping φ_C.

In the above definition, φ_C is a mapping from a set of variables in Q to a set of specialized variables in $h_C(V)$ obtained by applying the head homomorphism h_C to the original set of variables in V. G_C is the minimal set of subgoals of Q that are covered by $h_C(V)$ as required, given φ_C.

Property 1 below specifies the exact conditions that need to be satisfied when deciding whether an MCD can be used in a non-redundant rewriting of the query and which query subgoals should be included in G_C. The MiniCon algorithm considers only those MCDs in which h_C is the least restrictive head homomorphism necessary in order to unify the minimal set of subgoals in the query with subgoals in a view.

Property 1. Let C be an MCD for a query Q over a view V. Then C can only be used in a non-redundant rewriting of Q if the following conditions hold:

C1: For each distinguished variable X of Q which is in the domain of φ_C, $\varphi_C(X)$ is a distinguished variable in $h_C(V)$.

C2: If $\varphi_C(X)$ is an existential variable in $h_C(V)$, then for every g, subgoal of Q, that includes X (1) all the variables in g are in the domain of φ_C, and (2) $\varphi_C(g) \in h_C(V)$.

Clause C1 makes sure that every distinguished query variable in the query is substituted by a distinguished view variable in a view that is used in a rewriting of the query. Clause C2 guarantees that if a query variable X is part of a join predicate in the query, which is not enforced by the view, then $\varphi_C(X)$ must be a distinguished view variable so the join predicate can be applied in the rewriting.

Property 2 below states the conditions that need to be satisfied when the MiniCon algorithm combines MCDs to generate non-redundant rewritings of a query so that only the MCDs that cover pair-wise disjoint subsets of subgoals of the query are combined.

Property 2. Given a query q, a set of views $\mathcal{V}$, and the set of MCDs $\mathcal{C}$ for q over $\mathcal{V}$, the only combinations of MCDs that can result in non-redundant rewriting of q are of the form $C_1, ..., C_l$, where

D1. $G_{C_1} \cup ... \cup G_{C_l} = Subgoals(q)$, and
D2. for every $i \neq j$, $G_{C_i} \cap G_{C_j} = \emptyset$.

Example 3. Suppose we have the same mediated schema as in Example 1 and 2, and the following set of data sources:

$v_2(S', P') : -student(S', P', Y')$.
$v_4(S', Y') : -student(S', P', Y')$.
$v_5(P', D') : -taught(P', D')$.
$v_6(S', D') : -student(S', P', Y'), taught(P', D')$.

Consider the following query: $q(S, D) : -student(S, P, Y), taught(P, D)$.

The MiniCon algorithm creates the following MCDs[1]:

$V(Y)_C$	φ_C	G_C
$v_2(S', P')$	$S \rightarrow S'$	1
	$P \rightarrow P'$	
	$Y \rightarrow Y'$	
$v_5(P', D')$	$P \rightarrow P'$	2
	$D \rightarrow D'$	
$v_6(S', D')$	$S \rightarrow S'$	1,2
	$P \rightarrow P'$	
	$Y \rightarrow Y'$	
	$D \rightarrow D'$	

Combining the above MCDs, the MiniCon algorithm generates the following two rewritings only:

$q_1(S', D') : -v_2(S', P'), v_5(P', D').$
$q_3(S', D') : -v_6(S', D').$

4   Extending the MiniCon Algorithm

The MiniCon algorithm does not take into account the presence of functional dependencies in the mediated schema. As we indicated in Section 1, it sometimes misses query rewritings in the presence of such dependencies. In this section, we describe how the MiniCon algorithm can be extended to take into account the presence of functional dependencies and solve the problem of missing query rewritings.

Continue with the examples given in Section 1. In Example 1, we have the query:
$q(S, P, Y) : -student(S, P, Y).$

We also have the following three data sources:
$v_1(S', Y', D') : -student(S', P', Y'), taught(P', D').$
$v_2(S', P') : -student(S', P', Y').$
$v_3(P', C') : -program(P', C').$

The MiniCon algorithm, however, cannot generate the following rewriting:
$q'(S', P', Y') : -v_1(S', Y', D'), v_2(S', P').$

Though we can have a partial mapping so that the only subgoal in q can be covered by the *student* subgoal in v_1. It is easy to see that not all the distinguished variables in the query subgoal can be mapped to the distinguished variables in v_1. So Clause C1 of Property 1 is violated. No MCD for q over v_1 can be used in a non-redundant rewriting of q. However, we can construct a joint view $v_{1,2}$ of v_1 and v_2 that has all the distinguished variables in either v_1 or v_2 as its distinguished variables, and all the subgoals in either v_1 or v_2 as its subgoals. The joint view provides all the distinguished variables that the distinguished variables in the query subgoal can be mapped to. We can therefore have an MCD for q over $v_{1,2}$ covering the only subgoal in q, which satisfies Clause C1 of Property 1 and can be used to generate a non-redundant rewriting of q. Furthermore, when the functional dependencies $S' \rightarrow P'$ and $S' \rightarrow Y'$ hold in the mediated schema, the joint view $v_{1,2}$ is equivalent to the join of v_1 and v_2 because the

---

[1] These are simplified MCDs in which the head homomorphisms on the views are omitted, where each homomorphism simply maps a view variable to itself

join is a lossless-join decomposition of $v_{1,2}$. The join of v_1 and v_2 can then be used to rewrite $v_{1,2}$ in the rewriting to get q'.

In Example 2, we have the query:

$q(D) : -taught(P, D), program(P, C), C = cs401.$

The MiniCon algorithm again fails to generate the following rewriting:

$q'(D) : -v_1(S, D), v_2(S, P), v_3(P, C), C = cs401.$

First of all, we can have a partial mapping so that the *taught* subgoal in q is covered by the *taught* subgoal in v_1 and the only distinguished variable in the query subgoal can be mapped to a distinguished variable in v_1. So Clause C1 of Property 1 is satisfied. However, the existential variable P in the *taught* subgoal in q is in the join predicate with the *program* subgoal in q. But the join predicate has not been enforced in v_1, and the P variable in v_1, which the P variable in q is mapped to, is not a distinguished variable in v_1 either. So Clause C2 of Property 1 is violated. No MCD for q over v_1, can be used in a non-redundant rewriting of q.

Again we can use the joint view $v_{1,2}$ of v_1 and v_2, in which the P variable is a distinguished variable. We can therefore have an MCD for q over $v_{1,2}$ covering the *taught* subgoal in q, which satisfies both Clause C1 and C2 of Property 1 and can be used in a non-redundant rewriting of q. It is easy to see that another MCD for q over v_3 covering the *program* subgoal in q can also be used in a non-redundant rewriting of q. The rewriting q' of q can be generated by first combining both MCDs for q over $v_{1,2}$ and v_3 respectively. Furthermore, the joint view $v_{1,2}$ is equivalent to the join of v_1 and v_2 only when functional dependencies $S' \rightarrow P'$, $P' \rightarrow D'$ and $S' \rightarrow D'$ hold in the mediated schema. Note that the third functional dependency is a transitive functional dependency which can be derived from the first two functional dependencies. So the join of v_1 and v_2 can be used to rewrite $v_{1,2}$ in the generated rewriting to get q'.

In the above examples, what we have revealed is the following. Though we can have a partial mapping so that a subgoal in a query q can be covered by a subgoal in a view v_1, no MCD for q over v_1 can be used in a non-redundant rewriting of q because one of the clauses of Property 1 is violated. However, in the presence of functional dependencies in the mediated schema, it may be possible to create a joint view $v_{1,2}$ of v_1 and another view v_2, over which no MCD for q can be used in a non-redundant rewriting of q either, so that (1) the MCD for q over $v_{1,2}$ satisfies both clauses of Property 1 and therefore can be used in a non-redundant rewriting of q; (2) the joint view $v_{1,2}$ is equivalent to the join of v_1 and v_2, which can then be used to rewrite $v_{1,2}$.

In Section 4.1, we describe how to form an MCD for a query Q over a joint view, which can be used in a non-redundant rewriting of Q. In Section 4.2, we describe how to combine MCDs over either single or joint views to generate the conjunctive rewritings of a query. Our extension of the MiniCon algorithm retains the main properties of the MiniCon algorithm and its computational advantage over the other algorithms.

4.1   Forming MCDs over Joint Views

We first formally define the joint view.

Definition 7. *Given a set of views $v_1(\overline{X}_1)$, $v_2(\overline{X}_2)$, ..., and $v_n(\overline{X}_n)$, their joint view, $v_{1,2,...,n}(\overline{X})$, is formed by having all the distinguished variables in the given views as its distinguished variables and all the subgoals in the given views as its subgoals.*

When forming the joint view from the given views, we make sure that the subgoals in different views with the same predicate are unified to get a single subgoal. As a result, some variables in different views may be mapped to a representative variable in the joint view, where we choose a distinguished variable as the representative variable whenever possible. In Examples 1 and 2, we have the following two views:

$v_1(S', Y', D') : -student(S', P', Y'), taught(P', D').$
$v_2(S', P') : -student(S', P', Y').$

and we can form a joint view:

$v_{1,2}(S', Y', D', P') : -student(S', P', Y'), taught(P', D').$

Note that two $student$ subgoals in v_1 and v_2 are unified to get a single $student$ subgoal in the joint view $v_{1,2}$, in which the variables S', Y', D' and P' are all distinguished variables. Proposition 1 below specifies the exact conditions that we need to consider when we decide whether the join of a set of single views is equivalent to the joint view of the corresponding views.

Proposition 1. *Let $v_{1,2,...,n}(\overline{X})$ be the joint view of views $v_1(\overline{X}_1)$, $v_2(\overline{X}_2)$, ..., and $v_n(\overline{X}_n)$. Given that there exists a set of variables $X_1, ..., X_m$, where $X_1, ..., X_m \in \overline{X}_1$, $X_1, ..., X_m \in \overline{X}_2$, ..., and $X_1, ..., X_m \in \overline{X}_n$, and for any other variable X', where $X' \in \overline{X}_i$ for $1 \leq i \leq n$, the functional dependency $X_1, ..., X_m \to X'$ holds in $v_i(\overline{X}_i)$, then $v_{1,2,...,n}(\overline{X})$ is equivalent to the join of $v_1(\overline{X}_1)$, $v_2(\overline{X}_2)$, ..., and $v_n(\overline{X}_n)$, that is, $v_{1,2,...,n}(\overline{X}) \equiv v_1(\overline{X}_1), v_2(\overline{X}_2), ..., v_n(\overline{X}_n)$.*

It is straightforward that in the presence of the corresponding functional dependencies, the join of $v_1(\overline{X}_1), v_2(\overline{X}_2)$, ..., and $v_n(\overline{X}_n)$ is a lossless-join decomposition of the joint view $v_{1,2,...,n}(\overline{X})$. So we have the equivalence $v_{1,2,...,n}(\overline{X}) \equiv v_1(\overline{X}_1), v_2(\overline{X}_2)$, ..., $v_n(\overline{X}_n)$.

In Examples 1 and 2, as functional dependencies $S' \to Y'$, $S' \to D'$, and $S' \to P'$ hold in the mediated schema, we have the following equivalence:

$v_{1,2}(S', Y', D', P') \equiv v_1(S', Y', D'), v_2(S', P').$

Property 3 below specifies the exact conditions that we need to consider when we decide which views can be used to form a joint view over which an MCD for a query q can be used in a non-redundant rewriting of q.

Property 3. Let $\mathcal{F}$ be a set of functional dependencies in the mediated schema, q be a query, $v_1(\overline{X}_1)$ be a view containing a subgoal that a subgoal in q can be mapped to but no MCD for q over v_1 satisfies both Clause C1 and C2 of Property 1 hence can be used in a non-redundant rewriting of q; Let $v_2(\overline{X}_2)$, ..., and $v_n(\overline{X}_n)$ be some other views over each of which no MCD for q can be used in a non-redundant rewriting of q, and $v_{1,2,...,n}(\overline{X})$ be a joint view of $v_1(\overline{X}_1), v_2(\overline{X}_2)$, ..., and $v_n(\overline{X}_n)$; Let $C_{1,2,...n}$ be an MCD for q over $v_{1,2,...,n}(\overline{X})$. $C_{1,2,...,n}$ can only be used in a non-redundant rewriting of q if the following conditions hold:

C1: For each distinguished variable X of q which is in the domain of $\varphi_{C_{1,2,...,n}}$, $\varphi_{C_{1,2,...,n}}(X)$ is a distinguished variable in $h_{C_{1,2,...,n}}(v_{1,2,...n})$.

C2: If $\varphi_{C_{1,2,...,n}}(X)$ is an existential variable in $h_{C_{1,2,...,n}}(v_{1,2,...,n})$, then for every g, subgoal of q, that includes X, the following conditions must be satisfied: (1) all the variables in g are in the domain of $\varphi_{C_{1,2,...,n}}$, and (2) $\varphi_{C_{1,2,...,n}}(g) \in h_{C_{1,2,...,n}}(v_{1,2,...,n})$.

C3: $v_{1,2,...,n}(\overline{X}) \equiv v_1(\overline{X}_1), v_2(\overline{X}_2), ..., v_n(\overline{X}_n)$ holds in the presence of functional dependencies $\mathcal{F}$.

Clause C1 guarantees that for each distinguished variable X of q, which is in the domain of $\varphi_{C_{1,2,...,n}}$, $\varphi_{C_{1,2,...,n}}(X)$ is a distinguished variable in $h_{C_{1,2,...,n}}(v_{1,2,...,n})$. Clause C2 guarantees that if a variable X of q is part of a join predicate which is not enforced by the joint view $v_{1,2,...,n}$, then X must be a distinguished variable of $v_{1,2,...,n}$ so the join predicate can be applied in the rewriting. C3 guarantees that $v_{1,2,...,n}$ is equivalent to the join of $v_1(\overline{X}_1), v_2(\overline{X}_2), ..., v_n(\overline{X}_n)$ that can then be used to rewrite $v_{1,2,...,n}$. The extended MiniCon algorithm enforces the conditions in Property 3 to generate only those MCDs that satisfy these conditions and all the MCDs generated are used to form conjunctive rewritings.

In Example 1, we have the query: $q(S, P, Y) : -student(S, P, Y)$. and two views v_1 and v_2:

$v_1(S', Y', D') : -student(S', P', Y'), taught(P', D')$.

$v_2(S', P') : -student(S', P', Y')$.

each of which has a subgoal that the *student* subgoal in q can be mapped to. But neither of v_1 and v_2 actually satisfies Clause C1 of Property 1. However, we can have the following joint view:

$v_{1,2}(S', Y', D', P') : -student(S', P', Y'), taught(P', D')$.

and a mapping from q to $v_{1,2}$:

$\varphi_{C_{1,2}} = \{S \to S', P \to P', Y \to Y'\}$

It is easy to see that every distinguished variable in q has been mapped to a distinguished variable in $v_{1,2}$. So Clause C1 of Property 3 is satisfied. Clause C2 does not apply. We also have functional dependencies: $S' \to Y'$, $S' \to D'$, and $S' \to P'$ in the mediated schema. So $v_{1,2}$ is equivalent to the join of v_1 and v_2 and Clause C3 is also satisfied. Now an MCD for q over $v_{1,2}$ can be used in a non-redundant rewriting of q. Furthermore, the join of v_1 and v_2 can be used to rewrite $v_{1,2}$. Therefore, we can have the following rewriting:

$q'(S', P', Y') : -v_1(S', Y', D'), v_2(S', P')$.

In Example 2, we have the query: $q(D) :- taught(P, D), program(P, C), C = cs401$. and the view v_1 that covers the *taught* subgoal in q but does not satisfy Clause C2 of Property 1: $v_1(S', Y', D') :- student(S', P', Y'), taught(P', D')$. Again we can have the joint view $v_{1,2}$ $v_{1,2}(S', Y', D', P') :- student(S', P', Y'), taught(P', D')$. and a mapping from q to $v_{1,2}$: $\varphi_{C_{1,2}} = \{P \to P', D \to D'\}$

Now the variable P' in $v_{1,2}$ is a distinguished view variable. So Clause C2 of Property 3 is satisfied. In the presence of functional dependencies $S' \to Y'$, $S' \to D'$ and $S' \to P'$ in the mediated schema, Clause C3 of Property 3 is also satisfied. It is easy to see that another view v_3 covers the *program* subgoal in q and can also be used in a non-redundant rewriting of q. Therefore we have the following rewriting:

$q'(D') :- v_1(S', Y', D'), v_2(S', P'), v_3(P', C'), C' = cs401$.

Given a subgoal in the query, the extended MiniCon algorithm first finds every view containing a subgoal that the query subgoal can be mapped to and checks whether the view satisfies Property 1. If so an MCD for the query over the view is created, which can then be used in a non-redundant rewriting of the query. In this phrase, the extended MiniCon algorithm is the same as the MiniCon algorithm. Otherwise, if a view can be found which contains a subgoal that the query subgoal can be mapped to but the view does not satisfy either Clause C1 or C2 of Property 1, the algorithm finds other views to form, together with the given view, a joint view that satisfies Property 3. Clause C1 and C2 of Property 3 are the same as Clause C1 and C2 of Property 1 while Clause C3 of Property 3 further ensures that the joint view is equivalent to the join of the corresponding views.

When finding other views, together with the given view, to form a joint view, attention is paid to those views that can help to satisfy either Clause C1 or C2 of Property 1 which the given view failed to satisfy. We then also make sure that the joint view that consists of the selected views and the given view satisfies Clause C3 of Property 3. A joint view formed this way can therefore satisfy Property 3 and an MCD for the query over the joint view can be created, which can then be used in a non-redundant rewriting of the query. The joint view is added to the set of existing views.

4.2   Combining MCDs over Either Single or Joint Views

In the secodn phrase, the extended MiniCon algorithm finds valid combinations of MCDs formed in the first phrase and creates conjunctive rewritings of the query. The maximally-contained rewriting of the query is a union of conjunctive rewritings.

Property 4 specifies the exact conditions a combination of MCDs must satisfy so that it can be used to create a conjunctive rewriting of the query. The extended Mini-Con algorithm enforces the conditions in Property 4 to combine only those MCDs that satisfy these conditions.

Property 4. Given a query q, a set of views $\mathcal{V}$, a set of functional dependencies $\mathcal{F}$ in the mediated schema, and the set of MCDs $\mathcal{C}$ formed by the first phase of the extended algorithm for q over $\mathcal{V}'$ that may also contain joint views apart from the single views in $\mathcal{V}$ in the presence of $\mathcal{F}$, the only combinations of MCDs that can result in non-redundant rewriting of q are of the form $C_1,...,C_l$, where
   D1. $G_{C_1} \cup ... \cup G_{C_l} = Subgoals(q)$, and
   D2. for every $i \neq j$, $G_{C_i} \cap G_{C_j} = \emptyset$.

For creating the rewriting q', the extended MiniCon algorithm works the exactly the same as the second phase of the MiniCon algorithm, simply treating joint views as single views. In the last step of the extended MiniCon algorithm, it however needs to replace every joint view in q' with its correct rewriting.

Theorem 1 states the properties of the extended MiniCon algorithm.

Theorem 1. *Given a conjunctive query q and a set of conjunctive views $\mathcal{V}$, in the presence of functional dependencies $\mathcal{F}$ in the mediated schema, the extended MiniCon algorithm is sound in the sense that every conjunctive rewriting q' that is generated by the algorithm is contained in q. In terms of completeness, the algorithm can generate the union of conjunctive rewritings that is a maximally-contained rewriting of q using $\mathcal{V}$ in the presence of $\mathcal{F}$ only if there exists such a maximally-contained rewriting. Sometimes, such a maximally-contained rewriting may not exist and recursive rewritings may be necessary in order to obtain a maximally-contained rewriting.*

The proofs of Properties 3 and 4 follow the correctness proof of the extended Mini-Con algorithm. In terms of computational complexity of the extended MiniCon algorithm, creating extra joint views does not involve a significant increase of computational complexity compared to the MiniCon algorithm. Even in the worst case, in the first phase, the running time of the extended MiniCon algorithm is only roughly a number of times of the running time of the MiniCon algorithm. In the second phase, the running time of the extended MiniCon algorithm is virtually the same as that of the MiniCon algorithm. The correctness proof and complexity analysis of the extended MiniCon algorithm are omitted in this paper due to space limitation. For details, refer to the extended version of the paper.

5   Related Work

The problem of answering queries using views has relevance to a wide variety of data management problems [6]. In the context of data integration, a number of algorithms, such as the bucket algorithm [1], the inverse-rules algorithm [7, 8] and the MiniCon algorithm [5], have been developed for the problem of reformulating conjunctive queries using conjunctive views. However, these algorithms have not taken into account the presence of functional dependencies in the mediated schema. As a consequence, these algorithms may miss query rewritings in the presence of these integrity constraints.

Some algorithms have recently been developed for answering queries using views in the presence of functional dependencies [9–11]. These algorithms can in general be viewed as the extensions of the inverse-rules algorithm, and they inherit the performance costs of the inverse-rules algorithm. In [5], it has been proven that the inverse-rules algorithm does not scale up and is significantly outperformed by the scalable Mini-Con algorithm. In this paper, we have presented an extension of the MiniCon algorithm to handle the presence of functional dependencies while retaining the main properties of the MiniCon algorithm and its significantly lower performance costs.

In addition to these algorithms, algorithms have been developed for conjunctive queries with comparison predicates [12, 13], recursive queries [10], queries over disjunctive views [14], queries over conjunctive views with negation [15], queries and views with grouping and aggregation [16, 17], queries over semi-structured data [18, 19], and OQL queries [20]. Duschka et al. [10] showed that in the presence of functional and full dependencies there does not always exist a non-recursive maximally-contained query rewriting. An algorithm [10] has been developed that deals with limitations on data sources, which are described by a set of allowed binding patterns. In this case it is known that recursive query rewritings may be necessary [3]. The algorithm constructs a recursive maximally-contained query rewriting.

6   Conclusions

In this paper, we have considered the problem of answering queries using views in the presence of functional dependencies. We have presented an extension of the MiniCon algorithm to deal with the functional dependencies in the mediated schema. The underlying idea is that in the presence of functional dependencies, some views can be joined with other views to form joint views for which the corresponding MCDs can be used in the non-redundant rewritings of the query, thus avoiding the problem of missing queries in the presence of functional dependencies that the previous algorithms may have. Our extension of the MiniCon algorithm retains the main properties of the algorithm. The extension does not involve any significant increase in performance costs and retains the computational competitiveness of the MiniCon algorithm over the other algorithms.

In future work, we will further explore the possibilities of extending the MiniCon algorithm to deal with other types of integrity constraints in the mediated schema, such as inclusion dependencies and domain dependencies.

References

1. Levy, A.Y., Rajaraman, A., Ordille, J.J.: Querying heterogeneous information sources using source descriptions. In: VLDB. (1996) 251–262
2. Duschka, O.M., Genesereth, M.R.: Query planning in informaster. In: Proc. of the ACM Symposium on Applied Computing. (1997) 109–111
3. Kwok, C.T., Weld, D.S.: Planning to gather information. In: AAAI. (1996) 32–39
4. Lambrecht, E., Kambhampati, S., Gnanaprakasam, S.: Optimizing recursive information gathering plans. In: IJCAI. (1999) 1204–1211
5. Pottinger, R., Halevy, A.: Minicon: A scalable algorithm for answering queries using views. VLDB Journal **10** (2001) 182–198
6. Halevy, A.: Answering queries using views: a survey. VLDB Journal **10** (2001) 270–294
7. Qian, X.: Query folding. In: ICDE. (1996) 48–55
8. Duschka, O.M., Genesereth, M.R.: Answering recursive queries using views. In: PODS. (1997) 109–116
9. Duschka, O.M., Levy, A.Y.: Recursive plans for information gathering. In: IJCAI. (1997) 778–784
10. Duschka, O.M., Genesereth, M.R., Levy, A.Y.: Recursive query plans for data integration. Journal of Logic Programming **43** (2000) 49–73
11. Gryz, J.: Query rewriting using views in the presence of functional and inclusion dependencies. Information Systems **24** (1999) 597–612
12. Yang, H.Z., Larson, P.A.: Query transformation for psj-queries. In: VLDB. (1987) 245–254
13. Afrati, F.N., Li, C., Mitra, P.: Answering queries using views with arithmetic comparisons. In: PODS. (2002) 209–220
14. Duschka, O.M., Genesereth, M.R.: Query planning with disjunctive sources. In: Proc. of AAAI Workshop on AI and Information Integration. (1998)
15. Flesca, S., Greco, S.: Rewriting queries using views. IEEE Transactions on Knowledge and Data Engineering **13** (2001) 980–995
16. Gupta, A., Harinarayan, V., Quass, D.: Aggregate-query processing in data warehousing environments. In: VLDB. (1995) 358–369
17. Srivastava, D., Dar, S., Jagadish, H.V., Levy, A.Y.: Answering sql queries using materialized views. In: VLDB. (1996) 318–329
18. Papakonstantinou, Y., Vassalos, V.: Query rewriting for semi-structured data. In: SIGMOD. (1999) 455–466
19. Calvanese, D., Giacomo, G.D., Lenzerini, M., Vardi, M.: Rewriting of regular expressions and regular path queries. In: PODS. (1999) 194–204
20. Florescu, D., Raschid, L., Valduriez, P.: A methodology for query reformulation in cis using semantic knowledge. International Journal of Intelligent and Cooperative Information Systems **5** (1996) 431–468

LAX: An Efficient Approximate XML Join Based on Clustered Leaf Nodes for XML Data Integration

Wenxin Liang[1] and Haruo Yokota[2]

[1] Department of Computer Science, Tokyo Institute of Technology
2-12-1 Oh-okayama, Meguro-ku, Tokyo 152-8552, Japan
wxliang@de.cs.titech.ac.jp
[2] Global Scientific Information and Computer Center, Tokyo Institute of Technology
2-12-1 Oh-okayama, Meguro-ku, Tokyo 152-8552, Japan
yokota@cs.titech.ac.jp

Abstract. Recently, more and more data are published and exchanged by XML on the Internet. However, different XML data sources might contain the same data but have different structures. Therefore, it requires an efficient method to integrate such XML data sources so that more complete and useful information can be conveniently accessed and acquired by users.

The tree edit distance is regarded as an effective metric for evaluating the structural similarity in XML documents. However, its computational cost is extremely expensive and the traditional wisdom in join algorithms cannot be applied easily. In this paper, we propose LAX (**L**eaf-clustering based **A**pproximate **X**ML join algorithm), in which the two XML document trees are clustered into subtrees representing independent items and the similarity between them is determined by calculating the similarity degree based on the leaf nodes of each pair of subtrees. We also propose an effective algorithm for clustering the XML document for LAX. We show that it is easily to apply the traditional wisdom in join algorithms to LAX and the join result contains complete information of the two documents. We then do experiments to compare LAX with the tree edit distance and evaluate its performance using both synthetic and real data sets. Our experimental results show that LAX is more efficient in performance and more effective for measuring the approximate similarity between XML documents than the tree edit distance.

1 Introduction

The eXtensible Markup Language (XML) is increasingly recognized as the de facto standard for representing and exchanging data on the Internet, because it can represent different kinds of data from multiple sources. Recently, more and more data, especially bioinformatics and bibliography data such as MAGE [12], DBLP [19] and ACM SIGMOD Record [1], are published by XML on the Internet. However, the same data might have different structures and contents in different XML data sources. Thus, it is paramount to integrate such data sources so that users can conveniently access and acquire more complete and

M. Jackson et al. (Eds.): BNCOD 2005, LNCS 3567, pp. 82–97, 2005.

useful information. However, the integration of XML data from multiple sources is not an easy task, because XML documents from different sources might have different structures even though they represent the same information.

The Document Type Descriptor (DTD) is regarded as a useful tool to obtain the structural information from XML documents [2, 7]. However, even if XML data sources have the same DTDs, they may not have identical tree structures due to the repeating and optional elements and attributes [8, 9, 14]. Therefore, an effective approximate XML join algorithm, which is able to measure the similarity between XML documents without considering DTDs, becomes of great importance to solve the problem of integrating multiple XML data sources.

Example 1. Fig. 1 shows an example of two XML documents with different DTDs[1]. Although these two documents are structurally different, they represent the similar data. Moreover, in terms of the related data items of the two documents (i.e. "article" here in this example), one document may have some information what the other does not have. For instance, **pages** in (a); and **volume** in (b).

The tree edit distance is currently verified as an effective metric for measuring the structural similarity in XML documents [8, 14]. However, the computational cost of the tree edit distance is extremely high. Besides, the traditional wisdom in join algorithms (sort merge, hash joins etc) is of difficulty to be applied to this area [8].

The main contributions of this paper are as follows:

– Computing tree edit distance between two XML documents is a very expensive operation. To solve this problem, we propose an efficient join algorithm LAX (**L**eaf-clustering based **A**pproximate **X**ML join algorithm), in which the two XML document trees are clustered into subtrees representing independent items and the similarity between them is determined by calculating the similarity degree based on the leaf nodes of each pair of subtrees. We also present an algorithm for effectively clustering the XML document into independent items for LAX.

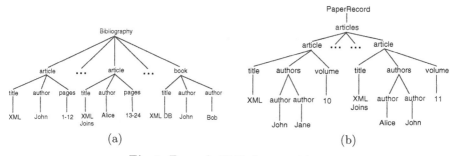

Fig. 1. Example XML document trees

---

[1] Associating to our interested real bibliography XML data, we make the DTD in Fig. 1(a) similar to that of DBLP, and the DTD in Fig. 1(b) similar to that of ACM SIGMOD Record

- The traditional wisdom in join algorithms can be easily applied to LAX, because the join operation of LAX is the same as traditional joins in RDBs. Besides, the integration of the hit subtrees can make the join results contain complete information from the two XML documents been joined.
- We do experiments to evaluate LAX using both synthetic and real data sets, investigating how the number of leaf nodes and the number of clustered subtrees affect the performance of LAX. We also do experiments to compare LAX with the tree edit distance. The experimental results show that our algorithm is more efficient in performance and more effecitive for measuring the approximate similarity between XML documents than the tree edit distance.

The rest of this paper is arranged as follows: Section 2 briefly introduces the work related to the issues addressed in this paper. In Section 3, we briefly introduce the tree edit distance, and we provide basic definitions necessary for the proposed algorithm and state the problem considered in this paper. In Section 4, we propose and discuss LAX. In Section 5, we compare LAX with the tree edit distance evaluate its performance by experiments. In the end, Section 6 concludes the paper and outlines the future work.

2   Related Work

An XML document can be modeled as an ordered labeled tree [18]. Each element in the XML document corresponds to a node in the ordered labeled tree labeled with the element tag name. A lot of work has been done to solve the problem of measuring the edit distance between such trees [3, 4, 13, 16, 17, 21, 22]. A general definition of the distance between ordered labeled trees is presented by using the tree edit distance that is defined as the minimum cost edit operations (insertions, deletions and substitutions) required to transform one tree to another [22]. The tree edit distance is considered to be an effective metric for calculating the structural similarity in XML documents [8, 14]. However, the tree edit distance is a very expensive operation and the traditional wisdom in join algorithms (sort merge, hash joins etc) is not easy to be extended to this application field [8].

To avoid the expensive tree edit distance operation as much as possible, S. Guha, et al. [8] developed lower and upper bounds as inexpensive filters for the tree edit distance operation. However, when the upper bound is greater than the threshold distance τ and, at the same time, the lower bound is less than τ, the expensive tree edit distance still must be calculated.

Besides, XML and its schema languages do not provide any semantic information. A number of work related to XML schema matching and integration has been studied by many researchers [5, 6, 11, 15, 20]. Generally, schema matching is an important and difficult problem for many database applications such as schema integration, data warehousing, and E-business [15]. From the XML data integration point of view, the problem of semantic heterogeneities is still a pervasive and paramount issue. However, many real XML documents contain repeating elements, `articlesTuple` in `SigmodRecord.xml` [1] for example. Taking such XML documents as the target, the approximate similarity degree between them can be effectively determined by computing the similarity degree of clustered subtrees (rooted at the repeating elements) even without considering the semantic heterogeneity. In Section 4, we will mention this problem associated with our algorithm.

3 Preliminaries

3.1 Tree Edit Distance

A well formed XML document can be parsed into an ordered labeled tree, in which the tree structure represents nesting of the elements and node labels records the contents of the elements by element tags, attribute names, attribute values and PCDATA values.

Definition 1 (XML Document Tree). An XML document tree T is an ordered labeled tree parsed from an XML document.

Let T_1 and T_2 be two XML document trees, the tree edit distance between them is defined as follows:

Definition 2 (Tree Edit Distance). Given two XML document trees T_1 and T_2, the tree edit distance, TEDist(T_1, T_2), is de ned as the m inim um cost edit operations (insertions, deletions and substitutions) that transform s one tree to the other.

Assume each node label is a symbol chosen from an alphabet Σ of size $|\Sigma|$. Let $\lambda \notin \Sigma$ denote the null symbol. An edit operation can be represented as $\gamma(a \rightarrow b)$. $\gamma(a \rightarrow b)$ is an insert operation if $a = \lambda$, a delete operation if $b = \lambda$, and a substitute operation if $a \neq \lambda$ and $b \neq \lambda$.

The tree edit distance TEDist(T_1, T_2) can be figured out by a mapping M between the nodes of the two trees. Formal description of the mapping and algorithms for computing the tree edit distance are available in [22].

Given an XML document tree T, let $d(T)$ denote its depth. For two document trees T_b and T_t, and let t_b and t_t be any pair of subtree. Then the time complexity of the computation of the tree edit distance can be bounded by the following equation [22]:

$$O(\sum_{i=1}^{|T_1|}\sum_{j=1}^{|T_2|}|t_{1i}|\times|t_{2j}|) = O(\sum_{i=1}^{|T_1|}|t_{1i}|\times\sum_{j=1}^{|T_2|}|t_{2j}|) = O(|T_1|\times|T_2|\times d(T_1)\times d(T_2)) \quad (1)$$

For document trees of size $O(n)$, in the worst case, it is an $O(n^4)$ operation.

3.2 Basic Definitions for LAX

Notation. Let T_b and T_t be two XML document trees, where b denotes base, and t denotes target. Assume T_b and T_t are clustered into k_b and k_t sub-trees $t_{bi}(1 \leq i \leq k_b)$ and $t_{tj}(1 \leq j \leq k_t)$, as shown in Fig. 2, respectively.

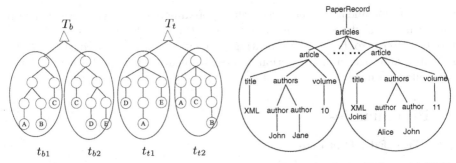

Fig. 2. Example clustering of XML document trees

Fig. 3. Example of a well-clustered XML document

Definition 3 (Subtree Similarity Degree). For each pair of subtrees t_{bi} and t_{tj}, let t_{bi} be the base subtree, and t_{tj} be the target one. Let n_{bi} and n_{tj} represent the number of leaf nodes of t_{bi} and t_{tj}. If there are n pairs of leaf nodes of the two subtrees having the same PCDATA values, then the similarity degree of subtrees t_{bi} and t_{tj}, $S(t_{bi}, t_{tj})$ is defined as follows:

$$S(t_{bi}, t_{tj}) = \frac{n}{n_{bi}} \times 100 \ (\%) \tag{2}$$

Definition 4 (Matched Subtree). In each join loop i, for the base subtree t_{bi} and each target subtree t_{tj} $(1 \leq j \leq k_t)$, the subtree similarity degree $S(t_{bi}, t_{tj})$ is computed one by one. The matched subtree T_{Mi} is defined as the pair of subtrees t_{bi} and t_{tj} that has the maximum subtree similarity degree in that join loop.

Definition 5 (Tree Similarity Degree). Let the base document tree T_b that has the less number of subtrees be the outer loop and the target one T_t be the inner loop. In each join loop i, let the similarity degree of each matched subtree be recorded into an array $S_M[i]$. The tree similarity degree $S(T_b, T_t)$ is defined as follows:

$$S(T_b, T_t) = \frac{\sum_{i=1}^{k_b} S_M[i]}{k_b} \times 100 \ (\%) \tag{3}$$

3.3   Problem Statement

Let S_b and S_t be two XML data sources. We are pursuing an algorithm to execute join operations, based on the leaf nodes of each pair of clustered subtrees of the XML documents, using similarity degree as a join predicate. The main problem addressed in this paper is formally defined as follows:

Problem 1 (Leaf-clustering based Approximate XML Joins). Given two XML data sources, S_b and S_t, a user defined threshold τ, and the tree similarity degree $S(T_b, T_t)$ accessing the distance between pairs of XML documents trees T_b and T_t parsed from two documents $d_b \in S_b$ and $d_t \in S_t$. The leaf-clustering based approximate join operation outputs all pairs of documents $(d_b, d_t) \in S_b \times S_t$, such that $S(T_b, T_t) \geq \tau$.

In the tree edit distance, for any two XML documents with different DTDs that have the same number of nodes, the tree edit distances of them do not change a lot when the PCDATA values of the leaf nodes change. However, in LAX, the change of the values of the leaf nodes might change the values of the tree similarity degrees in a large scale. Therefore, pairs of XML documents that have the same tree edit distance might have different tree similarity degrees. Besides, because in LAX the XML document is clustered into subtrees representing independent items, the matched subtrees that have large enough subtree similarity degrees still can be integrated even though the tree edit distance of the two whole documents exceeds the threshold.

4   LAX

4.1   Clustering

An XML document can be generally divided into many independent items by clustering it into subtrees at some specific element nodes. However, it is not easy to cluster an XML document tree into subtrees representing independent items. As a matter of fact, a well-clustered document requires that each clustered subtree meets the following conditions.

1. Each subtree represents only one independent item; that is, a subtree does not include any information of other items.
2. One independent item is clustered into one subtree; that is, one item does not have more than one corresponding subtrees.
3. Each subtree includes the information of an item as much as possible. In other words, the leaf nodes belonging to that item should be included in the subtree as much as possible.

Example 2. Fig. 3 shows an example of a well-clustered document. The document tree is clustered into two subtrees at the element nodes **article** so that each subtree represents complete information of an independent article.

In order to include more information of an independent item, an element is not supposed to be selected as the spot for clustering, if 1) it has only one child, and 2) the distance to its furthest child is less than 3. Before we treat of the algorithm for clustering XML document trees, we give the following definitions.

Definition 6 (Candidate Element). An element is a candidate element, if it has at least 2 children, or the distance to its furthest child is at least 3.

Definition 7 (Link Branch). A branch between two candidate elements is a link branch.

Definition 8 (Top-down Path). A top-down path is defined as a path from the top candidate element to the bottom one via link branches.

```
Algorithm ClusterXMLDoc(T) {
Input: XML document tree T
Output: Clustering spots for T
Let N be the number of top-down paths, and M[i] be the
number of candidate elements in the i-th path.
    for (i = 1 to N) {
        ClusteringSpot[i] = null;
        w_max[i] = 0;
        for (j = 1 to M[i]) {
            w=n[j] × d[j]^φ;
            if ( w_max[i] < w) {
                w_max[i] = w;
                ClusteringSpot[i] = E(n[j], d[j]);
            }
        }
        return CluteringSpot[i];
    }
}
```

Fig. 4. Algorithm ClusterXMLDoc

Only one candidate element should be selected as the place for clustering in one top-down path. Generally, we consider a candidate element as a proper spot for clustering, if it has more link branches (i.e. there are more candidate elements among its children), and it is at higher level of the document tree (i.e. it is far from its furthest child). To effectively find the most appropriate spot for clustering, we define the weighting factor for evaluating each candidate element in a top-down path as follows.

Definition 9 (Weighting Factor). For a candidate element $E(n, d)$, let n denote the number of link branches below it, and d denote the distance to its furthest child. The weighting factor w is defined as follows:

$$w = n \times d^\phi \qquad (0 < \phi \le 1) \qquad (4)$$

where ϕ is an adjustable constant[2].

Then we define the **clustering spot** that indicates the place for clustering using the weighting factor w as follows.

Definition 10 (Clustering Spot). In each top-down path of an XML document tree T, the clustering spot, indicating the place for clustering, is the candidate element $E(n, d)$ that has the maximum w in that top-down path. If two or more candidate elements have the same value of w in the same path, the one who has the maximum d is chosen as the clustering spot.

---

[2] For the sake of simplicity, we set $\phi = 1$ for the examples in this paper. In fact, documents from different sources may require different ϕ to achieve better clusterings. In the real application, ϕ can be dynamically optimized by experiments

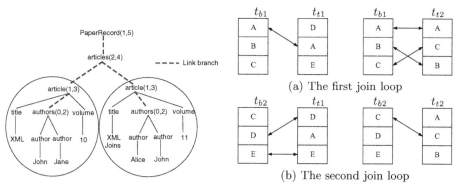

Fig. 5. Example of clustering using Algorithm *ClusterXMLDoc*

Fig. 6. Example of calculating subtree similarity degrees

In a top-down path, the subtree can be simply generated by deleting the link branch below the clustering spot; that is, the root of the subtree is the child element of the clustering spot in that top-down path. The algorithm for determining the clustering spots for an XML document tree is shown in Fig. 4 .

Example 3. Fig. 5 shows a simple example of clustering an XML document tree by Algorithm ClusterXMLDoc. There are two top-down paths in the document tree. In the left path, {PaperRecord(1,5), articles(2,4), article(1,3), authors(0,2)}, the clustering spot is the candidate element articles(2,4) because of the maximum $w = 2 \times 4 = 8$. Similarly, the clustering spot in the right path is the same element, articles(2,4). Therefore, the document tree can be clustered into the two circled subtrees shown in Fig. 5.

4.2 Join Algorithm

Let S_b and S_t be two XML data sources, and each $d_b \in S_b$ and $d_t \in S_t$ be parsed into XML document trees T_b and T_t. Assume T_b and T_t are clustered into k_b and k_t subtrees t_{bi} and t_{tj} by using Algorithm ClusterXMLDoc. Given a user-defined threshold τ, the **L**eaf-clustering based **A**pproximate **XML** join algorithm (LAX) is illustrated by Fig. 7.

Example 4. Fig. 6 shows the join process by LAX for the two XML documents trees T_b and T_t in Fig. 2. Let T_b be the outer loop and T_t be the inner loop for the join operation. In the first join loop shown in Fig. 6 (a), the similarity degrees of each pair of subtrees can be calculated as follows:

$$s(t_{b1}, t_{t1}) = \frac{1}{3} \times 100\% = 33.3\%$$

$$s(t_{b1}, t_{t2}) = \frac{3}{3} \times 100\% = 100\%$$

Then the similarity of the matched subtree,
$S_M[1] = Max\{S(t_{b1}, t_{t1}), S(t_{b1}, t_{t2})\} = 100\%$. In the same way, we have $S_M[2] =$

```
Algorithm LAX {
Input: XML data source S_b and S_t
Output: Pairs of XML documents (d_b, d_t)
    for each d_b ∈ S_b {
        Parse d_b into T_b;
        ClusterXMLDoc(T_b);
        for each d_t ∈ S_t {
            Parse d_t into T_t;
            ClusterXMLDoc(T_t);
            Sum = 0;
            for (i = 1 to k_b) {
                S_M[i] = 0;
                for (j = 1 to k_t) {
                    Calculate S(t_bi, t_tj);
                    S_M[i] = Max(S_M[i], S(t_bi, t_tj));
                }
                Sum = Sum + S_M[i];
            }
            if(Sum/k_b ≥ τ) {
                return (d_b, d_t);
            }
        }
    }
}
```

Fig. 7. Algorithm LAX

66.7% for the second join loop. Finally, the tree similarity degree $S(T_b, T_t)$ can be calculated by equation (3), i.e., $S(T_b, T_t) = \frac{S_M[1]+S_M[2]}{2} \times 100\% = \frac{1+0.667}{2} \times 100\% = 83.4\%$. If $S(T_b, T_t) \geq \tau$, the two documents should be output as the final result.

4.3   Discussion

Cost. Let two XML document trees T_b and T_t be clustered into k_b and k_t subtrees, respectively. For $i = 1$ to k_b, assume each subtree t_{bi} has α_i leaf nodes, and for $j = 1$ to k_t, each subtree t_{tj} has β_j leaf nodes. Then the total computational cost of LAX can be figured out by the following equation:

$$C = \sum_{i=1}^{k_b} \sum_{j=1}^{k_t} \alpha_i \times \beta_j \tag{5}$$

If the sizes of the two XML document trees are both $O(n)$, in the worst case, LAX is an $O(n^2)$ operation.

Traditional Wisdom in Join Algorithms. The traditional wisdom in join algorithm can be easily applied to LAX, because the join operations based on the

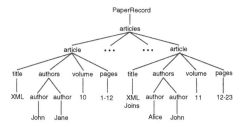

Fig. 8. Example of an output of *LAX*

clustered leaf nodes in LAX are just the same as the traditional joins in an RDB. Therefore, LAX may achieve more efficiency by using traditional techniques for join algorithms. For example, the total cost of LAX using hash joins can be calculated as follows:

$$C_{HASH} = \sum_{i=1}^{k_b} \sum_{j=1}^{k_t} (C_{gen}(\alpha_i) + C_{hash}(\alpha_i + \beta_j) + C_{comp}(\beta_j)) \qquad (6)$$

where, C_{gen} represents the cost of making entries for subtree t_{bi}; C_{hash} stands for the cost of using the hash function to the two subtrees; and C_{comp} means the cost of comparisons in the probe phase.

Output of LAX

Definition 11 (Hit Subtree). In the *ith* join loop, let the similarity degree of the matched subtree T_{Mi} be $S_M[i]$. Given a threshold T $(0 < T \leq 1)$, the matched subtree is a hit subtree, if $S_M[i] \geq T$.

Given two XML document trees T_1 and T_2, if the tree similarity degree of T_1 and T_2, $S(T_1, T_2) \geq \tau$, the two XML document trees can be integrated at each hit subtrees. Fig. 8 shows an example of the output XML document from joining the two XML documents in Fig. 1 using LAX, in which the whole information of the articles from the two documents been joined is included. Thus, users can conveniently acquire more complete and useful information of the articles by accessing the output document.

Issues to be Considered. In our algorithm, we just compare the PCDATA values of the leaf nodes without considering their semantic similarities. The more precise join can be achieved by using techniques of semantic matching. Another issue is that in case the similarity degrees of one subtree in the outer loop and several subtrees in the inner loop happen to be the same, how to choose the right pair? In this case, one effective solution is to compare the common parents of the leaf nodes to decide which subtree is the right one. However, there still exists semantic problem when comparing the common parents.

5   Experimental Evaluation

In this section, we conduct experiments to observe the efficiency and effectiveness of our algorithm comparing with the tree edit distance. We also perform experiments to investigate how the number of leaf nodes and the number of clustered subtrees affect the performance of our algorithm.

5.1   Data Set Used

We used both real and synthetic data sets to perform our experiments. For a synthetic data set, we used IBM XML generator available through AlphaWorks [10]. The XML generator can randomly generate XML documents by inputting DTDs. In our experiments, we utilized SigmodRecord.dtd [1] to randomly generate XML documents of different sizes by changing the two parameters: `MaxLevels` and `MaxRepeats`. The size range of the generated XML documents was from 1 to 150 KB (about 0 to 5000 nodes).

For the real data set, we made use of the XML documents of `OrdinaryIssue Page`, `ProceedingsPage` and `SigmodRecord` from the XML version of ACM SIGMOD record [1], and the XML document of the DBLP database [19].

5.2   Experimental Environment

Our experiments were done under the environment shown in Table 1.

Table 1. Experimental Environment

CPU	Intel Pentium IV 2.80GHz
Memory	1.0 GB
OS	MS Windows XP Professional
Programming Environment	Sun JDK 1.4.2

5.3   Comparing LAX with Tree Edit Distance

Efficiency. To evaluate the efficiency of our algorithm, we compared the time to computer the tree similarity degree for a pair of XML documents by our algorithm with that of tree edit distance using synthetic data sets. Because the tree edit distance is extremely time-consuming, in this paper we only used the pair of documents whose total number of nodes is less than 1200.

From Fig. 9, we observe that our algorithm is overwhelmingly faster comparing to the tree edit distance when the number of nodes is more than 500, corresponding with our analytical expectations. Therefore, we can consider that our algorithm is more efficient than the tree edit distance for measuring the similarity between XML documents.

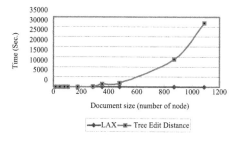
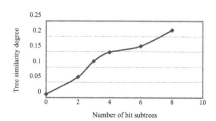

Fig. 9. Time for computing tree edit distance and tree similarity degree

Fig. 10. Tree similarity degree increases proportionally to the number of hit subtrees

Table 2. The number of nodes and clustered subtrees included in each fragment

	sigmod.xml	dblp1.xml	dblp2.xml	dblp3.xml	dblp4.xml	dblp5.xml	dblp6.xml
No. of nodes	194	196	196	193	202	198	202
No. of subtrees	17	9	9	9	9	9	9

Effectiveness. In our algorithm, the similarity degree is defined as the quantitative measurement for calculating the subtree similarity degree. The larger the similarity degree is, the higher the probability of the subtrees being the same is, even though the element nodes above the leaf nodes have different structures or values.

To verify the effectiveness of our algorithm for determining the similarity between XML documents, we calculated the tree similarity degrees using LAX and compared them with the tree edit distances of the same pairs of XML documents. In our experiments, we utilized the real XML documents, DBLP.xml [19] and SigmodRecord.xml [1]. Because the calculation of the tree edit distance is extremely time-consuming, we divided the SigmodRecord.xml into small fragments. Each fragment contains the entire articles of one issue. In the same way, we divided the DBLP.xml into fragments contains almost the same number of nodes as those of SigmodRecord.xml. Here we show the result of an example using one fragment of SigmodRecord.xml[3] and six fragments of DBLP.xml[4]. Table 2 shows the number of nodes and clustered subtrees (each subtree contains complete information of an article) included in each fragment. Table 3 shows the results of the tree edit distance and tree similarity degree of each pair of fragments. From the results, we can observe that the tree edit distance of each pair of fragments is almost the same. However, the tree similarity degree increases proportionally to the number of hit subtrees as shown in Fig. 10. That is to say, our algorithm can effectively distinguish the similarity differences between pairs of XML documents even they have the same tree edit distance. Table 4

---

[3] Vol.20, No.3, SIGMOD Record 1991

[4] To obtain different number of hit subtrees, in this paper we specially chose the fragments that contain different number of articles from Vol.20, No.3, SIGMOD Record 1991

Table 3. Result of each pair of fragments

	Tree edit distance	Tree similarity degree	No. of hit subtrees
$sigmod.xml \times dblp1.xml$	216	0.149	4
$sigmod.xml \times dblp2.xml$	216	0.120	3
$sigmod.xml \times dblp3.xml$	210	0.067	2
$sigmod.xml \times dblp4.xml$	219	0.011	0
$sigmod.xml \times dblp5.xml$	216	0.220	8
$sigmod.xml \times dblp6.xml$	220	0.169	6

Table 4. Result of the matched subtrees of $sigmod.xml \times dblp6.xml$

	$T_M[1]$	$T_M[2]^*$	$T_M[3]^*$	$T_M[4]$	$T_M[5]^*$	$T_M[6]^*$	$T_M[7]^*$	$T_M[8]$	$T_M[9]^*$
N_{sigmod}	25	21	21	23	23	21	23	23	21
N_{dblp}	12	10	10	12	12	10	12	14	10
S_M	0.083	0.2	0.2	0.091	0.273	0.2	0.273	0.0	0.2
$TEDist$	24	20	20	22	22	20	22	23	20

shows the detailed results of each matched subtree of $sigmod.xml \times dblp6.xml$, where $T_M[i]$ denotes the matched subtree, $*$ indicates the hit subtree, N_{sigmod} and N_{dblp} represent the number of nodes in each subtree of the matched subtree of $sigmod.xml$ and $dblp6.xml$, respectively, and S_M and TEDist denote the similarity degree and the edit distance of each matched subtree, respectively. From the results, we can see that it is difficult for the tree edit distance to determine the hit subtree. However, our algorithm can effectively determine the hit subtree by setting an appropriate threshold T. Therefore, by integrating the hit subtrees, the XML document that contains more complete information can be output.

5.4   Evaluating LAX

In our experiments, we took two XML documents from synthetic or real data sets as the input for our algorithm. And then we investigated how the number of leaf nodes and the number of clustered subtrees impacted the performance of our algorithm. The time for computing the tree edit distance using synthetic data sets are shown in Fig. 11. The X-axis in Fig. 11 (a) represents the total number of leaf nodes of the two documents to be joined, and the X-axis in (b) denotes the total number of clustered subtrees in the two documents. From Fig. 11, we observe that the runtime of our algorithm increases almost proportionally to the number of leaf nodes or the number of clustered subtrees, and the impacts on the time to computer the tree similarity degree by the two factors are almost the same. Fig. 11 also shows that for the total number of leaf nodes of the two documents less than 5000 (document size less than 300KB) or the total number of clustered subtrees less than 400, the computation of the tree similarity degree can be accomplished within 2 seconds.

We also investigated how the number of clustered subtrees changed when the document size increased. Fig. 12 indicates that the number of clustered subtrees

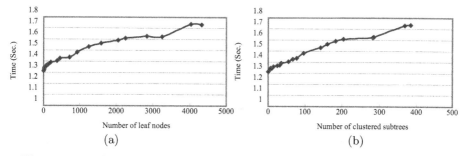

Fig. 11. Time for computing the tree similarity degree using synthetic data sets

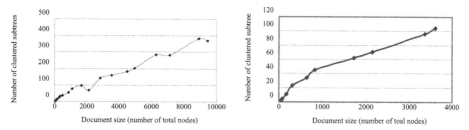

Fig. 12. Number of clustered subtrees of synthetic XML documents

Fig. 13. Number of clustered subtrees of real XML documents

generally increases, when the size of document becomes larger. However, the number of clustered subtrees does not always increase monotonously, because the clustered subtrees might contain different number of nodes due to different DTDs.

The results using real XML data sets are shown in Fig. 13 and 14. The runtime using real data sets increases faster than the one using synthetic data does under the same scale number of leaf nodes. Because the length of the PCDATA of real data is generally longer than that of synthetic data made by the XML generator.

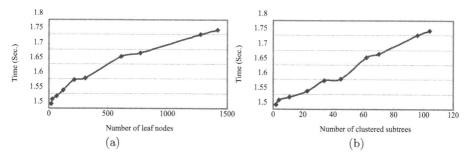

Fig. 14. Time for computing the tree similarity degree using real data sets

6 Conclusions and Future Work

It becomes more important to measure the approximate similarity between XML documents for integrating multiple XML data sources. Tree edit distance is currently recognized as a general metric for computing the structural similarity between XML documents. However, its computational cost is too expensive. Recognizing this problem, in this paper we have proposed LAX (**L**eaf-clustering based **A**pproximate **X**ML join algorithm), in which the two XML document trees are clustered into many subtrees representing independent items and the approximate similarity between them are determined by calculating the similarity degree based on the leaf nodes of each pair of subtrees. We have also proposed an effective algorithm for clustering the XML document for LAX.

The proposed algorithm has the following advantages: 1) it is an inexpensive and effective algorithm to determine the approximate similarity between XML documents; 2) the traditional wisdom in join algorithms can be applied to it without any difficulties; and 3) its output document contains complete information of the two documents been joined.

We have done experiments to compare our algorithm with the tree edit distance and evaluate its performance using both synthetic and real data sets. Our experimental results show that LAX, comparing with the tree edit distance, is more efficient in performance and more effective for measuring the approximate similarity between XML documents.

In our experiments, we just used XML data of small size generated by the DOM Parser. In the future, we plan to do further experiments with the real bioinformatics and large-scale knowledge-based XML data stored in RDBs.

Acknowledgements

We thank the anonymous reviewers for their valuable comments. We are also grateful to Mr. Xiangyong Ouyang for his assistance on programming. This work is supported in part by the Grant-in-Aid for Scientific Research of MEXT Japan (grant number 16016232), by CREST of JST (Japan Science and Technology Agency), and by the TokyoTech 21COE Program "Framework for Systematization and Application of Large-Scale Knowledge Resources".

References

1. ACM SIGMOD Record in XML. Available at http://www.acm.org/sigmod/record/xml/
2. M. Arenas and L. Libkin. A Normal Form for XML Documents. *ACM Transactions on Database Systems*, 29(1):195-232, March 2004.
3. S. Chawathe and H. Garacia-Molina. Meaningful Change Detection in Structured Data. In *Proc. of ACM SIGMOD 1997*, pages 26-37, 1997.
4. S. Chawathe, A. Tajaraman, H. Garacia-Molina and J. Widom. Change Detection in Hierarchically Structured Information. In *Proc. of ACM SIGMOD 1996*, pages 493-504, 1996.

5. I. F. Cruz, H. Xiao and F. Hsu. An Ontology-Based Framework for XML Semantic Integration. In *Proc. of IDEAS 2004*, pages 217-226, 2004.

6. A. Doan, P. Domingos and A. Halevy. Reconciling Schemas of Disparate Data Sources: A Machine-learning Approch. In *Proc. of ACM SIGMOD 2001*, pages 509–520, 2001.

7. W. Fan and L. Libkin. On XML Integrity Constraints in the Presence of DTDs. In *Proc. of PODS'01*, pages 114-125, 2001.

8. S. Guha, H.V. Jagadish, N. Koudas, D. Srivastava and T. Yu. Approximate XML Joins. In *Proc. of ACM SIGMOD 2002*, pages 287-298, 2002.

9. S. Guha, N. Koudas, D. Srivastava and T. Yu. Index-Based Approximate XML Joins. In *Proc. of ICDE 2003*, pages 708-710, 2003.

10. IBM XML Generator. Available at http://www.alphaworks.ibm.com/xml/

11. M. Lee, L. Yang, W. Hus and X. Yang. XClust: Clustering XML Schemas for Effective Integration. In *Proc. of CIKM'02*, pages 292-299, 2002.

12. MAGE (MicroArray and Gene Expression). Available at http://www.mged.org/ Workgroups/MAGE/mage.html

13. A. Marian, S. Abiteboul, G. Cobena and L. Mignet. Change-Centric Management of Versions in an XML Warehouse. In *Proc. of 27th VLDB*, pages 581-590, 2001.

14. A. Nierman and H. V. Jagadish. Evaluating Structural Similarity in XML Documents. In *Proc. of WebDB 2002*, pages 61-66, 2002.

15. E. Rahm and P. A. Bernstein. A Survey of approaches to automatic schema matching. *the VLDB Journal*, 10(1):334-350, 2001.

16. S. Selkow. The Tree-to-tree Editing Problem. *Information Processing Letters*, 6(6):184-186, December 1977.

17. Y. Wang, D. J. DeWitt and J. Cai. X-Diff: An Effective Change Detection Algorithm for XML Documents. In *Proc. of ICDE 2003*, pages 519-530, March 2003.

18. World Wide Web Consortium (W3C). The Document Object Model (DOM). http://www.w3.org/DOM/.

19. XML Version of DBLP. Available at http://dblp.uni-trier.de/xml/

20. X. Yang, M. Lee and T. Ling. Resolving Structural Conflicts in the Integration of XML Schemas: A Semantic Approach. In *Proc. of ER2003*, papges 520-533, 2003.

21. K. Zhang and D. Shasha. Simple Fast Algorithm for the Editing Distance Between Trees and Related Problems. *SIAM Journal of Computing*, 18(6):1245-1262, December 1989.

22. K. Zhang and D. Shasha. Tree Pattern Matching. *Pattern Matching Algorithms*, chapter 11. Oxford University Press, 1997.

Exploitation of Referential Integrity Constraints for Efficient Update of Data Warehouse Views

Carson Kai-Sang Leung[1] and Wookey Lee[2]

[1] The University of Manitoba, Winnipeg, MB, Canada
kleung@cs.umanitoba.ca
[2] Sungkyul University, Anyang, Korea
wook@sungkyul.edu

Abstract. Data warehouse (DW) views provide an efficient access to information integrated from source data. As changes are made to the source data, the corresponding views may be outdated. Hence, the maintenance of DW views is crucial for the currency of information. In this paper, we propose a novel method to efficiently self-maintain DW views that contain select-project-joins over relations modelled in a star schema. Specifically, our method avoids computing the views from scratch, which can be very costly. Instead, it exploits the referential integrity constraints that are imposed on the relations. Therefore, with our proposed method, DW views can be updated or refreshed by using only the old materialised views and the files that keep the truly relevant tuples in the "delta". The method avoids accessing the underlying source data, and hence, achieves efficient update of DW views that contain joins over relations modelled in a star schema.

Keywords: Data warehousing, view maintenance, referential integrity constraints, star schema, self-maintainability.

1 Introduction

A data warehouse (DW) is a subject-oriented, integrated, time-variant, and non-volatile collection of data organised in such a way that it supports the decision making process of the management. In general, DW views provide a fast access to integrated source data. As changes can be made to the source data, the corresponding views may be outdated. Hence, the maintenance of views is crucial for the currency of information. In other words, views need to be periodically refreshed so as to reflect those updates that have been made to the source data. In response to the changes to the source data, many existing DW views are refreshed by recomputing the contents from scratch (i.e., computing the new views from the updated source data), while some other DW views are incrementally maintained by accessing the source data. However, these approaches can be costly. Moreover, in many real-life situations, it is not uncommon that only a tiny fraction of some huge source data gets changed. The above approaches require an access to a huge amount of source data. Consequently, both CPU and I/O costs of these approaches can be extremely high. A better approach is to

M. Jackson et al. (Eds.): BNCOD 2005, LNCS 3567, pp. 98–110, 2005.

incrementally maintain views without accessing the source data. This calls for efficient view maintenance.

In this paper, our *key contribution* is the development of a novel method, which exploits referential integrity constraints, for self-maintaining DW views. With our method, the DW views can be self-maintained in the sense that the new views can be formed by using only (i) the old materialised views and (ii) referential integrity constraints, i.e., without requiring an access to any underlying databases. The method can be used in data warehousing environments to efficiently maintain views, and to effectively avoid concurrency control problems faced by many generic view maintenance strategies [2, 7, 13, 17, 19]. Specifically, we study the following problems:

1. How to efficiently update DW views containing a select-project-join (SPJ) operation over two relations (e.g., a fact table and a dimension table)?
2. How to efficiently update DW views containing a SPJ over a fact table and more than one dimension table?
3. How to efficiently update DW views containing a SPJ over a fact table and multiple dimension tables modelled in a star schema?

More specifically, we keep all and only those tuples that are relevant to the maintenance of views in files called referential integrity differential files (RIDFs). By using RIDFs and by exploiting properties of referential integrity constraints, our developed method provides self-maintainability to DW views that are modelled in a star schema. The method can be extended to self-maintain views that are modelled in other schemas (e.g., snowflake schema, galaxy schema). To avoid distraction, we focus on the star schema in this paper.

The outline of this paper is as follows. Section 2 gives related works and background. Sections 3, 4, and 5 describe how we exploit referential integrity constraints to self-maintain DW views involving joins over a fact table and n dimension tables (where $n \geq 1$) that are modelled in a star schema. Section 6 discusses further reduction in size for RIDFs. Experimental results are given in Section 7. Finally, conclusions are presented in Section 8.

2   Related Works and Background

Here, we first discuss the related works, and then present some background materials relevant to the rest of this paper.

2.1   Related Works

Many view maintenance approaches have been proposed (e.g., [1–6, 8–17, 19]) over the past decade. In this section, let us discuss some relevant ones.

Self-maintainability of DW views is a notion that views can be maintained, with respect to data warehouse objects, without requiring any accesses to any underlying databases. This notion was initially proposed as a Boolean expression with sufficient and necessary conditions on the view definition for autonomously computable updates [1]. To compute the updates, Blakeley et al. [1] applied a special case of a counting algorithm to SPJ expressions (with no negations, aggregations, or recursions). Several other researchers have developed algorithms related to the integration and maintenance of information extracted from heterogeneous or autonomous sources [9, 19]. Most of their works focused mainly on conventional database views, but not data warehouse views.

Over the past decade, several algebraic approaches for maintaining views have been proposed [1, 5, 6, 9, 15, 16]. Qian and Wiederhold [15] presented an algorithm for incremental view maintenance based on finite differencing techniques. Their algorithm uses source data, and thus, it lacks the notion of self-maintainability. Hyun [9] dealt with functional dependencies, while Gupta and Mumick [8] integrated outer joins. However, most of these works did not fully exploit referential integrity constraints for the maintenance of views. In this paper, we use – and extend – some notations from [5, 6, 11, 15] to present an efficient method to self-maintain DW views based on referential integrity constraints.

With respect to the maintenance of views based on referential integrity, the most relevant works include [10, 12, 14, 16], in which relevant tables are selected to form auxiliary structures – such as auxiliary views [16], auxiliary relations [14], auxiliary data [10], or complements [12] – for self-maintaining a SPJ view. Although the use of these auxiliary structures (e.g., auxiliary views) leads to self-maintenance of DW views, the construction cost of these structures can be quite high in some situations. Accesses of a large number of tuples may be required to construct these structures. As a preview, we will show in Section 7 that our proposed self-maintenance method incurs a lower cost.

2.2   Background

A referential integrity constraint is one of the most fundamental constraints in database and data warehousing environments. It can be specified between two relations, and used to maintain consistency among tuples in the two relations. Informally, the constraint states that a tuple r in a relation R (called the **referencing relation**) that refers to another relation S (called the **referenced relation**) must refer to an existing tuple s in S. More formally, the foreign key of R (denoted as $R.fk$) must "match" a candidate key of S (denoted as $S.ck$), that is, they must have the same domain and $R.fk = S.ck$ [1]. Without loss of generality, we assume in this paper that all relations in the data warehouse are "linked" by referential integrity constraints.

Whenever there is a change to a relation in an underlying database, the corresponding views need to be updated to reflect the change. This can be done using either an immediate mode or a deferred mode. For the former, the views are refreshed immediately; for the latter, all the changes are first recorded in some differential files, and the views are then updated periodically using these

---

[1] A *candidate key* of a relation is a minimal set of attributes whose values uniquely identify each tuple in the relation. A *foreign key* is a set of attributes (in a referencing relation R) that refers to a candidate key of the referenced relation S.

differential files. Whenever a tuple is inserted into, or deleted from, a referencing relation R or a referenced relation S, appropriate actions need to be taken as described below. (i) When a tuple r is **inserted into a referencing relation** R, a look-up in S is required to ensure the presence of a tuple $s \in S$ where $s.ck = r.fk$. If s is present, then r is inserted into R as well as the differential file ΔR [2]; otherwise, referential integrity is violated. It can be easily observed that the insertion into R does not affect S. (ii) When a tuple r is **deleted from a referencing relation** R, the tuple r is recorded in the differential file ∇R. Such a deletion from R also does not affect S. (iii) When a tuple s is **inserted into a referenced relation** S, the tuple s is recorded in the differential file ΔS. Such an insertion into S does not affect R. (iv) When a tuple s is **deleted from a referenced relation** S, a look-up in R is required (for the default mode of "on delete no action") to ensure the absence of a tuple $r \in R$ satisfying $r.fk = s.ck$. If r is absent, then s is safely removed from S; otherwise (i.e., r exists in R), referential integrity is violated, and the deletion is rejected. Note that there is no change in R.

3   Maintenance of Data Warehouse Views Involving a Dimension Table

In this section, we discuss the situation where the view contains a join over a fact table F and a dimension table D, where F references D. For example, F represents a sales relation (`Sales`) that contains sales information, and D represents an item relation (`Item`) that contains item information as described below:

- Item (<u>itemID</u>, name, type, description), and
- Sales (<u>invoiceID</u>, itemID, price) where itemID references Item.

The view $\pi_{\text{name,price}}\sigma_{\text{price}>100}(\text{Item} \bowtie \text{Sales})$ finds the item name and the selling price for each item whose price is over \$100.

3.1   A Naïve Method: Recompute Views from Scratch

Consider a SPJ view $\pi_A \sigma_C (F \bowtie D)$ where σ_C is the (usual) selection based on a Boolean condition C and π_A is the (usual) projection on a list of attributes A. When the underlying relations (namely, F and D) of the view are updated, we need to update the view in order to preserve consistency. A naïve method is to ignore the old view $\pi_A \sigma_C (F \bowtie D)$ and to compute the new view $\pi_A \sigma_C (F' \bowtie D')$ from scratch, where F' and D' are the updated F and D respectively. However, this method can be very costly, especially when updates are made very frequently or when only a tiny fraction of F or D is updated.

---

[2] Since the views can be updated using the deferred mode, it is more precise to say the following. An insertion of a tuple r into R requires a look-up in the "current" referenced relation $(S - \nabla S \cup S)$. If there exists a tuple $s \in (S - \nabla S \cup S)$ such that $s.ck = r.fk$, then r is inserted into R as well as ΔR.

3.2   An Improved Method: Update Views by Using Old Views, Differential Files, and Source Relations

A more efficient method is to obtain the new view from the old view, differential files, and source relations. It is well-known that the updated referencing relation F' can be expressed in terms of the old relation F, its insertion ΔF, and its deletion ∇F (i.e., $F' = F - \nabla F \cup \Delta F$). Similarly, the updated referenced relation D' can be expressed as $D' = D - \nabla D \cup \Delta D$. Therefore, the new view $\pi_A \sigma_C(F' \bowtie D')$ can be expressed in terms of the old view, differential files, and source relations. In the following expression, let us focus on how to efficiently update the join component because it dominates the SPJ operations (i.e., the select, project, and join operations):

$$
\begin{aligned}
v' &= F' \bowtie D' \\
&= (F - \nabla F \cup \Delta F) \bowtie (D - \nabla D \cup \Delta D) \quad\quad\quad (1) \\
&= (F \bowtie D) - (F \bowtie \nabla D) \cup (F \bowtie \Delta D) \\
&\quad - (\nabla F \bowtie D) - (\nabla F \bowtie \nabla D) - (\nabla F \bowtie \Delta D) \\
&\quad \cup (\Delta F \bowtie D) - (\Delta F \bowtie \nabla D) \cup (\Delta F \bowtie \Delta D). \quad\quad (2)
\end{aligned}
$$

Note that, among the $3^2 = 9$ terms in Equation (2), the first term $(F \bowtie D)$ is the old view. Hence, we do not need to compute the new view entirely from scratch; we can compute the new view by combining the old view with the results from the other eight terms. However, many of these eight terms, such as $(\Delta F \bowtie D)$, involve not only the differential files (e.g., ΔF) but also the source relations (e.g., D). Since source relations are required, this improved method still cannot efficiently self-maintain DW views.

3.3   An Efficient Self-maintainable Method

Equation (2) can be simplified by exploiting the properties of referential integrity constraints and the nature of the nine terms (e.g., by applying the propagation rules [13]):

- The term $(F \bowtie D)$ represents the old view, as mentioned in Section 3.2.
- The term $(F \bowtie \Delta D)$ gives an empty relation. Because of referential integrity constraints, for all $f \in F$, there must exist $d \in D$ such that $f.fk = d.ck$. In other words, there does not exist a tuple $d' \in \Delta D$ satisfying $f.fk = d'.ck$.
- All the terms involving ∇D (and similarly, all the terms involving ∇F) can be grouped together because they basically represent the action that all the tuples containing $d \in \nabla D$ (and $f \in \nabla F$) can be deleted.
- The term $(\Delta F \bowtie \Delta D)$ involves only the two differential files ΔF and ΔD. In other words, no access to the source data is required.

The computation of the only remaining term – namely $(\Delta F \bowtie D)$ – requires an access to the differential file ΔF and the source relation D. A natural question to ask is whether one can compute this term without accessing any source relations such as D? If so, how to compute it? Recall from Section 2.2 that when a tuple f is inserted into F, we check if there exists a tuple $d \in D$ such that $d.ck = f.fk$. If such d exists, the insertion is successful and f is then recorded in ΔF. Given that the search and check has been performed, one can record the tuple d in a file called **referential integrity differential file (RIDF)**. By so doing, the RIDF contains all those tuples (d) that are related to the tuples in ΔF. In other words, the RIDF contains all and only those tuples that could be joined with ΔF in the term $(\Delta F \bowtie D)$. Therefore, with this RIDF, the term $(\Delta F \bowtie D)$ can be rewritten as $(\Delta F \bowtie RIDF(D))$, which no longer requires an access to the source data. See the definition below.

Definition 1 (Referential integrity differential file (RIDF)). Let (i) a SPJ view $\pi_A \sigma_C (F \bowtie D)$ be created in terms of two relations F and D, and (ii) a referential integrity constraint be imposed on F and D such that $F.fk = D.ck$ where $F.fk$ denotes the foreign key of the referencing relation F and $D.ck$ denotes a candidate key of the referenced relation D. Then, when a tuple r is successfully inserted into F (i.e., f is put in ΔF), a **referential integrity differential file** $RIDF(D)$ keeps all and only those tuples (in D) that are truly relevant to the update of the view. Precisely, for each tuple $f \in \Delta F$, its corresponding $d \in D$ (such that $d.ck = f.fk$) is kept in $RIDF(D)$.

The following are some nice properties of the referential integrity differential file $RIDF(D)$. First, $RIDF(D)$ keeps all and only those tuples (in D) that are truly relevant to the join $(\Delta F \bowtie D)$. Thus, the number of tuples in $RIDF(D)$ is bounded above by the number of tuples in D, that is, $|RIDF(D)| \le |D|$. Second, for each candidate key of D, the number of tuples in $RIDF(D)$ is bounded above by the number of tuples in ΔF. This is due to referential integrity constraints. More specifically, because $f.fk = d.ck$, many f can reference one d (but each f can only reference one d). Hence, if D only has one candidate key (which is quite common for the dimension tables modelled in a star schema), then $|RIDF(D)| \le |\Delta F|$. Third, $RIDF(D)$ can be created without any significant cost (e.g., no extra searches in D). The file $RIDF(D)$ can be considered as a "by-product" of the referential integrity checks.

Therefore, by exploiting properties of referential integrity constraints and by using $RIDF(D)$, Equation (2) can be simplified to become the following (i.e., the new view can be computed as follows):

$$v' = F' \bowtie D' = v \cup (\Delta F \bowtie RIDF(D)) \cup (\Delta F \bowtie \Delta D) \ominus \nabla F \ominus \nabla D \quad (3)$$

where $v = (F \bowtie D)$ is the old view. Here, the fourth and the fifth terms $(\ominus \nabla F)$ and $(\ominus \nabla D)$ represent the deletion of all the tuples containing $f \in \nabla F$ and $d \in \nabla D$, respectively. It is important to note that, with this self-maintainable method, we no longer require accesses to the source data. The new view v' can be computed using (i) the old view v, (ii) the RIDF, and (iii) differential files $(\Delta F, \Delta D, \nabla F,$ and $\nabla D)$. See the following example.

Example 1. Consider the following two relations F and D:

F ($\underline{U}$, W, X)	D($\underline{X}$, Y, Z)
F: u1 w1 x1	D: x1 y1 z1
u2 w2 x2	x2 y2 z2
	x3 y3 z3
∇F: u2 w2 x2	∇D: x3 y3 z3
ΔF: u3 w3 x1	ΔD: x4 y4 z4
u4 w4 x2	
	$RIDF(D)$: x1 y1 z1
	x2 y2 z2

In this example, when tuples $\langle$u3, w1, x1$\rangle$ and $\langle$u4, w4, x2$\rangle$ are inserted into F, the corresponding tuples in D (namely, $\langle$x1, y1, z1$\rangle$ & $\langle$x2, y2, z2$\rangle$) are recorded in $RIDF(D)$. It is important to note that $(\Delta F \bowtie RIDF(D))$ gives the same result as $(\Delta F \bowtie D)$, but the former does not require any accesses to the source data D while the latter does. Hence, by keeping $RIDF(D)$, one can compute the join more efficiently. Moreover, the new view $v_1' \equiv (F' \bowtie D')$ can be computed using the old view $v_1 \equiv (F \bowtie D)$ with the differential files $(\Delta F, \Delta D, \nabla F, \nabla D)$ and $RIDF(D)$, according to Equation (3). $\square$

4   Self-maintenance of Data Warehouse Views Involving Two Dimension Tables

Given that our efficient method for view self-maintenance (as discussed in Section 3.3) is not confined to just two relations (one fact and one dimension tables), we show in this section how a new DW view containing a join over three relations (say, a fact table F and two dimensions tables D_1 & D_2) – where foreign keys of F references candidate keys of D_1, D_2 – can be computed using only the old view and the "delta" of the corresponding relations (i.e., without accessing base relations).

As we discussed in Section 3, an updated relation F' can be expressed in terms of the old relation F, its insertion ΔF, and its deletion ∇F (i.e., $F' = F - \nabla F \cup \Delta F$). Similar comments can be applied to D_1 and D_2. So, the new view $(F' \bowtie D_1' \bowtie D_2')$ can be expressed as follows:

$$v' = (F' \bowtie D_1' \bowtie D_2')$$
$$= (F - \nabla F \cup \Delta F) \bowtie (D_1 - \nabla D_1 \cup \Delta D_1) \bowtie (D_2 - \nabla D_2 \cup \Delta D_2). \quad (4)$$

This equation can be factored into $3^3 = 27$ terms. Fortunately, we can reduce the number of terms in the expression by grouping all terms involving ∇F (and those involving ∇D_1 and ∇D_2), as we did in Section 3.3. Moreover, some other terms – such as $(F \bowtie D_1 \bowtie \Delta D_2)$, $(F \bowtie \Delta D_1 \bowtie D_2)$, and $(F \bowtie \Delta D_1 \bowtie \Delta D_2)$ – can be eliminated because any join involving $F \bowtie \Delta D_j$ (for $j = 1$ or 2) would result in an empty relation. This is due to referential integrity constraints.

The exploitation of referential integrity constraints not only helps us to eliminate the three "join" terms mentioned above but also leads us to efficient self-maintainability. Specifically, due to the constraints, whenever we insert a tuple f

into the referencing relation F, we check to see if there exists a corresponding tuple in the referenced relations D_1 and D_2. So, we create $RIDF(D_1)$ and $RIDF(D_2)$ as "by-products" of the checks, and use them to compute the updated view as follows:

$$
\begin{aligned}
v' &= (F' \bowtie D_1' \bowtie D_2') \\
&= v \cup (\Delta F \bowtie RIDF(D_1) \bowtie RIDF(D_2)) \\
&\quad \cup (\Delta F \bowtie RIDF(D_1) \bowtie \Delta D_2) \cup (\Delta F \bowtie \Delta D_1 \bowtie RIDF(D_2)) \\
&\quad \cup (\Delta F \bowtie \Delta D_1 \bowtie \Delta D_2) \ominus \nabla F \ominus \nabla D_1 \ominus \nabla D_2
\end{aligned}
\tag{5}
$$

where $v = (F \bowtie D_1 \bowtie D_2)$ is the old view. Note that we do not need to access the source data. The new view can be computed by using v, the differential files (i.e., insertion files, deletion files), and RIDFs.

5 Generalization: Self-maintenance of Data Warehouse Views Involving Multiple Dimension Tables

In general, DW views may contain joins over several relations that are modelled in the form of a **star schema** – the most common modelling paradigm in data warehousing environments – in which the data warehouse contains a fact table and several dimension tables (say, m dimension tables). These tables are connected in such a way that, for each dimension table D_i, there exists a foreign key of the fact table F referencing a candidate key of D_i (where $1 \le i \le m$). Given a star schema consists of m dimension tables, a view may contain a join over some (but not necessary all) of these dimension tables. Without loss of generality, let us assume that the view contains a join over n dimension tables $D_1, \ldots, D_n$ (where $n \le m$). Then, the new view $v' = (F' \bowtie D_1' \bowtie \cdots \bowtie D_n')$ can be expressed as follows:

$$
\begin{aligned}
v' &= (F' \bowtie D_1' \bowtie \cdots \bowtie D_n') \\
&= (F - \nabla F \cup \Delta F) \bowtie (D_1 - \nabla D_1 \cup \Delta D_1) \bowtie \cdots \bowtie (D_n - \nabla D_n \cup \Delta D_n)
\end{aligned}
\tag{6}
$$

which can be factored into 3^{n+1} terms. As expected, the number of terms can be greatly reduced (in two steps) by exploiting properties of referential integrity constraints. First, there are $3^{n+1} - 2^{n+1}$ terms involving deletions, which can be grouped together to form $n + 1$ "deletion" terms (one "deletion" term for each table: $\nabla F, \nabla D_1, \ldots, \nabla D_n$). Second, there are 2^{n+1} "join" terms, out of which $2^n - 1$ terms contain F with at least one ΔD_j (for some $1 \le j \le n$). It is observed that any term containing $F \bowtie \Delta D_j$ results in an empty relation, due to referential integrity constraints. Thus, these terms can be eliminated; we only need to consider the remaining $2^n + 1$ "join" terms. Among them, we note the following:

- The term $(F \bowtie D_1 \bowtie \cdots \bowtie D_n)$ represents the old view v.
- The term $(\Delta F \bowtie \Delta D_1 \bowtie \cdots \bowtie \Delta D_n)$ involves only differential files ΔD_j (for $1 \le j \le n$).

- There are $2^n - 1$ terms contain ΔF, D_i and ΔD_j (for some $1 \leq i, j \leq n$, where $i \neq j$). The occurrence of D_i in the term implies an access to source data. Hence, in order to achieve self-maintainability, we replace each occurrence of D_i by $RIDF(D_i)$. As a result, we no longer need to access the source data.

In summary, the new view $v' = (F' \bowtie D'_1 \bowtie \cdots \bowtie D'_n)$ can be computed using the following $(n+1) + (2^n + 1) = 2^n + n + 2$ terms:

$$v' = v \cup \quad \Delta F \bowtie RIDF(D_i) \bowtie \Delta D_j$$
$$\cup (\Delta F \bowtie \Delta D_i \bowtie \cdots \bowtie \Delta D_n) \ominus \nabla F \ominus \nabla D_1 \ominus \cdots \ominus \nabla D_n, \quad (7)$$

where $1 \leq i, j \leq n$ and $i \neq j$. Since the star schema is the most common modelling paradigm in data warehousing environments, our proposed method can be very beneficial.

Example 2. Consider a DW view containing a join over a fact table and $n = 2$ dimension tables in a star schema (which contains $m \geq 2$ dimension tables). The new view can be computed, using Equation (7), as follows:

$$v' = (F' \bowtie D'_1 \bowtie D'_2)$$
$$= v \cup (\Delta F \bowtie RIDF(D_1) \bowtie RIDF(D_2)) \cup (\Delta F \bowtie RIDF(D_1) \bowtie \Delta D_2)$$
$$\cup (\Delta F \bowtie \Delta D_1 \bowtie RIDF(D_2)) \cup (\Delta F \bowtie \Delta D_1 \bowtie \Delta D_2) \ominus \nabla F \ominus \nabla D_1 \ominus \nabla D_2.$$

An observant reader may notice that this gives same expression as in Equation (5) – for the efficient self-maintenance of DW views involving two dimension tables and a fact table.   □

6   Discussion: Further Improvements

So far, we have shown that RIDFs keep all and only those tuples that are relevant for efficient self-maintenance of DW views modelled in a star schema. A careful analysis reveals that we do not need to keep all the attributes of those relevant tuples. Any attributes that do not contribute to the update of DW views can be discarded. For instance, reconsider Example 1, but with view $v_2 \equiv \pi_{W,Y}(F \bowtie D)$ where $F(\underline{U}, W, X)$ and $D(\underline{X}, Y, Z)$. When inserting $\langle u3, w3, x1 \rangle$ into F, we only need to keep $\langle x1, y1 \rangle$ in $RIDF(D)$ because the attribute Z does not contribute to the self-maintenance of v_2. Similarly, when inserting $\langle u4, w4, x2 \rangle$ into F, only $\langle x2, y2 \rangle$ needs to be kept in $RIDF(D)$. By so doing, only two (instead of three) attributes of the relevant tuples need to be stored in RIDFs.

The above shows the benefits on exploiting the project operator (π) – namely, the reduction in the number of attributes required for self-maintenance. Along this direction, we can also exploit the select operator (σ) in the SPJ to further reduce the size of RIDFs. For instance, reconsider Example 1, but with view $v_3 \equiv \pi_{W,Y} \sigma_{U \neq u3}(F \bowtie D)$ this time. When inserting $\langle u3, w3, x1 \rangle$ into F, we do not even need to keep the tuple $\langle x1, y1 \rangle$ because it does not contribute to the self-maintenance of v_3 (as $U = u3$, which violates the selection condition). So, we only need to keep $\langle x2, y2 \rangle$ in $RIDF(D)$.

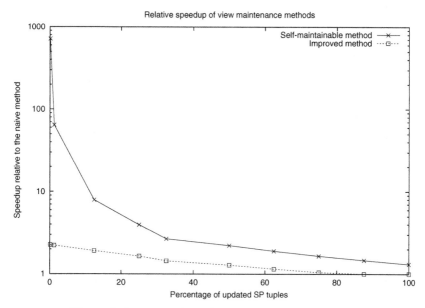

Fig. 1. Relative speedup of view maintenance methods

7   Experimental Results

The experimental results cited below are based on a database (from TPC-D [18]) that consists of a fact table (namely, SupPart (SP)) and two dimension ta- bles (namely, Product (P) and Supplier (S)), where the tables are logically "linked" by the following referential integrity constraints: (i) P(pID, pName, manufacturer, price), (ii) S(sID, sName, addr), and (iii) SP(pID, sID, qty, SPrice) where pID references P and sID references S. Notice that one could also add a "time" dimension to make the above star schema contain three dimension tables.

   In this experiment, we suppose that base relations P, S, and SP consist of 200,000 tuples, 10,000 tuples, and 800,000 tuples, respectively. We assume that the selectivity of P.pName='computer' is 0.70,   S.addr='CA' is 0.75, SP.SPrice>P.price*1.1 is 0.50, and the join selectivity is 0.50 of transactions with uniform distribution.

   We illustrate the effectiveness of our self-maintainable method by comparing the results of the following three implemented methods:

- The **naïve method**, which reads and sorts the base relations with a sort- merge join.
- The **improved method**, which is similar to the naïve method except that the improved method uses old views, di erential les, and source relations.
- Our efficient **self-maintainable method**, which uses only old views, dif- ferential files, and R ID F s. In other words, this method avoids accessing source relations.

Here, we first used view $v_4 \equiv \pi_A \sigma_{C_4}(\text{SP} \bowtie \text{P} \bowtie \text{S})$, where the list of attribute A is ⟨sName, price, SPrice, qty⟩, and the selection condition C_4 is "addr='CA' & pName='computer' & SPrice>price*1.1". We varied the percentage of SP tuples being updated/changed from 0.125% to 100% (i.e., varied the number of updated SP tuples from 1,000 to 800,000, and correspondingly varied the number of updated P tuples from 100 to 80,000 while keeping relation S unchanged). The x-axis of Fig. 1 shows the percentage of updated SP tuples; the y-axis, in logarithmic scale, shows the speedup of the improved method and our self-maintainable method against the naïve method. As observed from Fig. 1, the lower the percentage of updated tuples, the higher is the benefit of using our method. For example, the speedup of our method is above 700 times when 0.125% of SP tuples are updated. It is important to note that a low percentage of updated tuples is not uncommon. In many real-life applications, DW views need to be refreshed frequently (which usually leads to a low percentage of tuples get updated between each refresh) so as to facilitate accurate decision making.

While Fig. 1 shows the relative speedup, the table below gives some samples of the total runtime (i.e., both CPU and I/O times) for updating view v_4.

% updated SP tuples	Naïve	Improved	Self-maintainable
0.125%	9358s	4148s	13s
1.25%	9358s	4217s	145s
12.5%	9358s	4904s	1183s

Note that our proposed self-maintainable method requires a much shorter runtime than the other two methods. Moreover, when compared with some existing approaches that use auxiliary structures (e.g., auxiliary views), our method also incurs a much lower cost (e.g., an approach using auxiliary views requires more than 4,000 seconds to update v_4 when 1.25% of SP tuples get changed).

Next, let us count the numbers of tuples in the base relations, in the "delta" (i.e., being changed), and in RIDFs. One can easily observe from the following table that the number of tuples need to be stored in a RIDF is bounded above by the numbers of tuples in its corresponding base relation and "delta" (e.g., $|RIDF(\text{P})| \leq \min\{|\text{P}|, |\Delta\text{SP}|\}$ and $|RIDF(\text{S})| \leq \min\{|\text{S}|, |\Delta\text{SP}|\}$).

	Base relation	1.25% updated SP tuples "delta"	RIDF	87.5% updated SP tuples "delta"	RIDF
P	200,000	1,000	6,930	70,000	200,000
S	10,000	0	7,000	0	10,000
SP	800,000	10,000	0	700,000	0

In addition to applying the three view maintenance methods to view v_4, we have also applied these methods to other views (e.g., v_5, v_6 and v_7). These additional views, of the form $v_i = \pi_A \sigma_{C_i}(\text{SP} \bowtie \text{P} \bowtie \text{S})$, are similar to v_4 except for the selection condition C_i. More specifically, $C_5 \equiv$ "pName='computer' & SPrice>price*1.1", $C_6 \equiv$ "addr='CA' & SPrice>price*1.1", and $C_7 \equiv$ "SPrice>price*1.1". The table below shows the runtime of the three methods when 1.25% of SP tuples get updated.

	Naïve	Improved	Self-maintainable
v_5	9358s	3375s	144s
v_6	9358s	3574s	145s
v_7	9358s	8498s	212s

8 Conclusions

Data warehouse (DW) views provide an efficient access to integrated data. As changes are made to the source data, the corresponding views may be outdated. Hence, the maintenance of views is crucial for the currency of information. In this paper, we proposed a novel method to efficiently self-maintain the DW views that contain a select-project-join (SPJ) over multiple relations. Specifically, we exploit the referential integrity constraints imposed on the relations in the source data. With our proposed method, views can be updated by using only the old views, differential files (e.g., the insertion file ΔR and the deletion file ∇R), and referential integrity differential files (RIDFs). This method uses the RIDFs to keep the truly relevant tuples in the "delta"; it avoids accessing the underlying databases. The proposed method is applicable to the efficient self-maintenance of DW views that contain SPJ over relations modelled in a star schema – the most popular model for data warehousing environments.

Acknowledgement

This project is partially sponsored by Science and Engineering Research Canada (NSERC) and The University of Manitoba, as well as Korea Science and Engineering Foundation (KOSEF) through Advanced Information Technology Research Centre (AITrc), in the form of research grants.

References

1. Blakeley, J.A., Larson, P.-Å., Tompa, F.W.: Efficiently updating materialized views. In: Proc. SIGMOD 1986. 61–71
2. Bruckner, R.M., Tjoa, A.M.: Managing time consistency for active data warehouse environments. In: Proc. DaWaK 2001. 254–263
3. Engström, H., Lings, B.: Evaluating maintenance policies for externally materialised multi-source views. In: Proc. BNCOD 2003. 140–156
4. Fišer, B., Onan, U., Elsayed, I., Brezany, P., Tjoa, A.M.: On-line analytical processing on large databases managed by computational grids. In: Proc. DEXA Workshop (GLOBE) 2004. 556–560
5. Griffin, T., Libkin, L.: Incremental maintenance of views with duplicates. In: Proc. SIGMOD 1995. 328–339
6. Griffin, T., Libkin, L., Trickey, H.: An improved algorithm for the incremental recomputation of active relational expressions. IEEE TKDE **9** (1997) 508–511
7. Gupta, A., Mumick, I.S.: Maintenance of materialized views: problems, techniques, and applications. IEEE Data Engineering Bulletin **18**(2) (1995) 3–18

8. Gupta, H., Mumick, I.S.: Selection of views to materialize in a data warehouse. IEEE TKDE **17** (2005) 24–43
9. Hyun, N.: Multiple-view self-maintenance in data warehousing environments. In: Proc. VLDB 1997. 26–35
10. Khan, S., Mott, P.: LeedsCQ: a scalable continual queries system. In: Proc. DEXA 2002. 607–617
11. Kotidis, Y., Roussopoulos, N.: A case for dynamic view management. ACM TODS **26** (2001) 388–423
12. Laurent, D., Lechtenbörger, J., Spyratos, N., Vossen, G.: Monotonic complements for independent data warehouses. VLDB Journal **10** (2001) 295–315
13. Lee, W.: On the independence of data warehouse from databases in maintaining join views. In: Proc. DaWaK 1999. 86–95
14. Mohania, M., Kambayashi, Y.: Making aggregate views self-maintainable. DKE **32** (2000) 87–109
15. Qian, X., Wiederhold, G.: Incremental recomputation of active relational expressions. IEEE TKDE **3** (1991) 337–341
16. Quass, D., Gupta, A., Mumick, I., Widom, J.: Making views self-maintainable for data warehousing. In: Proc. PDIS 1996. 158–169
17. Theodoratos, D., Xu, W.: Constructing search spaces for materialized view selection. In: Proc. DOLAP 2004. 112–121
18. Transaction Processing Performance Council: TPC Benchmark D. www.tpc.org
19. Zhuge, Y., Garcia-Molina, H., Hammer, J., Widom, J.: View maintenance in a warehousing environment. In: Proc. SIGMOD 1995. 316–327

Correlation-Based Data Broadcasting
in Wireless Networks*

Keke Cai, Huaizhong Lin, and Chun Chen

Department of Computer Science, Zhejiang University, Hangzhou, China, 310027
{caikeke,linhz,chenc}@zju.edu.cn

Abstract. A key element in many mobile application systems is the realization of efficient data delivery from server to mobile clients. Although broadcast has been proved to be an efficient data dissemination technique, selection of broadcast data is still an active research area. In this paper, we mainly studied the functions of the implicit regularities attached to clients' request data in the selection of broadcast data. Furthermore, we put forward a correlation-based broadcast model, which selects broadcast data items according to data access frequencies as well as their correlations. The primary rationale underneath is the fact that some data are prone to be accessed if certain data are reached. The results from extensive simulation experiments shows that the correlation-based broadcast can significantly improve the mean response time and reduce the number of client requests.

1 Introduction

The explosion of global information makes it a critical issue that how to realize an efficient data delivery in the wireless environment. Among all existing transfer schemes, broadcast has been proved to be an effective solution. It can adapt better to the special constraints of wireless network. While there are many critical issues concerning data broadcast, our paper mainly focuses on the issue of that how to realize an effective selection of data for broadcast.

The broadcast schedule, which determines what should be broadcast and when [1], directly impacts the performance of broadcast. Obviously, it is desirable to broadcast data in which clients are most interested. Some conventional broadcast schedules utilize the precompiled profiles as the criteria during the selection. However, considering the dynamic nature of client demands, these techniques are inclined to be inapplicable in many cases. To resolve these problems, some other schemes called popularity-based broadcast have been proposed [2], [3], [4] to ague that date with high request frequency should be imposed high priority during selection Unfortunately, due to the difficulty of the communication between server and clients, some popular data without explicit requests cannot be fully identified by server. Our paper will focus on this problem and proposes a new efficient approach, which can intelligently identify the importance of data in the lacking of information of data requests.

---

* Supported by the Natural Science Foundation of Zhejiang Province, China (Grant no. M603230) and the Research Fund for Doctoral Program of Higher Education from Ministry of Education, China (Grant no. 20020335020).

M. Jackson et al. (Eds.): BNCOD 2005, LNCS 3567, pp. 111–119, 2005.

Although lots of factors have been considered during the process of broadcast data selection, correlations among data are often ignored. In this paper, based on the hybrid data delivery model proposed by [5], we brought forward a new correlation-based broadcast scheme. When dealing with the selection problem, it simultaneously considers the relationships among data in addition to data access frequencies. The primary rationale underneath is the fact that some data are prone to be accessed if certain data are reached. Finally, data selected for broadcasting consists of two parts. One part includes popular data that can be identified explicitly through clients' explicit requests; and another part contains items that have high probability to be popular.

The rest of this paper is organized as follows. Section 2 introduces some background information and relevant work. The related definitions are described in Section 3. The proposed algorithm is depicted in Section 4. The experimental study and results are presented in Section 5. Section 6 draws the conclusion.

2 Background

One of the most concerned issues of broadcast is the selection of broadcast data, in which domain there exist many different solutions.

For the push-based broadcast, data sent out on the broadcast channel are either the anticipated client requests according to some periodic schedules [6], or the whole database [7]. Most precompiled-based data dissemination schemes belong to this type. In [8], a selective information dissemination system is realized based on the precompiled profiles posted by clients. A similar method is also applied in [9], in which Shek proposed an adaptive algorithm that can dynamically select the disseminated data according to the aggregation of user profiles. Contrasting with the push-based broadcast, pull-based scheme can better satisfy each client special needs, and dynamically react to workload changes [1]. In such case, server is in charge of monitoring and recording client requests, from which the most prospective data are chosen and then broadcast [10].

Each approach aforementioned has its own benefits and shortcomings. Push-based data broadcasting cannot adapt well to client dynamic data demands. Pull-based data broadcasting needs to possess a great deal of scarce uplink bandwidth. Consequentially, its performance is easily influenced by the changing workload. To overcome their drawbacks and make full use of their strengths, the hybrid broadcast model was firstly proposed in [11]. It provides effective data service if the server maintains a good balance between "data push" and "data pull" [1]. In the model of [11], it is assumed that items are clearly classified into frequent or infrequent data. These two kinds of data are served by broadcast and on demand respectively. Another hybrid approach proposed by Acharya et al. [12] allows clients to send data requests to server through a backchannel and these requests will be broadcasted interleaving with other data selected by some special broadcast schedules. The deficiency of these approaches is that the content and the organization of the broadcast are comparatively static. To overcome this limitation, an adaptive hybrid model was introduced in [5], which periodically adjusts its broadcast content to match clients' demands. Measure of data selection is based on the frequency of each requested data. For each data, the more popular it is, the more chance it has to be broadcasted.

Our scheme takes a similar hybrid model as that stated in [5], but adopts a totally different data selection scheme. Although the application environment in our paper is hybrid broadcast, this solution is also applicable to other broadcast models.

3 Problem Proposed and Related Definitions

Traditionally, the selection of broadcast data is implemented merely based on the data of client requests. Hence, the inconsistency and inadequacy of the request information always leads to the omissions of some popular data. Current existing techniques cannot tickle such problem efficiently, which calls for some other solutions. Based on our observation, we find that there are some intrinsic regularities in data requests. Certain data are often requested together during client transactions. Such information, expressed in the form of correlations, can be fully utilized to improve the accuracy of data selection. In our scheme, we use the association rules mining technique to investigate such correlations.

Let $I = \{i_1, i_2, \ldots i_m\}$ be a set of distinct items and $T = \{t_1, t_2, \ldots t_n\}$ a set of variable length transactions, $t_i \subseteq I$. An association rule is an implication of the form $A \rightarrow C$, where $A, C \subseteq I$ and $A \cap C = \phi$. Confidence of the association rule is defined as:

$$CONF(A \rightarrow C) = sup(A \cup C)/sup(A). \tag{1}$$

Function $sup(B)$ describes the support of an item set, which is just the frequency of B.

$$sup(B) = |U| / |T|. \tag{2}$$

where U represents all the transactions that contain B, $\|$ denotes the size of a data set.

4 Correlation-Based Broadcast Algorithm

Our paper adopts a hybrid broadcast model for data delivery, based on which we investigate the effect of correlations among data during the process of broadcast data selection.

4.1 Hybrid Model

The hybrid model adopted in our data dissemination is shown in Fig. 1. It is an extension of the model proposed in [5]. In this model, there exist three communication channels, Broadcast Channel, Unicast Channel and Backchannel. Broadcast Channel is used for broadcasting data from server to clients. Unicast Channel is responsible for the point-to-point data delivery. Backchannel is in charge of the submission of clients' data requests. In our model, the popular data for broadcast are kept in the broadcast queue, whose content will be updated every each broadcast. Clients' requests, which are not broadcasted, will be served on demand through Unicast Channel.

Each data item allocated to broadcast queue is assigned with a popularity value, which is initially set to data access frequency and will be proportionally decreased for each following broadcast. Data will be excluded from the broadcast queue once its popularity is lower than the system-predefined popularity threshold. As pointed in [5], the inherent problem of this method is that it cannot completely capture client data requirements, which consequently results in a situation that some important data cannot be broadcasted.

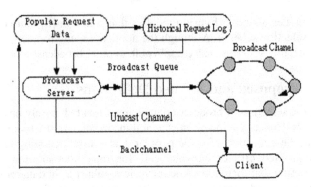

Fig. 1. Prediction-based broadcast model

4.2 Algorithm

Our proposed algorithm is primarily based on the identification of relationships among broadcast data. With the induction of the association rule mining technique, these relationships reflected by co-occurrence can be just extracted from client historic requests. Therefore, given the presence of certain data with affirmative popularity, we can infer some other data with the most popularity probability.

Request Session. In our paper, identification of relationships among data happens in the context of client request transactions. Client request transaction, known as request session, is a data unit consisting of data requested by a certain client to satisfy its local transaction. As introduced in section 4.1, data requests from client to server are transmitted through the Backchannel. They are initially collected in the form of data stream. To better understand the client data requirements, we should firstly separate this original data stream in terms of client-related requests, and further divide each of them into a number of data sets, each of which reflects an integrated data unit related to a client request transaction. In our paper, we assume that client requests can be differentiated according to their unique client ID. For each client, definition of client request transaction is similar to that defined in [14], which differentiates each two consecutive transactions according to the interval of client' requests. Given a set of continuous requests $Q = \{ q_1^i, q_2^i, \ldots q_m^i \}$ received from client i, if the access interval between requests q_i^i and q_{i+1}^i is more than δ, then q_i^i and q_{i+1}^i belong to different transactions. δ is the predefined maximal interval threshold. According to this definition, Q can be finally divided into a set of request transactions, which will be the basis of the later data analysis.

Identification of New Popular Data. Let $RS = \{rs_1, rs_2 \ldots rs_m\}$ be a set of clients' request transaction, $I = \{i_1, i_2, \ldots i_m\}$ includes distinct data RS involved. According to the support concept introduced in section 3, we can always identify a number of popular data $PD = \{pd_1, pd_2 \ldots pd_n\}$, where $pd_i \in I$ and $sup(pd_i) > \theta_0$, θ_0 is the predefined popularity threshold. Each element pd_i will be added to the broadcast queue with its popularity $sup(pd_i)$.

Prediction of Popular Data. According to the principle of [5], popularity of broadcast data will decrease gradually. For an item d with an initial popularity ρ, its popularity changes to ρ-n*σ after n times broadcast, where σ is the decrease factor. d will be excluded from broadcast once its popularity is lower than the popularity threshold θ_0. Obviously, there exist a potential problem under this method. It tends to discard some popular data, for that these popularities are just assumptions. As a remedy for these inaccuracies, "temperature probing" method was proposed by [5]. Although it decreases a certain number of clients' requests, data sometimes suffer repetitious exclusion and withdrawal, and it equally influences request respond time. In our method, according to the relationships identified above, we propose a new solution that tries to reduce the repetition of exclusion and withdrawal as more as possible.

In our scheme, data for broadcast will be updated periodically. Hence, it is inevitable to involve some add and deletion operations. We denote that data contained in the broadcast queue BQ is OD. After the identification of current popular data PD, BQ is denoted as $OD \cup PD$. For data belong to OD, they have two disposals, either excluded or retained. Different from the traditional treatment, our scheme considers not only the popularity of data themselves but also correlations among data when dealing with data of OD. An item opd of OD will be kept broadcasting if only it satisfies one of following conditions: $sup(opd) > \theta_0$ or there exist some closed relationships between it and some data in PD. The first condition is easy to judge according to the previous description, and the second condition is identification based on the correlations aforementioned. The whole process can be divided into the following steps:

1) Association rules mining. According to the confidence definition in section 3, identify all the valued association rules AR from clients' history request transaction. Each association rule ar in AR is formed as $A \rightarrow C, A \subseteq PD, C \subseteq OD$, and satisfies $CONF(ar) > \eta$, η is the minimum confidence threshold.
2) Identification of correlated data. Collect all data of C of any association rule $A \rightarrow C$ in AR, and construct a data set PPD.
3) Disposal of data of OD. Data simultaneously belong to PPD and OD as well as data satisfying the popularity requirement are kept in BQ, otherwise are excluded.

Prediction-Based Broadcast Algorithm. In general, this proposed scheme consists of five steps: Firstly, based on the algorithm of Apriori (refer to [14] for details) as well as client historical requests, dynamically identify a set of association rules, which reflect the characteristics of client requests within the latest period of time; Secondly, according to client current requests, construct a data set PD containing current popular data; Thirdly, recognize a set of satisfactory association rules, which can also indicate the relevance between data of PD and data of current broadcast queue; Fourthly, modify the popularities of current broadcast data by referring to the association rules identified above; Finally, update the broadcast queue. The detailed process is described in the algorithm 1. Among its parameters, HS is considered as a training data set that contains some historical requests data. NS represents clients' current request transactions, and Q is the broadcast queue. Functions $RuleIDF$ and $IsPop$ are respectively implemented to obtain the association rules inherent in client requests and current popular request data. The variable PD denotes a set of popular data gotten from current data requests, R represents a set of valued association rules obtained from HS, and CD contains data that exist in Q and simultaneously have most closed correlations with data in PD. $pop(d)$ represents the current popularity value of item d. The parameter θ_0 is the system predefined popularity threshold.

Algorithm 1.

```
prediction_based_broadcast(TrainRequestTransaction HS,
CurrentRequestTransactions NS, BQueue Q){

  AssociationRule R
  PopuarityData PD;
  CorrelatedData CD;

  R = RuleIDF(HS);
  PD = IsPop(NS);
  for each subset SD of PD {
    for each rule r in R{
      if r is formed as SD→ ED{
        for each item x in ED{
          if x does not exist in CD
            add x to CD;
        }
      }
    }
  }
  For each x in Q
    if(x exist in CD)
      increase pop(x);
    else{
      decrease pop (x);
      if(pop(x) < θ₀)
        remove x from Q;
    }
  For each data item x in PD
    append x to Q;
}
```

5   Experimental Study

In this section, we present the experimental results of our proposed scheme. We define two basic performance metrics. The first one is broadcast data hit ratio. It is defined as the fraction of clients' requests that can be satisfied by broadcast. The other one is the average response time of clients' requests. For the purpose of testing, we used a combination of synthetic and real data sets. The synthetic data is used as an ideal case. There are some predefined association rules and a set of fixed popular data items. The real data in our experiments are the historical data of the anonymous web from msnbc.com that are obtained from http://kdd.ics.uci.edu/. The source of the data came from the Internet Information Server logs at msnb.com, which described the page visits of 989,818 users during the twenty-four hour period. We assume that the broadcast and the unicast rates are 8Mbps while the uplink is 1Mbps. We performed experiments under various clients' request transactions. The number of each client's request transactions is range from 100 to 150.

In order to get a better understanding of the efficiency of this scheme, the first part of the experiments aims to demonstrate the effect of our approach on the average broadcast data hit ratio. To get a more clear comparison, we adopted the static work-loads and the ratio of request is 500 per second. For experiments executed on synthetic data, we set the minimum popularity support threshold to 30 percent and the minimum similarity confidence threshold to 60 percent. For other experiments applied to real data, due to the sparseness of clients' requests, we set those two parameters to 1 percent and 40 percent respectively. For comparative study, we contrasted our scheme (PB) with the optimal broadcast scheme (OB) that can periodically broadcast the theoretically optimal data and the base broadcast scheme (BASE) that does not any prediction. We randomly selected eight clients and illustrated their average hit ratio. As shown in Fig. 2 and Fig. 3, the extra information of correlations among data plays a strong assistant usage. It is help to make a better identification of data popularity, and thereby lead to a more accurate broadcast data selection.

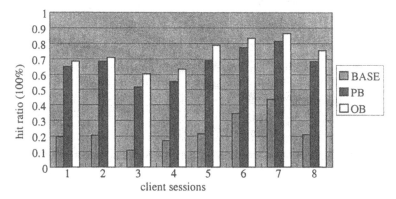

Fig. 2. Fixed workload with synthetic data

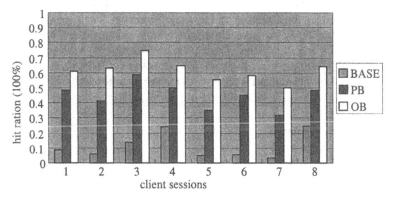

Fig. 3. Fixed workload with real data

In the experiments, we further evaluate the impact of the access ratio on the system response time with dynamic workloads. Considering the dynamic request ratio, we iterate our experiments with different popularity threshold. They are also inversely proportional to the request ratio. The minimum similarity confidence threshold is not change and is same to the previous set. Fig. 4 shows the average response time of requests under the synthetic data. We measure the performance by logical time units.

As shown in Fig. 4, performance of the system without prediction cannot accommodate well to the gradually increased workloads. Inversely, our prediction-based hybrid delivery approach can well scale to the workloads and exhibit a satisfied performance. This proposal is also evaluated with real experimental data. From the results shown in Fig. 5, we notice that there is a significant difference between our system and the optimal system. It is for the dynamic nature of clients' demands, which make the changes of client access pattern. However, in general, our proposal can still show good adaptability when request rate increases.

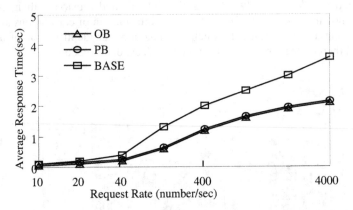

Fig. 4. Average response time as a function of request rate under synthetic data

6   Conclusions

In this paper, we sufficiently study the implicit regularities attached to clients' access behaviors, as well as their impact to broadcast selection. We extend a hybrid data delivery model and apply the association rule mining technique to disclose the correlations among different data items. These correlations exert an important influence on the selection of the content broadcasted. The experiments have showed that it is an effective method, which can achieve more exact data broadcasting.

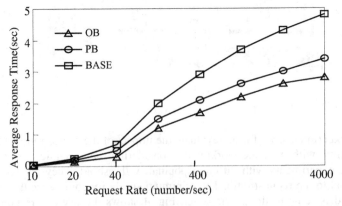

Fig. 5. Average response time as a function of request rate under real data

References

1. J. Xu, D. L. Lee, Q. Hu, and W.-C. Lee, Data Broadcast. Handbook of Wireless Networks and Mobile Computing. Chapter 11, Ivan Stojmenovic, Ed., New York: John Wiley & Sons, ISBN 0-471-41902-8, Jan (2002) 243-265
2. Acharya, S., Franklin, M., Zdonik, S, Dissemintanig Updates on Broadcast Disks. Proceedings of 22nd VLDB Conference. India (1996)
3. Datta, A., Celik, A., Kim, J. and VanderMeer, D.E., Adaptive Broadcast Protocol to Support Power Conservant Retrieval by Mobile Users. Proceedings of 13th International Conference on Data Engineering. (1997)
4. Leong, H.V. and Si, A., Database Caching over the Air-Storage. The Computer Journal. Volume 40, number 7. (1997) 401-415
5. K. Stathatos, N. Roujssopoulos and J.S. Baras, Adaptive data broadcast in hybrid networks. VLDB Conference. (1997) 326–335
6. A. Datta, A. Celik, J. Kim, D. VanderMeer and V. Kumar, Adaptive Broadcast Protocols to Support Efficient and Energy Conserving Retrieval from Databases in Mobile Computing Environments. In Proc. of the 13th International Conference on Data Engineering. April (1997) 124–134
7. Swarup Acharya, Rafael Alonso, Michael Franklin, and Michael Zdonik, Dissemination-based Data Delivery Using Broadcast Disks. IEEE Personal Communications Magazine, 2(6), December (1995)
8. Tak W. Yan and Hector Garcia-Molina, Distributed Selective Dissemination of Information. In Proceedings of the Third International Conference on Parallel and Distributed Information Systems (PDIS 94). Austin, Texas, September (1994) 89-98
9. Eddie C. Shek, Son Dao, Yongguang Zhang, Darrel J. Van Buer, Dynamic Multicast Information Dissemination in Hybrid Satellite-Wireless Networks. MobiDE (1999) 30-35
10. Demet Aksoy, Michael J. Franklin, Stanley B. Zdonik, Data Staging for On-Demand Broadcast. VLDB. (2001) 571-580
11. J. W. Wong, Broadcast delivery. Proceedings of the IEEE. December (1988) 76(12) 1566–1577
12. S. Acharya, M. Franklin and S. Zdonik, Balancing push and pull for data broadcast. In: Proc. ACM SIGMOD Conference. (1997) 183–194
13. Agrawal, R., Imielinski, T., Swami, A.N.: Mining association rules between sets of items in large databases. In Buneman, P., Jajodia, S., eds.: Proceedings of the 1993 ACM SIGMOD International Conference on Management of Data. Washington, D.C. (1993) 207–216
14. Y. Saygin, O. Ulusoy, Exploiting Data Mining Techniques for Broadcasting Data in Mobile Computing Environments. IEEE Transactions on Knowledge and Data Engineering, vol.14, no.6. November/December 2002

Hierarchical Group-Based Sampling

Rainer Gemulla, Henrike Berthold, and Wolfgang Lehner

Dresden University of Technology
Database Technology Group
{gemulla,henrike.berthold,lehner}@inf.tu-dresden.de

Abstract. Approximate query processing is an adequate technique to reduce response times and system load in cases where approximate results suffice. In database literature, sampling has been proposed to evaluate queries approximately by using only a subset of the original data. Unfortunately, most of these methods consider either only certain problems arising due to the use of samples in databases (e.g. data skew) or only join operations involving multiple relations. We describe how well-known sampling techniques dealing with group-by operations can be combined with foreign-key joins such that the join is computed after the generation of the sample. In detail, we show how senate sampling and small group sampling can be combined efficiently with the idea of join synopses. Additionally, we introduce different algorithms which maintain the sample if the underlying data changes. Finally, we prove the superiority of our method to the naive approach in an extensive set of experiments.

1 Introduction

As a result of rising computation and storage capacities, data acquisition has become simpler and more versatile. The amount of information stored on a wide range of different media has increased tremendously during the past years [1]. Data warehouse systems integrating different databases are capable of persistently storing this surge of information. However, it is rather difficult to extract knowledge from these voluminous databases, since the respective database queries usually suffer from long runtimes. Often an approximate but fast answer is the better alternative, e.g. to support interactivity. Sampling is a widely used technique which balances query result accuracy and response time.

The well-known simple random sampling (SRS) selects a fixed-sized random subset of a relation such that every possible subset has the same probability of being drawn. Approximate query evaluation using SRS assumes that the underlying data is uniformly distributed. In order to circumvent this restriction and to extend SRS to multiple relations, several techniques have been proposed. However, they only address either data distribution or join processing. We show how to combine sampling techniques developed to accurately answer group-by queries [2, 3] with the well known technique of join synopses [4] for foreign-key joins.

M. Jackson et al. (Eds.): BNCOD 2005, LNCS 3567, pp. 120–132, 2005.
© Springer-Verlag Berlin Heidelberg 2005

Related Work. The New Jersey Data Reduction Report [5] provides an overview of approximate query processing in general. Database-specific sampling techniques can be divided into two classes: online sampling, which computes the sample at query execution time, and offline sampling, which pre-computes the sample and materializes it in the database. Obviously, by using offline sampling it is possible to spend more effort in the computation of the sample in order to increase the accuracy of approximate results. However, the sample has to be maintained if the data is modified.

The method of online aggregation [6] belongs to the former of the two classes mentioned above. The main idea is to present the user with iteratively refined approximate results for aggregation queries. However, most sampling techniques generate the sample offline in order to deal with data skew (e.g. non-uniformly distributed value frequencies). Reservoir sampling [7, 8] allows the computation of a sample of predefined size. ICICLES [9], developed by Ganti et. al., attempts to generate and maintain a sample tailored to the actual query workload. The outlier indexing [10] detects outliers within the data and uses this knowledge for sample computation.

The main problem of bringing together sampling and join is the fact that these two operations do not commute. For two relations R_1 and R_2, it holds in general:

$$\mathrm{SRS}(R_1 \bowtie R_2) \neq \mathrm{SRS}(R_1) \bowtie \mathrm{SRS}(R_2)$$

Therefore, it is not possible to compute a sample of a join by only using the samples of the participating relations [11]. Fortunately, in the common case of an N:1-relationship as appearing in star and snowflake schemes the situation is less difficult, because it is possible to sample at least one of the involved relations:

$$\mathrm{SRS}(R_1 \bowtie_{N:1} R_2) = \mathrm{SRS}(R_1) \bowtie_{N:1} R_2$$

This property is the foundation of join synopses [4] which pre-calculate samples over foreign-key relationships. With the help of this technique, expensive joins are avoided at query execution time (sec. 2.1).

Typically, data is not uniformly distributed. This data skew causes enormous problems if sampling is not applied carefully. For instance, the small group problem appears: if the values of the grouping attributes are not uniformly distributed with regard to their frequency, groups consisting of only a few tuples appear infrequently in the sample and, thus, contribute to the approximate result infrequently. Group-based sampling techniques such as senate sampling [2] and small group sampling [3] deal with this problem.

Outline. The remainder of the paper is organized as follows. Section 2 provides an overview of fundamental techniques which deal with sampling, join and group-by. Additionally, we introduce the concept of a foreign-key tree which orders relations into a hierarchy (thus the name), and we explain a naive combination approach. In sections 3 and 4, we introduce algorithms superior to the naive one. Section 5 presents an extensive experimental evaluation. Finally, a summary concludes the paper in section 6.

2   Sampling, Join and Group-by

This section briefly introduces sampling techniques for join operations as well as group-based sampling. The new concept of foreign-key trees serves as the foundation for the combination of these techniques.

2.1   Join Synopses

Acharya et. al. combine sampling and foreign-key joins by creating so-called join synopses [4]. The foreign-key relationship of a relation R_1 with foreign key fk to a relation R_2 is denoted $R_1 \rightarrow_{fk} R_2$. The symbol $\Rightarrow$ denotes the transitive closure of $\rightarrow$, and $\Rightarrow^*$ the reflexive transitive closure. A foreign-key graph visualizes $\rightarrow$ over a schema (cf.

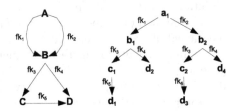

Fig. 1. F.k. graph (left) & tree (right)

Fig. 1, left). Every node represents a relation (and vice versa), every edge models a foreign-key relationship. The example shows a relation A which has two foreign keys fk_1 and fk_2 to relation B, i.e., A references B twice.

A join $R_1 \bowtie R_2$ is a foreign-key join (FKJ) with source relation R_1, if the join condition compares a foreign key of R_1 with the primary key of R_2 ($R_1 \rightarrow R_2$) for equality. The result of the FKJ consists of the primary key of the source relation, and the foreign keys of all involved relations. If it is joined with additional relations by using one of its foreign keys, another FKJ with the same source relation is created – thus, there is always exactly one source relation, which is used as a starting point. Between a relation R and an FKJ with source relation R, there is a 1:1-relationship. Informally, the FKJ looks up foreign keys in the respective relations and extends each tuple of the source relation by the result. A simple example scenario is shown in Figure 2. On the right, the result of the FKJ Emp $\bowtie$ Dep $\bowtie$ Loc is presented.

In the following, we assume that the foreign-key graph is free of cycles. In this case, a maximum foreign-key join (MFKJ) can be determined for every relation. It is free of redundancy; for example, it eliminates joins like $A \bowtie_{fk_1} B \bowtie_{fk_1} \ldots \bowtie_{fk_1} B$ (cf. Fig. 1, left). We introduce foreign-key trees to model such maximum foreign-key joins.

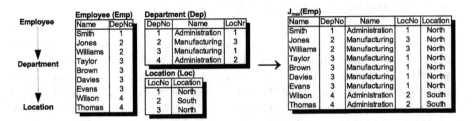

Fig. 2. Example scenario and maximum foreign-key join

Definition 1. The foreign-key tree $tree(R)$ of a relation R is made up of a root node r with associated relation $rel(r) = R$. For each foreign-key relationship of type $R \rightarrow_{fk} S$, the foreign-key tree of S is connected to r with the edge $r \rightarrow_{fk} tree(S)$.

Figure 1 (right) shows the foreign-key tree (FKT) of relation A. There is an N:1-relationship between nodes and relations. The MFKJ consists of one join operation per edge of the foreign-key tree. In detail, each node is joined with the MFKJ of its successors[1]. The MFKJ $J_{max}(A)$ of relation A is given by:

$$J_{max}(A) = A \bowtie_{fk_1} (B \bowtie_{fk_3} (C \bowtie_{fk_5} D) \bowtie_{fk_4} D)$$
$$\bowtie_{fk_2} (B \bowtie_{fk_3} (C \bowtie_{fk_5} D) \bowtie_{fk_4} D)$$

The join synopsis of a relation R resembles a random sample of $J_{max}(R)$. Due to the 1:1-relationship of tuples in R and $J_{max}(R)$, it is possible to sample R before executing the join, i.e., the sample $U = SRS(R)$ is computed and afterwards, it joined with all the relations of the FKT, yielding $J_{max}(U)$. This is crucial for the practicability of the method, since the complete MFKJ is very expensive to obtain. If a join synopsis is created for every relation of a schema, it is possible to approximately answer all queries with FKJs by using the appropriate synopsis.

2.2   Senate Sampling

Senate sampling [2] attacks the problem of sampling small groups; it ensures that all groups appear in the sample. This is achieved by assigning the same amount of space in the sample to each group. Therefore, it is necessary that all potential grouping attributes are already known in advance. Furthermore, the number of the non-empty groups has to be smaller than the size of the sample. Thus, it is guaranteed that for every group there is at least one tuple reserved in the sample.

The sampling process requires one scan of the relation. For each group, the algorithm creates an independent reservoir [7], i.e. a temporary relation usually stored in main memory. At any time, the reservoir contains a random sample of all tuples of its group. If m groups have been seen so far, the size of each reservoir is limited to $s_g = \frac{n}{m}$ tuples with n being the sample size. Therefore, each first occurrence of a group yields to a decrease of the size of all reservoirs. After all tuples have been processed, the reservoirs are written into a single sample table.

By using the senate sample, group-by queries can be answered approximately and without losing any group. However, the procedure has some inherent difficulties: it is often the case that the number of groups is too high because of the consideration of all potential grouping attributes and, thus, no useful sample can be generated. Alternatively, it is possible to compute multiple samples, each

---

[1] In the following, the term "node" is used synonymously for the relation associated with it; e.g., the tuples of a node a refers to the tuples of the relation A assigned to that node, actually

for a subset of the grouping attributes. Furthermore – if we limit the number of grouping attributes – small groups contain usually far less tuples than they have space in the sample. As a result, parts of the sample remain unused.

2.3   Small Group Sampling

Another approach to solve the small-group problem has been developed by Babcock et.al. and is called small group sampling (SGS, [3]). It generates multiple sample tables and selects an adequate subset of them at query evaluation time. The basic idea of SGS is to create a so-called small group table (SGT) for each attribute of the base relation. These small group tables include all tuples which have a rare value in the respective attribute. Therefore, the SGTs of a query's grouping attributes consist of tuples belonging to small groups. Additionally, a random sample of the base relation is generated. In general, this base sample covers tuples which belong to large groups.

The user has to define three parameters for the generation of the small group sample. First, the base sampling rate r $(0 < r \leq 1)$ determines the size n of the base sample in dependency of the number N of the tuples in the base relation $(n = N \cdot r)$. Second, if an attribute has more than τ distinct values, no SGT is generated. Therefore, τ is used to determine which attributes are likely to appear in a group-by clause. Finally, the small group fraction f defines the upper size limit of an SGT $(n_{SGT} \leq N \cdot f)$. Only the most rare attribute values appear in the SGT. Thus, f implicitly draws the line between rare and frequent.

The computation of the SGS consists of two phases, each requiring one table scan. First, a histogram is generated for each attribute. With their help, it is possible to decide which values are rare. In the second phase, this knowledge is used to generate the base sample and the SGTs. At query processing time, the base sample and the SGTs of the respective grouping attributes are used for approximate query evaluation. All tuples of groups which consist of at least one rare value in a grouping attribute are completely covered by an SGT – their aggregate is calculated exactly. All other groups are served by the base sample and evaluated approximately.

Dependencies between attributes may cause the SGS to miss some groups. Often, small groups which consist of frequent values only are not represented in the sample. But in contrast to senate sampling, the grouping attributes do not have to be known in advance and, thus, a small group sample is designed for arbitrary grouping attributes. However, the parametration is quite difficult. Additionally, functional dependencies between attributes lead to redundant SGTs, e.g., the SGT of an attribute country_name is likely to be equal to that of the attribute country_code.

2.4   Naive Combination

By combining join synopses and group-based sampling, we are able to answer queries with foreign-key joins and/or group-by approximately. It is not meaningful to simply use the MFKJ of a senate or small group sample, since thereby only attributes of the source relation would be considered as potential grouping attributes. Alternatively, the complete MFKJ of the source relation could be calculated and sampled afterwards. This naive approach is not feasible in most cases due to its high computation costs. Instead, we introduce new algorithms called hierarchical senate sampling (HSEN) and hierarchical small group sampling (HSGS), which result in samples identical to that of the naive approach but which are more efficient to obtain. Therefore, we show how to pull sampling before the join as done for join synopsis computation.

3   Hierarchical Senate Sampling

HSEN requires the FKT of the source relation as its input. Unlike in regular senate sampling, grouping attributes are defined at node level. Therefore, it is possible to assign different grouping attributes to relations that appear more than once within the tree. Throughout the paper, we use the scenario shown in Figure 2 as an example. Note that the foreign-key graph and the foreign-key tree of Emp are equal. Futhermore, let Loc.Location and Dep.Name be grouping attributes. In the following, we describe the computation of HSEN, which is divided into two phases.

3.1   Phase 1: Group Tables

Regular senate sampling determines the group of each tuple by extracting the values of the grouping attributes. Unfortunately, this is not possible if multiple relations are involved. Therefore, additional information has to be gathered from the data before sampling the source relation.

Definition 2. The group table GT_u of a node u contains one entry for every tuple of u. Each of these entries consists of a primary key and a group identifier (GID).

Thus, the group table (GT) captures the relationship between tuples and groups (cf. Fig. 3, left), which in turn are represented by a unique group identifier (GID). With their help, the group of a tuple of the source relation can be determined by looking up its foreign keys in the GTs of the respective referenced nodes. The actual values of the grouping attributes are not of interest. It is sufficient that tuples belonging to the same group have the same GID, and that tuples belonging to different groups have a different GID as well.

The group table does not have to be calculated for every node. A node is called directly grouping-relevant if at least one grouping attribute has been defined on it. In the example, this applies to the nodes Loc and Dep. Additionally, a node is called indirectly grouping-relevant if one of its successor nodes is grouping-relevant. This holds for Dep and Emp.

The first phase of HSEN computes the GTs of all grouping-relevant, direct successor nodes of the source relation. The algorithm starts with those nodes

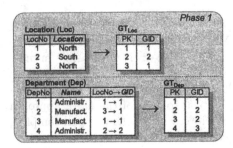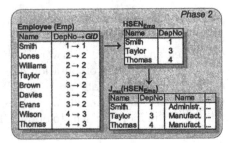

Fig. 3. Computation of the hierarchical senate sample

which do not have any grouping-relevant successor, and subsequently, proceeds backwards along the foreign-key relationships to the root node (bottom-up).

Let u be the node currently processed and let $v_1, \ldots, v_k$ be its direct, grouping-relevant successors. The computation of GT $_u$ requires one scan of u. If $k = 0$, i.e. u has no successor nodes with grouping attributes, each tuple's group is determined by simply using the values of the grouping attributes defined on it. A unique GID is assigned to each group. Thereby, a temporary data structure captures the 1:1-relationship between groups and GIDs. For each tuple, an entry consisting of its primary key and its GID is included in the GT. For instance, Fig. 3 shows the GT of Loc. The relationship between groups and GIDs is $\{(\text{North}, 1), (\text{South}, 2)\}$.

In order to calculate the GT of an indirectly grouping-relevant node ($k > 0$), the GTs of all its direct, grouping-relevant successors must be known. For example, GT $_{Loc}$ is required to calculate GT $_{Dep}$. In general, the procedure is identical to the one for $k = 0$. However, the value of every foreign key to a successor node is looked up in the respective group table. Afterwards, the obtained GID is used as an additional grouping attribute. Therefore, groups generated by successor nodes are considered, too. The complete algorithm is presented in more detail in the full paper [12].

The GT of the node Dep is shown in the lower left of Fig. 3. For its computation, the attribute Name and the GID out of GT $_{Loc}$ have been used as grouping attributes. By now, GT $_{Loc}$ is not needed anymore and is therefore deleted. The first phase is finished at this point, since there is no need to calculate a GT for the root node.

3.2 Phase 2: Sampling

The sampling of the source relation is almost identical to regular senate sampling. The only difference is that foreign keys have to be looked up in the GT of the respective successor node, and the obtained GID has to be used as additional grouping attribute. Due to space restrictions, this algorithm is not presented here.

Figure 3 (right) depicts a possible sample of size $n = 3$. One tuple is sampled from each of the groups (Adm, N), (Man, N), and (Adm, S). Finally, the MFKJ of this sample has to be calculated. In the full paper [12], we discuss several optimizations of the algorithm presented here and describe how to maintain the sample incrementally.

4   Hierarchical Small Group Sampling

As with senate sampling, SGS can be naively extended to multiple relations using the MFKJ of the source relation. By proceeding hierarchically, the computation costs are lowered noticeably and, thus, the method becomes practicable. Two core problems have to be solved: the determination of rare values on the one hand and of all tuples with these values on the other hand. The hierarchical approach is structured into 3 phases: phase 1 deals with the former of the two problems, phase 2 with the latter. In Phase 3 the base sample and the SGTs are computed.

4.1   Phase 1: Histogram Calculation

As explained in section 2.3, the determination of rare values requires a histogram for each attribute. If there is only one relation R, their calculation is simple. However, if multiple relations have to be considered, it is not possible to calculate the histograms[2] of every relation separately, since the influence of the foreign keys is lost otherwise. Instead, the number of references to every tuple has to be considered during histogram calculation.

Definition 3. The reference table $RT_{u \Rightarrow v}$ contains the primary key of every tuple of node v together with the number of tuples of node u that reference it via foreign keys $(u \Rightarrow v)$. Non-referenced tuples do not appear in the reference table.

For example, Fig. 4 (upper left part) shows the reference table $RT_{Emp \Rightarrow Dep}$, which captures the number of references of every tuple in Dep. For instance, the department with the number 3 is referenced four times. Subsequently, the reference table is used for histogram calculation. Let w be the root node of the FKT. Then, the reference table $RT_{w \Rightarrow v}$ is required for the computation of the histograms of a node v. The reference count is used as a weight for each tuple. For instance, the tuple $(3, Adm, 1)$ of Dep is counted four times.

The computation of histograms and reference tables is done simultaneously. In fact, the RT of a node v equals the (weighted) histogram of the foreign key attributes of its predecessor x, that is, the reference table $RT_{w \Rightarrow v}$ is computed together with the histograms of x. Since the root node w has no predecessor, its histograms and reference tables to successor nodes are computed first and without any weighting. Subsequently, the FKT is traversed top-down. For each tuple of a node v, its primary key is looked up in the reference table $RT_{w \Rightarrow v}$, and the obtained reference count is used as tuple weight, i.e. as scale factor. Therefore, the histograms are identical with those of the respective attributes in the MFKJ $J_{max}(rel(w))$. Please refer to the full paper [12] for a more detailed description of this algorithm.

---

[2] The histogram of the attribute i of node u is denoted $H_{u,i}$

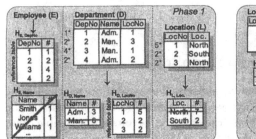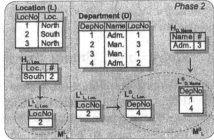

Fig. 4. Phase 1 and 2 of the computation of the hierarchical small group sample

After processing a node u, $RT_{w \Rightarrow u}$ is not needed anymore and therefore deleted. Furthermore, all histograms are restricted to rare values, i.e. iteratively, the most frequent value is removed until the number of tuples represented by the histogram does not exceed the upper size limit anymore. All remaining tuples will be included in the SGT later on (cf. sec. 2.3). Attributes with more than τ distinct values or without any rare values do not require a histogram anymore.

In the left of Figure 4, the first phase of hierarchical small group sampling is illustrated. In the example, the maximum number of distinct values is set to 2, the upper size limit of an SGT to 3. Therefore, only the histograms of the attributes Dep.Name and Loc.Location remain.

4.2   Phase 2: Key Sets and Assignment Sets

An SGT has to be generated for each attribute for which there is a non-empty histogram remaining after the first phase. Now, we have to determine which tuples of the source relation have to be included in which SGTs. Thus, the restricted histograms are converted step by step to so-called key sets (KS, per attribute), which consist of the primary keys of all tuples with rare values.

Definition 4. The key set $L_{u,i}^u$ of a histogram $H_{u,i}$ contains the primary keys of all tuples of u, whose value of the attribute i appears in the histogram.

Since the restricted histograms contain rare values only, this applies to the key sets, too. All histograms but those of the root node have to be converted to key sets according to definition 4. Thereby, the FKT is traversed bottom-up and a second table scan is performed at every node with at least one non-empty histogram. Figure 4 (right) shows the key sets $L_{Loc,Loc}^{Loc}$ and $L_{Dep,Name}^{Dep}$ for the example scenario. According to these key sets, the location with primary key 2 as well as the departments with primary keys 1 or 4 have a rare value in the attribute Location and Name respectively (cf. Fig. 2).

Additionally, when processing a node v the key sets of its direct successor nodes have to be converted to the primary keys of v.

Definition 5. Let v, u, and x be three nodes in the foreign-key tree with $v \neq u$ and $v \to u \Rightarrow^* x$, and assume that $L_{x,i}^u$ is known. Then, the key set $L_{x,i}^v$ contains the primary keys of all tuples from v, whose foreign keys to u appear in the key set $L_{x,i}^u$.

To summarize, the key set $L_{x,i}^v$ contains all those primary keys of v which lead to rare values of the attribute i of node x. The key sets of the leaf nodes (covered by definition 4) are used as a starting point. In this case, v and x refer to the same node. For instance, it holds Dep $\to$ Loc $\Rightarrow^*$ Loc in the example scenario. Therefore, the key set $L_{Loc,Loc.}^{Loc}$ is converted to $L_{Loc,Loc.}^{Dep}$ according to definition 5. It contains the primary keys of all tuples of Dep whose foreign key to Loc is present in the key set $L_{Loc,Loc.}^{Dep}$. In other words, the department with the primary key 4 leads to a rare value in the Loc.Location attribute.

An assignment set (AS, per node) integrates all the key sets of a specific node.

Definition 6. The assignment set M_L^u of a node u consists of the key sets $L_{u,i}^u$ of all restricted histograms $H_{u,i}$. If u has the direct successor nodes $v_1, \ldots, v_k$, M_L^u additionally contains all key sets out of $M_L^{v_1}, \ldots, M_L^{v_k}$ converted to primary keys of u according to definition 5.

Thus, all key sets of the assignment set M_L^u contain primary keys of u only. In the example scenario, there are two AS: $M_L^{Loc} = \{L_{Loc,Loc.}^{Loc}\}$ and $M_L^{Dep} = \{L_{Dep,Name}^{Dep}, L_{Loc,Loc.}^{Dep}\}$ (cf. Fig. 4). The computation of an AS requires the AS of all successor nodes. This is the reason why the FKT has to be processed bottom-up. Note that after the assignment set of a node u has been created, neither its histograms nor the assignment sets of its successors are needed anymore. Please refer to the full paper [12] for further details.

Only the assignment sets of the direct successors of the root node are the output of the second phase. Subsequently, they are used to sample the source relation.

4.3   Phase 3: Sampling

Just as with regular SGS, the source relation is scanned once to compute the base sample and the SGTs. For each attribute of the source relation, the assignment of tuples to SGTs is done with the help of its histogram. For all other attributes, the assignment sets are used, that is, for each direct successor node v the respective foreign key of the current tuple is extracted and looked up

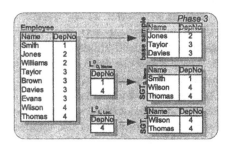

Fig. 5. Phase 3 of HSGS

in every key set $L_{x,i}^v$ within M_L^v. If it is present in there, the current tuple is copied to the SGT of attribute i of node x. For example, only the tuples with department number 1 or 4 are included in the SGT of Dep.Name (Fig. 5) since $L_{Dep,Name}^{Dep}$ contains the keys 1 and 4 only.

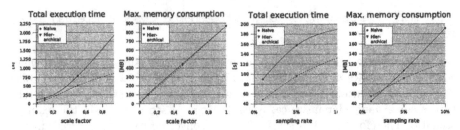

Fig. 6. DB size & computation costs   **Fig. 7.** Sampling rate & computation costs

Finally, the MFKJ of the base sample and the SGTs has to be computed. Since a tuple may appear in more than one sample table, it is worth computing the join before writing the sample tables in order to avoid unnecessary effort. Again, the discussion of several optimizations as well as sample maintenance is postponed to the full paper [8].

5   Evaluation

The hierarchical sampling techniques have been prototypically implemented and compared to the naive approach. The database (IBM UDB v8.1) has been addressed by a Java middleware, in which the sampling techniques have been integrated. The naive techniques have been implemented by using a view, and the hierarchical techniques have been implemented as described in the previous sections. The test system has been an AMD Athlon^{TM}XP 3000+ with 2 GB main memory. All tests have been executed with the TPC-D benchmark [13] and artificially skewed data. The size of the processed data is expressed by a scale factor. The relations Nation and Region have been excluded, since they only contain few tuples and do not scale. The skewness of the data has been simulated by a Zipf distribution with Zipf factor z. The Zipf factor $z = 1$ represents a uniform data distribution. A higher value of z yields more skewed data.

For an evaluation of the quality of the hierarchical senate sample, we used Customer.Nationkey and Part.Type as grouping attributes. The sampling rate has been 5%, the Zipf factor $z = 1.5$. Figure 6 compares the computation time of the sample and the main memory requirements. For large amounts of data, the hierarchical approach requires about 40% of the time the naive approach takes. The main memory requirements are almost identical for both approaches, even though the hierarchical approach uses additional data structures. The reason lies in the different use of the temporary reservoirs: on the one hand, they only consist of tuples from the source relation (hierarchical); on the other hand, these tuples are joined with all referenced relations in advance, and thus, become much bigger (naive).

Figure 7 depicts the influence of the sampling rate on the computation time and the memory requirements. The scale factor 0.1 has been used. The hierarchical approach accelerates the naive approach by a constant amount, i.e. it is

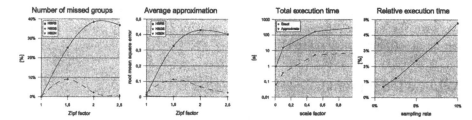

Fig. 8. Data skew & accuracy   **Fig. 9.** Approximate computation costs

mostly independent from the sample size. However, the naive approach needs considerably more main memory with increasing sampling rates.

The same measurements have also been done for hierarchical small group sampling. The results are almost identical. The only difference is the fact that small group sampling needs considerably less main memory space both in the naive and the hierarchical variant, but requires more computation time instead. Due to space restrictions, these results are not shown in here.

As can be seen in Figure 8 (left), group-based sampling decreases the amount of non-recognized groups considerably. A grouping by Custom er.N ationkey and Supplier.N ationkey has been done, the scale factor has been set to 0.1, and the metrics from [3] have been used. For a uniform data distribution ($z = 1$), all three sampling techniques offer comparable quality. But with increasing data skew, simple join synopses (HSRS) lose almost all small groups, while the HSGS only misses a few. The higher the data skew, the fewer middle-sized groups exist and the better small group sampling works. Finally, the HSEN recognizes all groups. It draws an advantage from the fact that it knows the grouping attributes in advance. The accuracy of the different techniques (cf. Figure 8, right) is evaluated similarly. For each group, the average revenue (price minus discount) has been calculated. Its root mean square error is shown in the figure.

Figure 9 (left) depicts the speed increase by approximate query processing with a sample size of 5% (logarithmic scale units). A scale factor of 0.1 has been used. The response time of join synopses and hierarchical group-based techniques is identical. On average, it is about 2.5% of the time required to compute the exact answer. As can be seen in Figure 9 (right), the sampling rate has a linear effect on the response time of an approximate query, relative to the one of an exact query.

6 Summary

We have shown how to efficiently combine foreign-key joins and group-based sampling. The resulting samples can be used to approximately answer queries, in which a relation and the relations referenced by it via foreign-key relationships are joined and/or in which groupings appear. It is not necessary to access the base data; all the required information is present in the sample.

Our approaches can also be applied to other sampling techniques. For example, with the help of reference tables, the outliers detected by outlier indexing can be determined more efficiently.

Acknowledgement

This work has been supported by the German Research Society (DFG) under LE 1416/3-1.

References

1. University of California at Berkeley: How much Information? (2003) http://www.sims.berkeley.edu/research/projects/how-much-info-2003/.
2. Acharya, S., Gibbons, P., Poosala, V.: Congressional Samples for Approximate Answering of Group-By Queries. In: Proc. ACM SIGMOD. (2000) 487–498
3. Babcock, B., Chaudhuri, S., Das, G.: Dynamic sample selection for approximate query processing. In: Proc. ACM SIGMOD. (2003) 539–550
4. Acharya, S., Gibbons, P., Poosala, V., Ramaswamy, S.: Join synopses for approximate query answering. In: Proc. ACM SIGMOD. (1999) 275–286
5. Barbará, D., DuMouchel, W., Faloutsos, C., Haas, P., Hellerstein, J., Ioannidis, Y., Jagadish, H., Johnson, T., Ng, R., Poosala, V., Ross, K., Sevcik, K.: The New Jersey Data Reduction Report. IEEE Data Eng. Bull. **20** (1997) 3–45
6. Hellerstein, J., Haas, P., Wang, H.: Online Aggregation. In: Proc. ACM SIGMOD. (1997) 171–182
7. Vitter, J.: Random Sampling with a Reservoir. ACM Transactions on Mathematical Software **11** (1985) 37–57
8. Gemulla, R., Lehner, W.: On Incremental Maintenance of Materialized Offline Samples (2005) Submitted for publication.
9. Ganti, V., Lee, M., Ramakrishnan, R.: ICICLES: Self-Tuning Samples for Approximate Query Answering. In: The VLDB Journal. (2000) 176–187
10. Chaudhuri, S., Das, G., Datar, M., Motwani, R., Narasayya, V.: Overcoming Limitations of Sampling for Aggregation Queries. In: Proc. ICDE. (2001) 534–544
11. Chaudhuri, S., Motwani, R., Narasayya, V.: On Random Sampling over Joins. In: Proc. ACM SIGMOD. (1999) 263–274
12. Gemulla, R., Berthold, H., Lehner, W.: Hierarchical Group-based Sampling (2005) Full version available at http://wwwdb.inf.tu-dresden.de/files/team/gemulla/files/hgs-fullversion.pdf.
13. Transaction Processing Performance Council: TPC-D Benchmark Version 2.1. (1998) http://www.tpc.org.

Using Schema Transformation Pathways for Data Lineage Tracing

Hao Fan and Alexandra Poulovassilis

School of Computer Science and Information Systems, Birkbeck College,
University of London, Malet Street, London WC1E 7HX
{hao,ap}@dcs.bbk.ac.uk

Abstract. With the increasing amount and diversity of information available on the Internet, there has been a huge growth in information systems that need to integrate data from distributed, heterogeneous data sources. Tracing the lineage of the integrated data is one of the problems being addressed in data warehousing research. This paper presents a data lineage tracing approach based on schema transformation pathways. Our approach is not limited to one specific data model or query language, and would be useful in any data transformation/integration framework based on sequences of primitive schema transformations.

1 Introduction

A data warehousing system collects data from distributed, autonomous and heterogeneous data sources into a central repository to enable analysis and mining of the integrated information. However, sometimes what we need is not only to analyse the data in the integrated database, but also to investigate how certain integrated information was derived from the data sources, which is the problem of *data lineage tracing* (DLT). Supporting DLT in data warehousing environments has a number of applications: in-depth data analysis, on-line analysis mining (OLAM), scientific databases, authorization management, and materialized view schema evolution [2, 8, 9, 13, 18].

AutoMed[1] is a heterogeneous data transformation and integration system which offers the capability to handle data integration across multiple data models. In the AutoMed approach, the integration of schemas is specified as a sequence of primitive schema transformation steps, which incrementally add, delete or rename schema constructs, thereby transforming each source schema into the target schema. We term the sequence of primitive transformations steps defined for transforming a schema S_1 into a schema S_2 a *transformation pathway* from S_1 to S_2.

In [11] we discussed how AutoMed metadata can be used to express the schemas and the cleansing, transformation and integration processes in heterogeneous data warehousing environments. In this paper, we focus on how AutoMed metadata can be used for tracing the lineage of data in an integrated database.

The outline of this paper is as follows. Section 2 gives a review of related work. Section 3 gives an overview of AutoMed, as well as a data integration example. Section 4 presents our DLT techniques, including the DLT formulae developed to handle virtual intermediate lineage data and the DLT algorithm operating along a general schema transformation pathway. Section 5 gives our concluding remarks.

---

[1] See http://www.doc.ic.ac.uk/automed/

M. Jackson et al. (Eds.): BNCOD 2005, LNCS 3567, pp. 133–144, 2005.
© Springer-Verlag Berlin Heidelberg 2005

2   Related Work

The problem of data lineage tracing in data warehousing environments has been formally studied by Cui *et al.* in [6–8]. In particular, the fundamental definitions regarding data lineage, including *tuple derivation for an operator* and *tuple derivation for a view*, were developed in [8], as were methods for derivation tracing with both set and bag semantics. Their work has addressed the derivation tracing problem using bag semantics and has provided the concept of *derivation set* and *derivation pool* for tracing data lineage with duplicate elements. Reference [6] also introduces a way to trace data lineage for complex views in data warehouses. However, the approach is limited to the relational data model.

Another fundamental concept of data lineage is discussed by Buneman *et al.* in [4], namely the difference between "why" provenance and "where" provenance. Why-provenance refers to the source data that had some influence on the existence of the integrated data. Where-provenance refers to the actual data in the sources from which the integrated data was extracted.

In our approach, both why- and where-provenance are considered, using bag semantics. Our previous work [10] defines the notions of *affect-pool* and *origin-pool* for data lineage tracing in AutoMed – the former derives all of the source data that had some influence on the tracing data, while the latter derives the specific data in the sources from which the tracing data is extracted. In that work we develop formulae for deriving the affect-pool and origin-pool of a data item in the extent of a materialised schema construct created by a single schema transformation step. Our DLT approach is to apply these formulae on each transformation step in a transformation pathway in turn, so as to obtain the lineage data in stepwise fashion.

Cui and Widom in [7] also discuss the problem of tracing data lineage for general data warehousing transformations, that is, the considered operators and algebraic properties are no longer limited to relational views. However, without a framework for expressing general transformations in heterogeneous database environments, most of algorithms in [7] are recalling the view definition and examining each item in the data source to decide if the item is in the data lineage of the data being traced. This can be expensive if the view definition is a complex one and enumerating all items in the data source is impractical for large data sets.

Reference [18] proposes a general framework for computing *fine-grained* data lineage, *i.e.* a specific derivation in the data source, using a limited amount of information, *weak* and *verified inversion*, about the processing steps. Based on weak and verified inversion functions, which must be specified by the transformation definer, the paper defines and traces data lineage for each transformation step in a database visualization environment. However, the system cannot obtain the exact lineage data, only a number of guarantees about the lineage is provided. Further, specifying weak and verified inversion functions for each transformation step is onerous work for the data warehouse definer. Moreover, the DLT procedures cannot straightforwardly be reused when the data warehouse evolves. Our approach considers the problem of data lineage tracing at the tuple level and computes the exact lineage data. Moreover, AutoMed's ready support for schema evolution (see [12]) means that our DLT algorithms can be reapplied if schema transformation pathways evolve.

One limit of our earlier work described in [10] is that we assumed the transformation pathway used by our DLT algorithm is fully materialised, *i.e.* new schema constructs created along the pathway are materialised. In practice, we need to handle the situation of virtual or partially materialised transformation pathways, in which intermediate schema constructs may or may not be materialised. In this paper, we describe an approach for tracing data lineage along a general schema transformation pathway.

3   Overview of AutoMed

AutoMed supports a low-level hypergraph-based data model (HDM). Higher-level modelling languages are defined in terms of this HDM. For example, previous work has shown how relational, ER, OO [15], XML [19], flat-file [3] and multidimensional [11] data models can be so defined. An HDM schema consists of a set of nodes, edges and constraints, and each modelling construct of a higher-level modelling language is specified as some combination of HDM nodes, edges and constraints. For any modelling language $\mathcal{M}$ specified in this way, via the API of AutoMed's Model Definitions Repository [3], AutoMed provides a set of primitive schema transformations that can be applied to schema constructs expressed in $\mathcal{M}$. In particular, for every construct of $\mathcal{M}$ there is an **add** and a **delete** primitive transformation which add to/delete from a schema an instance of that construct. For those constructs of $\mathcal{M}$ which have textual names, there is also a **rename** primitive transformation.

In AutoMed, schemas are incrementally transformed by applying to them a sequence of primitive transformations $t_1, \ldots, t_r$. Each primitive transformation adds, deletes or renames just one schema construct, expressed in some modelling language. Thus, the intermediate (and indeed the target) schemas may contain constructs of more than one modelling language.

Each **add** or **delete** transformation is accompanied by a query specifying the extent of the new or deleted construct in terms of the rest of the constructs in the schema. This query is expressed in a functional query language IQL[2]. The queries within **add** and **delete** transformations are used by AutoMed's Global Query Processor to evaluate an IQL query over a global schema in the case of a virtual data integration scenario. In the case that the global schema is materialised, AutoMed's Query Evaluator can be used directly on the materialised data.

3.1   Simple IQL

In order to illustrate our DLT algorithm, we use a subset of IQL, *Simple IQL* (SIQL), as the query language in this paper. More complex IQL queries can be encoded as a series of transformations with SIQL queries on intermediate schema constructs. We stress that although illustrated within a particular query language syntax, our DLT algorithms could also be applied to schema transformation pathways involving queries expressed in other query languages supporting operations on set, bag and list collections.

---

[2] IQL is a comprehensions-based functional query language. Such languages subsume query languages such as SQL and OQL in expressiveness [5]. We refer the reader to [14, 17] for details of IQL and references to work on comprehension-based functional query languages

Supposing D, D_1 ..., D_n denote bags of the appropriate type (base collections), SIQL supports the following queries: group D groups a bag of pairs D on their first component. distinct D removes duplicates from a bag. f D applies an aggregation function f (which may be max, min, count, sum or avg) to a bag. gc f D groups a bag D of pairs on their first component and applies an aggregation function f to the second component. ++ is the bag union operator and $--$ is the bag *monus* operator [1]. SIQL comprehensions are of three forms: $[\overline{x}|\overline{x_1} \leftarrow D_1; \ldots; \overline{x_n} \leftarrow D_n; C_1; \ldots; C_k]$, $[\overline{x}|\overline{x} \leftarrow D_1;$ member $D_2 \ \overline{y}]$, and $[\overline{x}|\overline{x} \leftarrow D_1;$ not(member $D_2 \ \overline{y})]$. Here, each $\overline{x_1}$, ..., $\overline{x_n}$ is either a single variable or a tuple of variables. $\overline{x}$ is either a single variable or value, or a tuple of variables or values, and must include all of variables appearing in $\overline{x_1}, ..., \overline{x_n}$. Each $C_1, ..., C_k$ is a condition not referring to any base collection. Also, each variable appearing in $\overline{x}$ and $C_1, ..., C_k$ must also appear in some $\overline{x_i}$, and the variables in $\overline{y}$ must appear in $\overline{x}$. Finally, a query of the form map $(\lambda \overline{x}.e)$ D applies to each element of a collection D an anonymous function defined by a lambda abstraction $\lambda \overline{x}.e$ and returns the resulting collection.

Comprehension syntax can express the common algebraic operations on collection types such as sets, bags and lists [5] and such operations can be readily expressed in SIQL. In particular, let us consider *selection* (σ), *projection*(π), *join* ($\bowtie$), and *aggregation* (α) (*union* ( ) and *difference* ($-$) are directly supported in SIQL via the ++ and $--$ operators). The general form of a Select-Project-Join (SPJ) expression is $\pi_A(\sigma_C(D_1 \bowtie ... \bowtie D_n))$ and this can be expressed as follows in comprehension syntax: $[A|\overline{x_1} \leftarrow D_1; \ldots; \overline{x_n} \leftarrow D_n; C]$. However, since in general the tuple of variables A may not contain all the variables appearing in $\overline{x_1}, ..., \overline{x_n}$ (as is required in SIQL), we can use the following two transformation steps to express a general SPJ expression in SIQL, where $\overline{x}$ includes all of the variables appearing in $\overline{x_1}, ...\overline{x_n}$:

```
v1 = [x̄|x̄₁ ← D₁;...;x̄ₙ ← Dₙ; C]
v  = map (λx̄.A) v1
```

The algebraic operator α applies an aggregation function to a collection and this functionality is captured by the gc operator in SIQL. E.g., supposing the scheme of a collection D is D(A1,A2,A3), an expression $\alpha_{A2,f(A3)}(D)$ is expressed in SIQL as:

```
v1 = map (λ{x1,x2,x3}.{x2,x3}) D
v  = gc f v1
```

3.2   An Example Data Integration

In this paper, we will use schemas expressed in a simple relational data model to illustrate our techniques. However, we stress that these techniques are applicable to schemas defined in *any* data modelling language having been specified within AutoMed's Model Definitions Repository, including modelling languages for semi-structured data [3, 19].

In our simple relational model, there are two kinds of schema construct: Rel and Att. The extent of a Rel construct $\langle\!\langle R \rangle\!\rangle$ is the projection of relation R onto its primary key attributes $k_1, ..., k_n$. The extent of each Att construct $\langle\!\langle R, a \rangle\!\rangle$ where a is a non-key attribute of R is the projection of R onto $k_1, ..., k_n, a$. We refer the reader to [15] for an encoding of a richer relational data model, including the modelling of constraints.

Suppose that MAtab(CID, SID, Mark) and IStab(CID, SID, Mark) are two source relations for a data warehouse respectively storing students' marks for two departments

MA and IS, in which CID and SID are the course and student IDs. Suppose also that a relation CourseSum(<u>Dept</u>, <u>CID</u>, Total, Avg) is in the data warehouse which gives the total and average mark for each course of each department.

The following transformation pathway expresses the schema transformation and integration processes in this example. Due to space limitations, we have not given the steps for removing the source relation constructs (note that this 'growing' and 'shrinking' of schemas is characteristic of AutoMed schema transformation pathways). Schema constructs $\langle\!\langle$Details$\rangle\!\rangle$ and $\langle\!\langle$Details, Mark$\rangle\!\rangle$ are temporary ones which are created for integrating the source data and then deleted after the global relation is created.

addRel $\langle\!\langle$Details$\rangle\!\rangle$ $[\{\texttt{'MA'},\texttt{k1},\texttt{k2}\}|\{\texttt{k1},\texttt{k2}\}\leftarrow\langle\!\langle\mathsf{MAtab}\rangle\!\rangle]$
                                        $\texttt{++}[\{\texttt{'IS'},\texttt{k1},\texttt{k2}\}|\{\texttt{k1},\texttt{k2}\}\leftarrow\langle\!\langle\mathsf{IStab}\rangle\!\rangle];$
addAtt $\langle\!\langle$Details, Mark$\rangle\!\rangle$ $[\{\texttt{'MA'},\texttt{k1},\texttt{k2},\texttt{x}\}|\{\texttt{k1},\texttt{k2},\texttt{x}\}\leftarrow\langle\!\langle\mathsf{MAtab},\mathsf{Mark}\rangle\!\rangle]$
                                        $\texttt{++}[\{\texttt{'IS'},\texttt{k1},\texttt{k2},\texttt{x}\}|\{\texttt{k1},\texttt{k2},\texttt{x}\}\leftarrow\langle\!\langle\mathsf{IStab},\mathsf{Mark}\rangle\!\rangle];$
addRel $\langle\!\langle$CourseSum$\rangle\!\rangle$ $\texttt{distinct}\;[\{\texttt{k},\texttt{k1}\}|\{\texttt{k},\texttt{k1},\texttt{k2}\}\leftarrow\langle\!\langle\mathsf{Details}\rangle\!\rangle]$
addAtt $\langle\!\langle$CourseSum, Total$\rangle\!\rangle$ $[\{\texttt{x},\texttt{y},\texttt{z}\}|\{\{\texttt{x},\texttt{y}\},\texttt{z}\}\leftarrow(\texttt{gc sum}$
                                        $[\{\{\texttt{k},\texttt{k1}\},\texttt{x}\}|\{\texttt{k},\texttt{k1},\texttt{k2},\texttt{x}\}\leftarrow\langle\!\langle\mathsf{Details},\mathsf{Mark}\rangle\!\rangle])];$
addAtt $\langle\!\langle$CourseSum, Avg$\rangle\!\rangle$ $[\{\texttt{x},\texttt{y},\texttt{z}\}|\{\{\texttt{x},\texttt{y}\},\texttt{z}\}\leftarrow(\texttt{gc avg}$
                                        $[\{\{\texttt{k},\texttt{k1}\},\texttt{x}\}|\{\texttt{k},\texttt{k1},\texttt{k2},\texttt{x}\}\leftarrow\langle\!\langle\mathsf{Details},\mathsf{Mark}\rangle\!\rangle])];$
delAtt $\langle\!\langle$Details, Mark$\rangle\!\rangle$ $[\{\texttt{'MA'},\texttt{k1},\texttt{k2},\texttt{x}\}|\{\texttt{k1},\texttt{k2},\texttt{x}\}\leftarrow\langle\!\langle\mathsf{MAtab},\mathsf{Mark}\rangle\!\rangle]$
                                        $\texttt{++}[\{\texttt{'IS'},\texttt{k1},\texttt{k2},\texttt{x}\}|\{\texttt{k1},\texttt{k2},\texttt{x}\}\leftarrow\langle\!\langle\mathsf{IStab},\mathsf{Mark}\rangle\!\rangle];$
delRel $\langle\!\langle$Details$\rangle\!\rangle$ $[\{\texttt{'MA'},\texttt{k1},\texttt{k2}\}|\{\texttt{k1},\texttt{k2}\}\leftarrow\langle\!\langle\mathsf{MAtab}\rangle\!\rangle]$
                                        $\texttt{++}[\{\texttt{'IS'},\texttt{k1},\texttt{k2}\}|\{\texttt{k1},\texttt{k2}\}\leftarrow\langle\!\langle\mathsf{IStab}\rangle\!\rangle];$
...

Note that some of the queries appearing in the above transformation steps are not SIQL but general IQL queries. In such cases, for the purposes of lineage tracing, we decompose a general IQL query into a sequence of SIQL queries by means of a depth-first traversal of the IQL query tree. For example, the IQL query
$$[\{\texttt{x},\texttt{y},\texttt{z}\}|\{\{\texttt{x},\texttt{y}\},\texttt{z}\}\leftarrow(\texttt{gc avg}\;[\{\{\texttt{k},\texttt{k1}\},\texttt{x}\}|\{\texttt{k},\texttt{k1},\texttt{k2},\texttt{x}\}\leftarrow\langle\!\langle\mathsf{Details},\mathsf{Mark}\rangle\!\rangle])]$$
is decomposed into following sequence of SIQL queries:
$$\texttt{v1} = \texttt{map}\;(\lambda\{\texttt{k},\texttt{k1},\texttt{k2},\texttt{x}\}.\{\{\texttt{k1},\texttt{k2}\},\texttt{x}\})\;\langle\!\langle\mathsf{Details},\mathsf{Mark}\rangle\!\rangle$$
$$\texttt{v2} = \texttt{gc avg v1}$$
$$\texttt{v}\;\; = \texttt{map}\;(\lambda\{\{\texttt{x},\texttt{y}\},\texttt{z}\}.\{\texttt{x},\texttt{y},\texttt{z}\})\;\texttt{v2}$$
In the rest of the paper, our discussion assumes that all queries in transformation steps are SIQL queries.

4   Data Lineage Tracing with AutoMed Schema Transformations

In heterogenous data integration environments, the data transformation and integration processes can be described using AutoMed schema transformation pathways (see [11]). Our DLT approach is to use the individual steps of these pathways to compute the lineage data of the tracing data by traversing the pathways in reverse order one step at a time. In particular, suppose a data source LD with schema LS is transformed into a global database GD with schema GS, and the transformation pathway LS $\rightarrow$ GS is $ts_1, ..., ts_n$. Given tracing data td belonging to the extent of some schema construct in GD, we firstly find the transformation step ts_i which creates that construct and obtain td's lineage, dl_i, from ts_i. We then continue by tracing the lineage of dl_i from the

Table 1. DLT Formulae for MtMs

v	$DL(t)$
group D	$[\{x,y\}\mid\{x,y\}\leftarrow D; x=\overline{a}]$
sort D	$D\mid t$
distinct D	$D\mid t$
aggFun D	D
gc aggFun D	$[\{x,y\}\mid\{x,y\}\leftarrow D; x=\overline{a}]$
D_1 ++ D_2 ++ ... ++ D_n	$\forall i.D_i\mid t$
D_1 -- D_2	$D_1\mid t, D_2$
$[\overline{x}\mid\overline{x_1}\leftarrow D_1;\ldots;\overline{x_n}\leftarrow D_n; C]$	$\forall i.[\overline{x_i}\mid\overline{x_i}\leftarrow D_i; \overline{x_i}=((\lambda\overline{x}.\overline{x_i})\,t)]$
$[\overline{x}\mid\overline{x}\leftarrow D_1;\ \text{member}\ D_2\ \overline{y}]$	$D_1\mid t, [\overline{y}\mid\overline{y}\leftarrow D_2; \overline{y}=((\lambda\overline{x}.\overline{y})\,t)]$
$[\overline{x}\mid\overline{x}\leftarrow D_1;\ \text{not(member}\ D_2\ \overline{y})]$	$D_1\mid t, D_2$
map $(\lambda\overline{x}.e)$ D	$[\overline{x}\mid\overline{x}\leftarrow D, e=t]$

remaining transformation pathway $ts_1,\ldots,ts_{i-1}$. We continue in this fashion, until we obtain the final lineage data from the data source LD.

Since delete transformations do not create schema constructs, they can be ignored in the DLT process. Tracing data lineage with respect to a transformation rename (O,O') is simple – the lineage data in O is the same as the tracing data in O'. It only remains to consider add transformations. A single add transformation step can be expressed as v=q, in which v is the new schema construct created by the transformation and q is an SIQL query over the current schema constructs. We have developed a DLT formula for each type of SIQL query which, given tracing data in v, evaluates the lineage of this data from the extents of the schema constructs referenced in v=q. If these extents and the tracing data are both materialised, Table 1 gives the DLT formulae for tracing the affect-pool of a tuple t, $DL(t)$. The DLT formulae for tracing the origin-pool are similar and we refer the reader to [10] for a discussion of the difference between the affect-pool and the origin-pool.

In Table 1, $D\mid t$ denotes all instances of the tuple t in the bag D (i.e. the result of the query $[x\mid x\leftarrow D; x=t]$). Since the results of queries of the form group D and gc f D are a collection of pairs, in the DLT formulae for these two queries we assume that the tracing tuple t is of the form $\{\overline{a},\overline{b}\}$.

The DLT formulae in Table 1 either provide a *derivation tracing query* [8] specifying the lineage data of t or, in some cases, give the lineage data directly. If a formula returns a derivation tracing query, we need to evaluate the query to obtain the lineage data. If a formula returns the lineage data directly, no such evaluation is needed.

If all schema constructs created by add transformations are materialised, a simple way to trace the lineage of data in the global database GD is to apply the above DLT formulae on each transformation step in the transformation LS $\rightarrow$ GS in reverse from GS, finally ending up with the lineage data in the original data source LD. Such a DLT method has been described in our previous work [10]. However, in general transformation pathways not all schema constructs created by add transformations will be materialised, and the above simple DLT approach is no longer applicable because it does not obtain lineage data from a virtual schema construct. In this paper, we propose a DLT approach that handles such general transformation pathways.

4.1   The Approach

One approach to solving the problem of virtual schema constructs would be to use AutoMed's Global Query Processor to evaluate the query creating the virtual construct and compute its extent, so that the above simple DLT approach could be applied. However, this approach is impractical due to the space and time overheads it incurs.

Instead, our approach is to use a data structure, **Lineage**, to denote lineage data from the extent of a schema construct. If the construct is materialised, **Lineage** contains the actual lineage data. If the construct is virtual, **Lineage** contains relevant information for deriving the lineage data. This information will be used by subsequent DLT steps to evaluate the final lineage data. Each **Lineage** object contains five attributes: (i)data, which is a collection of materialised lineage data or, if the lineage data is virtual, the value $null$; (ii) construct, which is the name of the schema construct whose extent contains the lineage data; (iii) isVirtual, stating if the lineage data is virtual or not; (iv) elemStruct, describing the structure of the data in the extent of a virtual schema construct, $e.g.$ a 2-item tuple $\{$x1,x2$\}$, or a 3-item tuple $\{$x1,x2,x3$\}$; (v) constraint, expressing the constraint specifying the lineage data from a virtual schema construct.

For example, suppose lineage data in a schema construct D is derived from the query $[\{x,y\}|\{x,y\} \leftarrow D; x = 5]$, and lp is a **Lineage** object expressing the lineage data. If D= $[\{1,2\},\{5,1\},\{5,2\},\{3,1\}]$ is materialised, then lp will be: lp.data = $[\{5,1\},\{5,2\}]$; lp.construct= "D"; lp.isVirtual = false; lp.elemStruct= null; and lp.constraint= null. On the other hand, if D is a virtual schema construct, then lp will be: lp.data = null; lp.construct= "D"; lp.isVirtual = true; lp.elemStruct = "$\{$x,y$\}$"; and lp.constraint= "x=5".

We denote by O|d1 a **Lineage** object in which O is the name of the schema construct and d1 is the data lineage. If the lineage data is materialised, d1 will be the data itself, otherwise d1 will be the form of (S, C), where S denotes the *elemStruct* and C the *constraint*. For example, the above two **Lineage** objects are denoted by D|$[\{5,1\},\{5,2\}]$ and D|$(\{x,y\},$x=5$)$, respectively.

4.2   The DLT Formulae

It is necessary that our DLT formulae can handle the following four cases: MtMs – both the tracing data and the source data are materialised; MtVs – the tracing data is materialised and the source data is virtual; VtMs – the tracing data is virtual and the source data is materialised; and VtVs – both the tracing data and the source data are virtual. The DLT formulae for the case of MtMs were given in Table 1, and from these we have derived the DLT formulae for the other three cases:

Case MtVs. There were two kinds of DLT formulae in Table 1: tracing queries and real lineage data. Since with MtVS the source data is virtual, we cannot evaluate tracing queries and so **Lineage** objects are required to store the information about these queries. For example, the tracing query $[\{x,y\}|\{x,y\} \leftarrow D; x = \bar{a}]$ is expressed as $D|(\{x,y\}, x = \bar{a})$. In the case of real lineage data, the lineage data might be the tracing data, t, itself or all the items in a source collection D. If the lineage data is t, it is available no matter whether D is materialised or not. If the the lineage data is all items in

Table 2. DLT Formulae for MtVs

v	$DL(t)$
group D	$D\vert(\{x,y\}, x = \overline{a})$
sort D	$D\vert t$
distinct D	$D\vert t$
aggFun D	$D\vert(any, true)$
gc aggFun D	$D\vert(\{x,y\}, x = \overline{a})$
$D_1 \, \texttt{++} \, D_2 \, \texttt{++} \ldots \texttt{++} \, D_n$	$\forall i. D_i \vert t$
$D_1 \, \texttt{--} \, D_2$	$D_1\vert t, D_2\vert(any, true)$
$[\overline{x}\vert\overline{x_1} \leftarrow D_1; \ldots; \overline{x_n} \leftarrow D_n; C]$	$\forall i. D_i\vert(\overline{x_i}, \overline{x_i} = ((\lambda \overline{x}.\overline{x_i}) \, t))$
$[\overline{x}\vert\overline{x} \leftarrow D_1; \text{ member } D_2 \, \overline{y}]$	$D_1\vert t, D_2\vert(\overline{y}, \overline{y} = ((\lambda \overline{x}.\overline{y}) \, t))$
$[\overline{x}\vert\overline{x} \leftarrow D_1; \, \text{not}(\text{member } D_2 \, \overline{y})]$	$D_1\vert t, D_2\vert(any, true)$
map $(\lambda \overline{x}.e)$ D	$D\vert(\overline{x}, e = t)$

a virtual collection D, it is expressed by D| (any,true). Table 2 illustrates the DLT formulae for the case of MtVs.

Case VtMs. Virtual tracing data can be created by virtual source data. In particular, there are three kinds of virtual lineage data created in Table 2: (any,true), $(\{x,y\}, x=\overline{a})$, and $(\overline{x}, e=t)$ [3]. The DLT formulae for VtMs can be derived by applying these three kinds of virtual tracing data to the formulae given in Table 1. In this case, all source data is materialised, there is no virtual intermediate lineage data created.

For example, suppose the query is v=group D. If the virtual tracing tuple t is (any,true), the lineage data $DL(t)$ is all data in D, *i.e.* $DL(t) = $ D. If t is $(\{x,y\}, x=\overline{a})$, $DL(t)$ is all tuples in D with first component equal to $\overline{a}$, which is the result of the query $[\{x,y\}\vert\{x,y\} \leftarrow D; x = \overline{a}]$. If t is $(\overline{x}, e=t)$, $DL(t)$ is all tuples in D with first component equal to the first component of the tracing data t, which is the result of the query $[\{x,y\}\vert\{x,y\} \leftarrow D; member \, [first \, \overline{x}\vert\overline{x} \leftarrow v; e = t]]$. We can see that the virtual view, v, is used in this query. Since the source data is materialised, we can easily recover v and evaluate the tracing query.

Table 3 gives the whole list of formulae for the case of VtMs with virtual tracing data of the form $(\overline{x}, e=t)$. The formulae for the other two kinds of virtual tracing data can easily be derived.

Case VtVs. The DLT formulae for VtVs are similar to the formulae for VtMs but in this case the source data are unavailable. Thus, we use Lineage objects to store the virtual intermediate lineage data.

For example, suppose the query is v=group D. If the virtual tracing tuple t is (any,true), the virtual lineage data $DL(t)$ is D| (any,true). If t is $(\{x,y\}, x=\overline{a})$, the virtual $DL(t)$ is D|$(\{x,y\}, x=\overline{a})$. If t is $(\overline{x}, e=t)$, the virtual $DL(t)$ is D|$(\{x,y\}, member \, [first \, \overline{x}\vert\overline{x} \leftarrow v; e=t] \, x)$. Note that, the virtual view v is used

---

[3] Note that in Table 2 the lineage data $(\overline{x_i}, \overline{x_i} = ((\lambda \overline{x}.\overline{x_i}) \, t))$ and $(\overline{y}, \overline{y} = ((\lambda \overline{x}.\overline{y}) \, t))$ in the 8th and 9th lines are not virtual. Since t is real data and variable tuple $\overline{x}$ contains all variables appearing in $\overline{x_i}$, the expression $(\lambda \overline{x}.\overline{x_i}) \, t$ returns real data too. For example, supposing $\overline{x} = \{x_1, x_2, x_3\}$, $\overline{x_i} = \{x_1, x_3\}$, and $t = \{1, 2, 3\}$, then $(\lambda \overline{x}.\overline{x_i}) \, t = (\lambda\{x_1, x_2, x_3\}.\{x_1, x_3\}) \, \{1, 2, 3\} = \{1, 3\}$

Table 3. DLT Formulae for VtMs with tracing data $(\overline{x}, e = t)$

v	$DL(t)$
group D	$[\{x, y\} \mid \{x, y\} \leftarrow D;\ member\ [first\ \overline{x} \mid \overline{x} \leftarrow v; e = t]\ x]$
sort D	$[\overline{x} \mid \overline{x} \leftarrow D; e = t]$
distinct D	$[\overline{x} \mid \overline{x} \leftarrow D; e = t]$
aggFun D	D
gc aggFun D	$[\{x, y\} \mid \{x, y\} \leftarrow D;\ member\ [first\ \overline{x} \mid \overline{x} \leftarrow v; e = t]\ x]$
$D_1 +\!+ D_2 +\!+ \ldots +\!+ D_n$	$\forall i.[\overline{x} \mid \overline{x} \leftarrow D_i; e = t]$
$D_1 -\!- D_2$	$D_1 \mid [\overline{x} \mid \overline{x} \leftarrow v; e = t], D_2$
$[\overline{x} \mid \overline{x_1} \leftarrow D_1; \ldots; \overline{x_n} \leftarrow D_n; C]$	$\forall i.[\overline{x_i} \mid \overline{x_i} \leftarrow D_i;$ $member\ (map\ (\lambda \overline{x}.\overline{x_i})\ [\overline{x} \mid \overline{x} \leftarrow v; e = t])\ \overline{x_i}]$
$[\overline{x} \mid \overline{x} \leftarrow D_1; member\ D_2\ \overline{y}]$	$[\overline{x} \mid \overline{x} \leftarrow D_1; member\ D_2\ \overline{y}; e = t],$ $[\overline{y} \mid \overline{y} \leftarrow D_2; member\ (map\ (\lambda \overline{x}.y)\ [\overline{x} \mid \overline{x} \leftarrow v; e = t])\ \overline{y}]$
$[\overline{x} \mid \overline{x} \leftarrow D_1; not(member\ D_2\ \overline{y})]$	$D_1 \mid [\overline{x} \mid \overline{x} \leftarrow v; e = t], D_2$
$map\ (\lambda \overline{x_1}.e_1)\ D$	$[\overline{x_1} \mid \overline{x_1} \leftarrow D; e = t]$

in this virtual lineage data expression. However, since the source data D is virtual, we cannot recover v by just evaluating the query v=group D. In this case, AutoMed's Global Query Processor can be used to materialise v. Once v is materialised, the virtual tracing data t can also be recovered and this situation reverts to the case of MtVs which we discussed earlier. Alternatively, the view definition of v can be propagated through the remaining DLT steps until the end of the process. So far we have only implemented the first approach and it remains to implement the second approach and investigate their trade-offs.

4.3   DLT for General Transformation Pathways

Having obtained the DLT formulae for above four cases, lineage data based on a single transformation step is obtained by applying the appropriate formula to the step's query. Our DLT procedure for a single transformation step is DLT4AStep(td, ts) and its output is the lineage of td in ts's data sources i.e. a list of Lineage objects which might contain either materialised or virtual lineage data. In our DLT algorithms for a general transformation pathway, there are two further procedures: tracing the lineage of a single tuple along a transformation pathway and tracing the lineage of a set of tuples along a transformation pathway. This is because the lineage of one Lineage object based on a single transformation step might be a list of Lineage objects, if the transformation step has multiple data sources. Figure 1 gives the two procedures: oneDLT4APath$(td, [ts_1, ..., t_n])$ traces the lineage of a single tracing tuple td along a transformation pathway $[ts_1, ..., t_n]$, and listDLT4APath$([td_1, ..., td_m], [ts_1, ..., ts_n])$ traces the lineage of a list of tracing tuples along a transformation pathway.

oneDLT4APath firstly finds the transformation step, ts_i, which creates the schema construct containing td and then calls the procedure DLT4AStep to obtain the lineage of td based on this transformation step. DLT4AStep returns a list of Lineage objects. After that, the procedure oneDLT4APath calls the procedure listDLT4APath to further trace the lineage of this list of Lineage objects along the rest of the transformation

```
Proc oneDLT4APath(td, [ts₁, ..., tsₙ])
{  lpList = ø;
    for i = n downto 1, do
       if (td.construct is created by tsᵢ)
          Num = i;
          lpList = DLT4AStep(td, tsᵢ);
          continue; //* End the for loop
       restTP = [ts₁, ..., ts_Num];
       return listDLT4APath(lpList, restTP);
}

Proc listDLT4APath([td₁, ..., td_m], [ts₁, ..., tsₙ])
{  lpList = ø;
    for i = 1 to m, do
       lpList = merge(lpList, oneDLT4APath(tdᵢ, [ts₁, ..., tsₙ]));
    return lpList;
}
```

Fig. 1. DLT Algorithms for a general transformation pathway

pathway (i.e. the steps prior to ts_i). oneDLT4APath also returns a list of Lineage objects. listDLT4APath itself calls oneDLT4APath for each item td_i in the tracing data list to find the entire lineage of the whole list based on the transformation pathway. The merge function is used to avoid duplication of lineage data: A tuple, dl, might be in the lineage of two different tracing tuples, td_i and td_j ($i \neq j$). If dl and all its copies in a source collection have already been added to $lpList$ as the lineage of td_i, we do not add them again into $lpList$ as the lineage of td_j.

The complexity of the overall DLT process is $O(n \times m)$ where n is the number of add transformations in the transformation pathway and m is the number of different schema constructs referenced in the pathway.

4.4 Example

We use the example described in Section 3.2 to illustrate our DLT approach. Recall that some queries appearing in the example are not SIQL queries but general IQL queries. In such situations, we firstly decompose these IQL queries into sequences of SIQL queries.

Supposing $td = \{\text{'MA'}, \text{'MAC01'}, 81\}$ is a tuple in the extent of the construct $\langle\!\langle \text{CourseSum}, \text{Avg} \rangle\!\rangle$ in the global database GD, the transformation pathway generating $\langle\!\langle \text{CourseSum}, \text{Avg} \rangle\!\rangle$ construct can be expressed as following sequence of view definitions, where the intermediate constructs v1, ..., v4 and $\langle\!\langle \text{Details}, \text{Mark} \rangle\!\rangle$ are virtual:

v1	$= [\{\text{'IS'}, \text{k1}, \text{k2}, \text{x}\} \mid \{\text{k1}, \text{k2}, \text{x}\} \leftarrow \langle\!\langle \text{IStab}, \text{Mark} \rangle\!\rangle]$
v2	$= [\{\text{'MA'}, \text{k1}, \text{k2}, \text{x}\} \mid \{\text{k1}, \text{k2}, \text{x}\} \leftarrow \langle\!\langle \text{MAtab}, \text{Mark} \rangle\!\rangle]$
$\langle\!\langle \text{Details}, \text{Mark} \rangle\!\rangle$	$= \text{v1} ++ \text{v2}$
v3	$= \text{map} (\lambda\{\text{k}, \text{k1}, \text{k2}, \text{x}\}.\{\{\text{k}, \text{k1}\}, \text{x}\}) \langle\!\langle \text{Details}, \text{Mark} \rangle\!\rangle$
v4	$= \text{gc avg v3}$
$\langle\!\langle \text{CourseSum}, \text{Avg} \rangle\!\rangle$	$= \text{map} (\lambda\{\{\text{x}, \text{y}\}, \text{z}\}.\{\text{x}, \text{y}, \text{z}\}) \text{v4}$

Traversing this transformation pathway in reverse, we obtain td's lineage data, dl, with respect to each view as follows:

$$
\begin{aligned}
td &= \langle\!\langle \mathsf{CourseSum, Avg}\rangle\!\rangle\,|\,\{\,'\mathtt{MA}'\,,\,'\mathtt{MAC01}'\,,\,81\} \\
\overset{\mathsf{MtVs}}{\Longrightarrow} v4\,|\,\mathtt{dl} &= v4\,|\{\{\,'\mathtt{MA}'\,,\,'\mathtt{MAC01}'\,\}\,,81\} \\
\overset{\mathsf{MtVs}}{\Longrightarrow} v3\,|\,\mathtt{dl} &= v3\,|(\{\mathtt{x},\mathtt{y}\},\mathtt{x}=\{\,'\mathtt{MA}'\,,\,'\mathtt{MAC01}'\,\}) \\
\overset{\mathsf{VtVs}}{\Longrightarrow} \langle\!\langle \mathsf{Details, Mark}\rangle\!\rangle\,|\,\mathtt{dl} &= \langle\!\langle \mathsf{Details, Mark}\rangle\!\rangle\,|(\{\mathtt{k},\mathtt{k1},\mathtt{k2},\mathtt{x}\},\{\mathtt{k}='\mathtt{MA}'\,;\mathtt{k1}='\mathtt{MAC01}'\,\}) \\
\overset{\mathsf{VtVs}}{\Longrightarrow} v2\,|\,\mathtt{dl} &= v2\,|(\{\mathtt{k},\mathtt{k1},\mathtt{k2},\mathtt{x}\},\{\mathtt{k}='\mathtt{MA}'\,;\mathtt{k1}='\mathtt{MAC01}'\,\}), \\
v1\,|\,\mathtt{dl} &= v1\,|(\{\mathtt{k},\mathtt{k1},\mathtt{k2},\mathtt{x}\},\{\mathtt{k}='\mathtt{MA}'\,;\mathtt{k1}='\mathtt{MAC01}'\,\}) \\
\overset{\mathsf{VtMs}}{\Longrightarrow} \langle\!\langle \mathsf{MAtab, Mark}\rangle\!\rangle\,|\,\mathtt{dl} &= \langle\!\langle \mathsf{MAtab, Mark}\rangle\!\rangle\,|(\{\mathtt{k1},\mathtt{k2},\mathtt{x}\},\{\,'\mathtt{MA}'='\mathtt{MA}'\,;\mathtt{k1}='\mathtt{MAC01}'\,\}) \\
\langle\!\langle \mathsf{IStab, Mark}\rangle\!\rangle\,|\,\mathtt{dl} &= \langle\!\langle \mathsf{IStab, Mark}\rangle\!\rangle\,|(\{\mathtt{k1},\mathtt{k2},\mathtt{x}\},\{\,'\mathtt{IS}'='\mathtt{MA}'\,;\mathtt{k1}='\mathtt{MAC01}'\,\})
\end{aligned}
$$

In conclusion, we can see that the lineage from $\langle\!\langle \mathsf{IStab, Mark}\rangle\!\rangle$ is empty and the lineage form $\langle\!\langle \mathsf{MAtab, Mark}\rangle\!\rangle$ is obtained by evaluating the final tracing query $[\{\mathtt{k1},\mathtt{k2},\mathtt{x}\}\,|\,\{\mathtt{k1},\mathtt{k2},\mathtt{x}\}\leftarrow\langle\!\langle \mathsf{MAtab, Mark}\rangle\!\rangle;\,'\mathtt{MA}'='\mathtt{MA}'\,;\mathtt{k1}='\mathtt{MAC01}'\,]$.

5   Concluding Remarks

AutoMed schema transformation pathways can be used to express data transformation and integration processes in heterogeneous data warehousing environments. This paper has discussed techniques for tracing data lineage along such pathways and thus addresses the general DLT problem for heterogeneous data warehouses.

We have developed a set of DLT formulae using virtual arguments to handle virtual intermediate schema constructs and virtual lineage data. Based on these formulae, our algorithms perform data lineage tracing along a general schema transformation pathway, in which each add transformation step may create either a virtual or a materialised schema construct. The algorithms described in this paper have been implemented and tested over simple relational data source and integrated schemas. We are currently deploying them as part of a broader bioinformatics data warehousing project (BIOMAP).

One of the advantages of AutoMed is that its schema transformation pathways can be readily evolved as the data warehouse evolves [12]. In this paper we have shown how to perform data lineage tracing along such evolvable pathways.

Although this paper has used IQL as the query language in which transformations are specified, our algorithms are not limited to one specific data model or query language, and could be applied to other query languages involving common algebraic operations on collections such as selection, projection, join, aggregation, union and difference.

Finally, since our algorithms consider in turn each transformation step in a transformation pathway in order to evaluate lineage data in a stepwise fashion, they are useful not only in data warehousing environments, but also in any data transformation and integration framework based on sequences of primitive schema transformations. For example, [19, 20] present an approach for integrating heterogeneous XML documents using the AutoMed toolkit. A schema is automatically extracted for each XML document and transformation pathways are applied to these schemas. Reference [16] also discusses how AutoMed can be applied in peer-to-peer data integration settings. Thus, the DLT approach we have discussed in this paper is readily applicable in peer-to-peer and semi-structured data integration environments.

References

1. J. Albert. Algebraic properties of bag data types. In *Proc. VLDB'91*, pages 211–219. Morgan Kaufmann, 1991.
2. P. A. Bernstein and T. Bergstraesser. Meta-data support for data transformations using microsoft repository. *IEEE Data Engineering Bulletin*, 22(1):9–14, 1999.
3. M. Boyd, S. Kittivoravitkul, and C. Lazanitis. AutoMed: A BAV data integration system for heterogeneous data sources. In *Proc. CAiSE'04*, LNCS. Springer-Verlag, 2004.
4. P. Buneman, S. Khanna, and W.C. Tan. Why and Where: A characterization of data provenance. In *Proc. ICDT'01*, volume 1973 of *LNCS*, pages 316–330. Springer, 2001.
5. P. Buneman *et al.* Comprehension syntax. *SIGMOD Record*, 23(1):87–96, 1994.
6. Y. Cui and J. Widom. Practical lineage tracing in data warehouses. In *Proc. ICDE'00*, pages 367–378. IEEE Computer Society, 2000.
7. Y. Cui and J. Widom. Lineage tracing for general data warehouse transformations. In *Proc. VLDB'01*, pages 471–480. Morgan Kaufmann, 2001.
8. Y. Cui, J. Widom, and J.L. Wiener. Tracing the lineage of view data in a warehousing environment. *ACM Transactions on Database Systems (TODS)*, 25(2):179–227, 2000.
9. C. Faloutsos, H.V. Jagadish, and N.D. Sidiropoulos. Recovering information from summary data. In *Proc. VLDB'97*, pages 36–45. Morgan Kaufmann, 1997.
10. H. Fan and A. Poulovassilis. Tracing data lineage using schema transformation pathways. In *Knowledge Transformation for the Semantic Web*, volume 95 of *Frontiers in Artificial Intelligence and Applications*, pages 64–79. IOS Press, 2003.
11. H. Fan and A. Poulovassilis. Using AutoMed metadata in data warehousing environments. In *Proc. DOLAP'03*, pages 86–93. ACM Press, 2003.
12. H. Fan and A. Poulovassilis. Schema evolution in data warehousing environments – a schema transformation-based approach. In *Proc. ER'04*, LNCS, pages 639–653, 2004.
13. H. Galhardas, D. Florescu, D. Shasha, E. Simon, and C.A. Saita. Improving data cleaning quality using a data lineage facility. In *Proc. DMDW'01*, page 3, 2001.
14. E. Jasper, A. Poulovassilis, and L. Zamboulis. Processing IQL queries and migrating data in the AutoMed toolkit. Technical Report 20, Automed Project, 2003.
15. P. McBrien and A. Poulovassilis. A uniform approach to inter-model transformations. In *Proc. CAiSE'99*, volume 1626 of *LNCS*, pages 333–348. Springer, 1999.
16. P. McBrien and A. Poulovassilis. Defining peer-to-peer data integration using both as view rules. In *Proc. DBISP2P, Berlin, Germany, September 7-8*, LNCS. Springer, 2003.
17. A. Poulovassilis. A Tutorial on the IQL Query Language. Technical Report 28, Automed Project, 2004.
18. A. Woodruff and M. Stonebraker. Supporting fine-grained data lineage in a database visualization environment. In *Proc. ACDE'97*, pages 91–102. IEEE Computer Society, 1997.
19. L. Zamboulis. XML data integration by graph restrucring. In *Proc. BNCOD'04*, volume 3112 of *LNCS*, pages 57–71. Springer-Verlag, 2004.
20. L. Zamboulis and A. Poulovassilis. Using automed for xml data transformation and integration. In *DIWeb*, volume 3084 of *LNCS*, pages 58–69. Springer-Verlag, 2004.

XDGL: XPath-Based Concurrency Control Protocol for XML Data*

Peter Pleshachkov[1], Petr Chardin[2], and Sergei Kuznetsov[3]

[1] Institute for System Programming RAS, Russia
peter@ispras.ru
[2] Moscow State University, Russia
pchardin@acm.org
[3] Institute for System Programming RAS, Russia
kuzloc@ispras.ru

Abstract. Today XML has become the most important data exchange technique on the World Wide Web. As a consequence the interest in concurrent XML processing has greatly increased.

In this paper we propose a new XPath-based DataGuide Locking protocol (XDGL), which generalizes on and extends the hierarchical data locking protocol. This new protocol takes into account the semantics and nature of XML. It can be easily implemented on top of traditional databases as well as in a native XML DBMS.

1 Introduction

The eXtensible Markup Language (XML) [1] has emerged as the de facto standard for storing and exchanging information in the Internet Age. As the amount of XML data on the World Wide Web is constantly increasing, concurrent access to XML documents becomes a more and more important issue. Usually we are interested in the case when several transactions are working with the same document concurrently. Then we need to check that these transactions have been serialized properly.

Serializability [2] requires that concurrent transactions produce the same result that we would get if they were executed in a certain sequential order. Different protocols have been proposed to ensure serializability.

A number of concurrency control protocols has been proposed. The most popular class is locking-based protocols. Locking-based protocols use various types of locks to determine whether a transaction can proceed. Shared locks and exclusive locks are two basic types of locks. A transaction can proceed if the lock on the desired object is compatible with locks held by other transactions on the same object.

Locking mechanisms such as predicate locking [3], hierarchical locking [4] and tree-based locking [5] have been introduced to suit special needs and increase the level of concurrency provided by multi-user data management systems.

---

* This work was partially supported by the grant of the Russian Basic Research Foundation (RBRF) N 05-07-90204

M. Jackson et al. (Eds.): BNCOD 2005, LNCS 3567, pp. 145–154, 2005.

Two-phase locking protocol (2PL) [6] is the most widely used one. 2PL uses locks to prevent conflicting transactions from modifying the shared objects. To ensure serializability, transaction should obtain locks only in the growing phase and release locks only in the shrinking phase.

There has been proposed a number of concurrency control methods, which are tailored to XML data. Most of them provide node-level locking [7], [8], [9]. On the one hand, these methods provide a high degree of concurrency. On the other hand, their problem is that for large documents the lock manager should manage a large number of locks. It leads to significant increase of the lock manager table, which results in the system performance loss. To alleviate this problem, lock escalation procedure should be employed. The procedure handles the conversion of many fine-granularity locks into fewer coarse-granularity locks. Unfortunately, this method usually leads to a major concurrency decrease. Another problem is that these approaches rely on the assumption that the whole document is available. Unfortunately, for most XML applications this is not the case. Our protocol does not impose this restriction and requires only summary of the DataGuide structure [10] instead.

Obviously it is possible to use these well-known results to provide concurrency control for XML data. However, it has been shown [11] that the above-mentioned conventional concurrency control methods do not suite XML data well. These methods do not provide high enough degree of concurrency for XML. There is a need for synchronization method utilizing the semantics and nature of XML data.

We present XPath-based DataGuide Locking protocol (XDGL), which guarantees serializability and provides high degree of concurrency within the same XML document. In the proposed method we use a subset of well-known XPath [12] language to access the document nodes and insert/delete operators to modify document. In our locking method we employ the DataGuide structure for locking purposes rather than document itself. We use combination of hierarchical and node locks on DataGuide. Besides, we utilize the knowledge of XML document prescriptive schema (e.g. given as a Document Type Definition (DTD) [1] specification). We also take into account the semantics of update operations to increase concurrency. Our locking method enforces strict serializability and prevents appearance of phantoms [3].

The rest of the paper is organized as follows. In Section 2 we introduce the XML query and update languages, which are of interest in this paper. Section 3 is devoted to proposed locking protocol. It contains a number of examples, which show the benefits of our method. In Section 4 we give a brief overview of related work. Particularly, we discuss similar locking methods. Section 5 contains a summary and a discussion of future research.

2   Preliminary Notes

This section gives an overview of query and update languages. We also describe the DataGuide structure employed for locking purposes. To illustrate these notions we will use the example document D containing information about various people and their families. It is shown in Fig. 1(a). The document conforms to the DTD depicted in Fig. 1(b).

```
<doc>
<person age = '66'>
  <name>Vadim Petrov</name>
  <addr>Red Street, 25</addr>
  <child>
    <person>
      <name>Ivan Petrov</name>
      <addr>Polskaya Street, 16</addr>
      <hobby>walking</hobby>
      <hobby>cycling</hobby>
    </person>
  </child>
  <child>
    <person>
      <name>Anna Karenina</name>
      <addr>Red Street, 25</addr>
    </person>
  </child>
</person>
<person>
  <name>Pavel Morozov</name>
  <addr>Volhonka, 34</addr>
  <hobby>writing</hobby>
</person>
</doc>
```

(a)

```
<!ELEMENT doc (person)*>
<!ELEMENT person (name, addr, (hobby)*,
(child)*)>
<!ATTLIST person age CDATA  #IMPLIED>
<!ELEMENT child person>
<!ELEMENT name #PCDATA>
<!ELEMENT addr #PCDATA>
<!ELEMENT hobby #PCDATA>
```

(b)

Fig. 1. (a) an XML document D, (b) its DTD

2.1   Query Language

The user can access the documents through XPath queries. Location path is the most important construction in the XPath language. A location path consists of several location steps, separated by '/'. There is a set of nodes (called context nodes) from which each location step starts with. A location step then generates its result, which is a set of nodes. This set provides context nodes for the next location step in the path. The result of the location path is the result of the last location step.

Each location step is represented by the following construction: axis:node-test[predicate], where axis specifies the step direction (e. g. child, parent, ancestor, descendant, attribute), node-test specifies the selected node type and predicate refines the selected nodes.

In this paper we will consider only restricted version of location steps, which do not contain predicates. There is also an abbreviated syntax which is widely used: instead of explicit axis specification parent, descendant and attribute axises could be referred as '..', '//', '@' abbreviations respectively. In all our examples we will follow an abbreviated syntax of location paths.

Let us consider the document shown in Fig. 1(a), the location path /doc/person starts from the root / and consists of two location steps. The context node of the first step is the root and context node of the second step is the doc node. The result of this location path is person elements.

2.2 Update Language

To change the document one should use update operators. We define two kinds of update operators: insert and delete operators. It is obvious, that arbitrary update operation could be expressed as a combination of inserts and deletes.

- insert-operator: INSERT constructor (INTO | BEFORE | AFTER) path-expr
- delete-operator: DELETE path-expr

Here constructor is an element or attribute constructor. We specify an element constructor as element{elem-name} {content} (or as <elem-name>content</elem-name>); meaning of the elem-name and content is straightforward. There are complex element constructors. In such constructor content itself is the nested element constructor. In a simple case content could be just a text.

One can specify the attribute constructor as attribute {name} {text}. Here name and text specifies the name and the value of the attribute.

We introduce three types of insert operators: insert-into, insert-before and insert-after. These operators insert new node defined by constructor as the last child, previous sibling and next sibling for each node selected by path-expr respectively. If constructor specifies an attribute constructor, then we could only use insert-into operator that adds new attribute to each node selected by path-expr. It also means that each of the selected nodes should be of element type.

Delete operator removes subtrees of all nodes specified by path-expr from the document. That is to say, our delete operator uses the deep deletion semantics.

Now we will study a simple example to make the above clear. Consider the document shown in Fig. 1(a). The following update statement adds new hobby element to each person located inside the doc element: INSERT element{hobby}{'skating'} INTO /doc/person.

2.3 DataGuide

DataGuide is a concise synopsis of the XML document. DataGuide is a tree and it is defined as follows: every path of the document has exactly one path in the DataGuide, and every path in the DataGuide is the path in the document. Fig. 2 depicts DataGuide of the document D shown in Fig. 1(a).

3 Locking Method

In order to define a locking method we need to define the locks and locking rules for transactions to follow. Every transaction should obtain a certain number of locks to access an object. If transactions need to lock the same objects, they should check whether the locks are compatible. Our protocol requires transaction to follow strict two-phase locking protocol (S2PL). According to S2PL a transaction, acquired a lock, keeps it until the end.

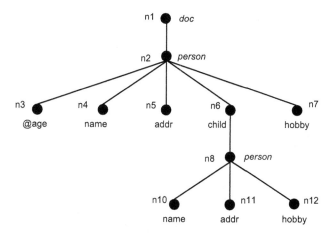

Fig. 2. DataGuide of the document D

We introduce granular locking protocol on DataGuide. The protocol defines intentional locks in addition to shared and exclusive locks. To set a shared lock on an object a transaction T must firstly set an intention locks on its ancestors. But there are a number of use cases when the locking of the entire subtree, as the common granular locking protocol does, is not necessary. Use Case 1 is intended to explain it.

Exam ple 1 (U se C ase 1). Let us suppose that transaction $T1$ has issued the XPath query /doc/person/nam e. It should be possible for transaction $T2$ to insert empty element <person/> as a child of doc element. According to the granular locking protocol $T1$ must lock nam e subtree while $T2$ must lock the entire person subtree including nam e element. Thus, $T1$ and $T2$ cannot be executed concurrently.

In fact, transactions $T1$ and $T2$ do not conflict. They would conflict if $T2$ inserted <person><nam e>Tanya</nam e></person> element inside doc element.

To avoid locking of the entire subtree, we use locks on the DataGuide's nodes. This way we can provide high degree of concurrency and, in particular solve the above problem. Besides, we introduce some special shared locks on DataGuide's nodes, utilized by insert operations.

To remedy the phantom problem we introduce special logical locks. They allow to lock name under the DataGuide's node. These locks are useful for such queries as //addr. According to the DTD of document D, person element is defined recursively. Therefore, D 's DataGuide could contain random number of the addr nodes. A logical lock on the addr name on the D 's DataGuide denies other transactions to insert any element with the name addr.

In next subsection we describe in detail our locking method and give a couple of examples to emphasize the benefits of our protocol.

3.1   The XDGL Protocol

Logical locks add a great deal of complexity to the XDGL protocol. Hence, at first we will describe a simplified variant of XDGL without logical locks. However, we will note that this variant does not ensure serializability.

Simplified XDGL Method. Concurrent operations may result in inconsistent data unless controlled properly. To avoid this kind of problems we must serialize concurrent operations. We employ locks as a mean of synchronization. Let us define the kinds of locks we need.

- SI, SA and SB locks. These special shared locks are used by insert operations. They provide high degree of concurrency that could be achieved because of the insert operator semantics. As we have already mentioned, there are three types of insert operators: insert-into, insert-after and insert-before. Insert-into operator adds a child or an attribute to a node. Insert-after operator creates a sibling for a node. Thus, we add a node to the parent next to our node in the document order [12]. Insert-before operator defined in a similar way. SI (shared insert), SA (shared after) and SB (shared before) locks block concurrent insert operations of the sam e type. These locks also protect the very node. For instance, a transaction cannot delete this node while such a lock is held.
- X   lock. The lock sets exclusive mode on a DataGuide node. For instance, this lock is obtained for a newly created node.
- ST lock. The lock sets shared mode on a DataGuide's subtree. XPath queries require this kind of locks. Due to the semantics of XPath the results of the location path are the subtrees selected by the last location step. It implies the request of the ST (shared tree) lock for subtrees retrieved by location path.
- X T   lock. The lock sets exclusive mode on a DataGuide's subtree. We use it for delete operations. The delete operator drops the subtrees defined by location path. It implies the request of the X T (exclusive tree) locks for these subtrees.
- IS lock. According to the granular locking protocol we have to obtain these locks on each ancestor of the node which is to be locked in a shared mode.
- IX lock. According to the granular locking protocol we have to obtain these locks on each ancestor of the node which is to be locked in an exclusive mode.

Fig. 3 shows compatibility matrix for the lock modes defined above. A compatibility matrix indicates whether a lock of mode M_1 may be granted to a transaction, while a lock of mode M_2 is presently held by another transaction.

Note, that IX and X locks are compatible since IX lock on a node only implies the intention to lock the descendants of the node. But it does not imply the lock on the node itself. SI (SA, SB) lock is not compatible with SI (SA, SB) lock, which prevents concurrent insert-into (insert-after, insert-before) operations upon the same node.

	granted							
requested	SI	SA	SB	X	ST	XT	IS	IX
SI	-	+	+	-	+	-	+	+
SA	+	-	+	-	+	-	+	+
SB	+	+	-	-	+	-	+	+
X	-	-	-	-	-	-	+	+
ST	+	+	+	-	+	-	+	-
XT	-	-	-	-	-	-	-	-
IS	+	+	+	+	+	-	+	+
IX	+	+	+	+	-	-	+	+

Fig. 3. Lock compatibility matrix

Now we will show that both transactions in the Use Case 1 can proceed with proposed locking method. According to XDGL, transaction $T1$ must obtain IS lock on nodes $n1$, $n2$ and ST lock on node $n4$. At the same time $T2$ must obtain IX lock on $n1$ and X lock on $n2$. As all locks are compatible transactions $T1$ and $T2$ could be executed concurrently. This is illustrated in Fig. 4(a).

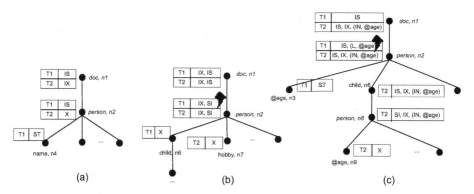

Fig. 4. (a) XDGL for Use Case 1, (b) incompatibility of insert operations, (c) logical locks and XDGL

To make the locking mechanism more clear we will consider several examples.

Example 2 (conflict of two insert operations). Let us suppose that transaction $T1$ inserts new child element: INSERT <child/> INTO /doc/person, while transaction $T2$ inserts new hobby element: INSERT <hobby/> INTO /doc/person. Fig. 4(b) shows that transactions $T1$ and $T2$ cannot run concurrently since SI lock is not compatible with itself.

Logical Locks and XDGL. In XPath language we can get nodes at any level of the document using descendant axis. Thus, we should prevent phantom appearance in such queries.

Inserts performed by concurrent transactions are the only source of phantoms. One way to prevent phantoms is to request locks of the coarser granules. It is obvious that this would lead to significant decrease in concurrency.

For this reason, we introduce logical locks. Logical lock (L, node-name) is requested for the name of the DataGuide's node.

For instance, the query /doc/person//addr requires logical lock (L, addr) on node $n2$, as well as delete statement DELETE //hobby requires logical lock (L, hobby) on the DataGuide's root.

In turn, a transaction, which wants to insert new node in the document should obtain (IN, node-name) lock on the all ancestors of the node to be inserted. IN is short for Insert New Node. (IN, node-name1) lock is compatible with (L, node-name2) lock if and only if node-name1 differs from node-name2. Note, that L and IN locks do not conflict with locks introduced in the previous section.

Example 3 (phantom prevention). Let us suppose that transaction $T1$ retrieves all age attributes found at any level inside person elements which can be found themselves inside doc. In XPath such query looks like this: /doc/person//@age. At the same time transaction $T2$ inserts new age attribute into the person element by the following statement: INSERT attribute{age}{'54'} INTO /doc/person/child/person.

It is easy to see that the second transaction might add a phantom node for the first one. However, our locking rules prevent this situation. This is shown in the Fig. 4(c): (L, @age) lock is not compatible with (IN, @age) lock. Thus, the insertion of the age attribute is denied.

3.2 Unordered XML Documents

We can adopt our locking method to unordered XML documents, when the order between nodes in the document is not important. In this case SI, SA and SB locks are not necessary, but instead of them conventional S lock is needed. It locks the DataGuide node in the shared mode. By definition S lock is compatible with itself, which allows to improve concurrency. For instance, two insert operations which add elements with different names into the same element do not conflict.

4   Related Work

There were proposed several locking schemes for synchronizing concurrent XML operations. Here is a brief overview of these methods.

Grabs et al. [13] proposed a DGLOCK protocol, which is a combination of well-known granular and predicate locking on the DataGuide. This work has much in common with our one. But DGLOCK has several disadvantages: (1) as a consequence of granular locking we have a conflict in the Use Case 1, (2) DGLOCK does not guarantee serializability and has no phantom prevention mechanism, (3) the descendant axis, which is widely used in applications, is not supported.

In [7], the synchronization of concurrent transactions is considered in the context of DOM API. The authors present three types of locks: node locks, navigational locks and logical locks. Node and navigational locks are acquired for context nodes and virtual navigation edges respectively. In turn, logical locks are introduced to prevent phantoms. Authors offer variety options to enhance transaction concurrency. But synchronization of other APIs (e.g. XPath) is part of the future work.

There are a number of isolation protocols for the DOM API proposed in the work [8]. Unfortunately, these locking protocols were developed for DOM API only, and it is not clear whether they will also perform well if most access is done by XPath expressions.

Dekeyser et al. [11] proposed the fine-grained (node-level) XPath-based locking protocol, which ensures serializability. But this method does not use the DataGuide. Instead all the locks are obtained on the document itself. Disadvantages of this approach have been already noted in this paper.

5 Conclusions and Further Work

Efficient processing of concurrent operations on XML data is an important problem. We have presented the XDGL, a locking method for concurrent processing of XML data. The XDGL protocol is based on the previous works upon locking of hierarchical data. It takes into account the semantics and nature of XML query and update operations. XDGL is a generic method and its application is not limited to native XML databases. It could be implemented on top of any existing system. Besides, the growth of XML document usually results in relatively small increase of the locking structures with our method. This happens, since the size of the DataGuide structure grows slowly.

We plan to extend XDGL with predicates. Then it would be possible to support the full version of XPath language and improve the degree of concurrency.

References

1. F. Yergeau, T. Bray, J. Paoli, C. M. Sperberg-McQueen and E. Maler. Extensible Markup Language, W3C Recommendation, http://w3.org/TR/2004/REC-xml-20040204, 4th February 2004.
2. J. Gray, A. Reuter. Transaction processing: concepts and techniques. Morgan Kaufmann, 1993.
3. K. P. Eswaran, J. Gray, R. Lorie and I. Traiger. The notions of consistency and predicate locks in a database systems. Comm of ACM, Vol. 19, No 11, pp. 624-633, November 1976.
4. J. Gray, R. Lorie. Granularity of locks in a large shared databases. International Conference on Very Large Data Bases, 1975.
5. A. Silberschatz and Z. Kedem. Consistency in hierarchical database systems. Journal of the ACM, 27(1), pp. 72-80, 1980.
6. P. Bernstein, V. Hadzilacos and N. Goodman, Concurrency Control and Recovery in Database System. Addison-Wesley, 1987.

7. M. P. Haustin, and Theo Harder. taDOM: a Tailored Synchronization Concept with Tunable Lock Granularity for the DOM API. In Proceedings of ADBIS Conference, LNCS 2798, Springer, 2003.
8. S. Helmer, C.C Kanne and G. Moerkotte. Evaluating lock-based protocols for cooperation on XML documents. ACM SIGMOD Record, Vol. 33, Issue 1, March 2004.
9. S. Dekeyser, J. Hidders. Conflict Scheduling of Transactions on XML Documents. In proceedings of the Fifteenth Australasian Database Conference, ADC 2004.
10. R. Goldman and J. Widom. DataGuides: Enabling Query Formulation and Optimization in Semistructured Databases. International Conference on Very Large Data Bases, 1997.
11. S. Dekeyser, J. Hidders. Path Locks for XML Document Collaboration. In Proceedings of the Third WISE Conference, 2002.
12. J. Clark, S. DeRose. XML path language (XPath) version 1.0. World Wide Web Consortium (W3C) Recommendation, Nov. 1999.
13. T. Grabs, K. Bohm and H.-J. Schek. XMLTM: efficient transaction management for XML documents, ACM CIKM 2002, McLean, Virginia, USA.

Updating XML
Using Object-Relational Database

Pensri Amornsinlaphachai, M. Akhtar Ali, and Nick Rossiter

University of Northumbria at Newcastle, UK
{pensri.amornsinlaphachai,akhtar.ali,nick.rossiter}@unn.ac.uk

Abstract. Presently, the area of updating XML is immature since XQuery has not provided update features. Thus this area has not been investigated as fully as it should have been. Moreover existing researches focus on updating native XML database so that everything must be created from scratch. Furthermore, an XML document is often treated as a database by keeping all data in one document, leading invariably to data redundancy. Such redundancy in XML documents can lead to data inconsistency and low performance when updates are performed. Therefore, we exploit the power of traditional database systems, which are fully developed to update XML documents. We present a mechanism to link non-redundant data kept in multiple XML documents. The data is held in an object-relational database (ORDB) and an update language is proposed, an extension to XQuery, which is translated into SQL for updating XML data stored in an ORDB. Finally, we present a technique to propagate the changes in an ORDB to XML documents.

1 Introduction

The emergence of XML as an effective standard for representation of (semi-) structured data on the Web has motivated a host of researches in the area related to XML such as storing [6], publishing [5], querying [1], and updating [9] XML documents. In the area of querying XML documents, several query languages, such as Lorel, XQL, and XQuery have been proposed and implemented while in the area of updating XML documents, several researchers pay attention to designing update languages such as XUpdate [11], SiXDML [8], and XML Update Extension [9] of which only a few have been implemented such as XUpdate. However, these update languages can perform only simple updates. For example, they may update an XML document without checking constraints and they cannot perform joins between documents in update commands. This indicates that at present the research in this area is underdeveloped.

Our research concentrates on developing a methodology to update linked XML documents. Our motivation comes from three reasons as follows. Firstly, research in the area of updating XML is not fully developed since XQuery, a standard from W3C, has not provided update features. However, there is a suggestion from W3C [3] for the imminent arrival of an update version in XQuery. Secondly, when updates are made directly on XML documents in the form of

M. Jackson et al. (Eds.): BNCOD 2005, LNCS 3567, pp. 155–160, 2005.

native XML database, many other tasks need to be performed such as preserving constraints. However, developing the mechanism for handling this work from the current starting point may take a long time. Thirdly, an XML document is usually treated as a database keeping all data in one document; thus data redundancy can occur. This redundancy may lead to data inconsistency and poor performance when updates are performed. To reduce data redundancy, data is sometimes kept separately in several documents. However, presently, this means that joins between XML documents in update commands cannot be performed.

In our methodology, we update XML documents via ORDB and let the database engine handle the preservation of constraints; thus structure and constraints of XML are mapped to an ORDB. To solve the problem of data redundancy, data is kept in several separated documents. These documents will be linked together by a mechanism called 'rlink'. This mechanism is then mapped to an ORDB. We propose an XML update language, which is an extension to XQuery. The proposed update language is translated into SQL to update XML data stored in an ORDB. Finally, the change in an ORDB is propagated to XML documents.

For the rest of the paper, we investigate issues relating to the design of our methodology. Section 2 describes how XML documents are mapped onto an ORDB. Section 3 presents our XML update language and its translation into SQL. Section 4 describes how changes are propagated into original XML documents. Preliminary conclusions and future work are discussed in section 5.

2   Mapping XML Documents

To update XML documents via traditional databases, XML must be mapped onto a database. We map XML onto an ORDB by using a shredding approach since hierarchical structures as well as constraints of XML can be represented in an ORDB. Presently, according to published work [6, 7], full mapping of XML structures and constraints onto ORDBs cannot be fully achieved due to limited constraints-handling capabilities in existing object-relational database management systems (ORDBMSs). Therefore, we propose new mapping rules and apply some existing rules [6] that are practicable using available ORDB technologies.

We use three features of ORDBs in our mapping rules: abstract data type, object table and nested table. Some of our rules are as follows. Firstly, elements having only one complex child-element are mapped to object tables, and their complex child-elements are mapped to abstract data type fields. Secondly, complex elements which have * or + occurrence and have siblings are mapped to nested tables if they comply with the following conditions: (a) all of their children are simple elements and all attributes have no type IDREF(s), (b) they have no references to other elements and no references from other elements to them, and (c) they have no recursive structure. Thirdly, complex elements which have ? or 1 occurrence, have a sibling and have children all of which are simple elements are mapped to abstract data type fields. Fourthly, complex elements which do not correspond to the above rules are mapped to object tables. Fifthly, for parent-child relationship and recursive structure with ? or 1 occurrence, the primary key of the table of parent-element is mapped to a table of child-element. Finally, for recursive structure with + or * occurrence, a separate table is created to store the primary keys of tables of a parent-element and a child-element. For attributes and simple elements, rules are similar to the work of [6].

For associating the relationship between elements from different XML documents, an rlink mechanism is used to provide information to identify which documents and/or elements are linked to others. Although this may be extended to XLink the main purposes of XLink and rlink are different. Mapping rlink mechanism to ORDB is the same as mapping IDREF(s). If an element referred by IDREF or occurrence of elements containing rlink is 1 or ?, the primary key of the table of a referred element is mapped to a table of a referring element. If an element is referred by IDREFs or occurrence of elements containing rlink is + or *, a separate table is created to keep primary keys of tables of a referring element and a referred element.

Most of XML constraints can be mapped onto ORDB constraints; however, a cardinality constraint is unavailable in any (O)RDBMSs. Therefore, we add a method for preserving this constraint when updates are performed.

3   XML Update Language and Its Translation

Our XML update language is adapted from the update language proposed, but not yet implemented, by Tatarinov et al. [9], and is based on the syntax of XQuery [10]. The syntax of our language is shown in Fig. 1.

When compared with existing XML query languages, XQuery is the most powerful, providing many features [4, 10]. Moreover, since XQuery is a functional language and SQL is a declarative language, this translation cannot be performed in a straightforward manner. In our research, five important constructs of the update language are inherited from XQuery: FLW(R—I—D), conditional expression, quantifier, aggregate functions and user-defined functions. These constructs are translated into SQL using four techniques: update/delete join commands, rewriting rules, graph mapping and optimisation. At here, only the first three techniques are presented while optimisation is presented in [2].

Update/delete join commands: In the SQL standard, joins in update/delete commands cannot be performed; however, translating XML update commands can produce a join of several tables. Thus we will translate XML update commands into update/delete join commands and then rewrite these commands in SQL. Syntax of the commands is shown in Fig. 2.

Rewriting rules: There are six categories of rewriting rules: For-Let-Where-Replace-Insert-Delete (FLWRID) expression, aggregate function, quantifier, conditional expression, (non-recursive) user-defined function and SQL rewriting rules. The first five categories are classified according to features of the update language. These rules will rewrite update commands as SQL functions. Such

```
(ForClause | LetClause)+

WhereUpdateClause|IfUpdateClause

where each clause is:

ForClause            ::= For $var in XPathExp(,$var in XPathExp)*
LetClause            ::= Let $var := XPathExp(,$var := XPathExp)*
WhereUpdateClause    ::= WhereClause? UpdateClause
WhereClause          ::= Where Condition
UpdateClause         ::= DeleteClause|ReplaceClause|InsertClause
DeleteClause         ::= Delete node WhereClause? (,Delete node WhereClause?)*
ReplaceClause        ::= Replace node with content WhereClause?
                         (, Replace node with content WhereClause?)*
InsertClause         ::= Insert content Into node (Before|After condition basedon XPath)?
                         (,Insert content Into node (Before|After condition basedon XPath)?)*
IfUpdateClause       ::= If Condition Then UpdateClause
                         (ElseIf Condition Then UpdateClause)*
                         (Else UpdateClause)?
```

Fig. 1. Syntax of XML Update Language

Syntax of joins in update command	Syntax of joins in delete command
Update *table whose fields will be updated* **From** *all related tables* **Set** *field1 =value1, field2 = value2,* **Where** *Condition;*	**Delete** *table whose data will be deleted* **From** *all related tables* **Where** *Condition;*

Fig. 2. Syntax for Update/Delete Join Commands

functions are sometimes conceptual, i.e., the function serves a purpose not currently existing in SQL. The last category is SQL rewriting rules, which rewrite update/delete join commands to SQL commands.

In translating XML update commands by using the rewriting rules, all clauses of the commands must be rewritten as SQL functions, which are used to group update clauses and their conditions together since one update command can consist of several update clauses, and each update clause can have its own conditions. These update clauses are grouped together using funcNo, a parameter of every SQL function. A funcNo of 0 for ForClause, LetClause, and WhereClause of the update command means that these clauses will be shared clauses of an UpdateClause. Each update clause will have its own funcNo, being a sequential number starting from 1. The update clause and its own condition(s) will have the same funcNo. Some of the SQL functions used are shown in Fig. 3.

Some functions have the parameter value| :funcNo (literal or variable) since the value in the predicate or in an insert or update command is sometimes not a

```
1. select(node, funcNo)        2. insert (node, value | :funcNo, funcNo)

3. delete(node, funcNo)        4. update(node, value | :funcNo, funcNo)

5. where | logical-operator (node, comparison-operator, value|:funcNo, funcNo)
```

Fig. 3. Examples of some SQL Functions

constant value but may come from selecting a value in other nodes. Hence in this case, :funcNo has the same value as the funcNo of select() function. Details of rewriting rules including additional rules for translating recursive functions into SQL can be found in [2].

Graph mapping: Graph mapping is used to determine the type of a node and hence which SQL functions can be performed on the structure of the ORDB, obtained as a result of mapping XML documents.

The process of graph mapping starts from creating a graph whose nodes correspond to nodes in SQL functions. The graph is then mapped into the database schema graph (a graph representing database schema) to identify which node is table, nested table, abstract data type field or simple field. Foreign keys for joins between tables are added to the graph. The SQL functions are then mapped to the graph. Then the graph may be split into several sub-graphs. The number of sub-graphs corresponds to the number of update operations performed on different tables. Finally, the (sub-)graphs are optimised and SQL commands or update/delete join commands are generated from the (sub-)graphs.

4   Propagating the Change in ORDB to XML Documents

The purpose of propagating the change in ORDB to XML documents is to reflect the change of data. Usually updating affects only some small parts of the documents; thus propagating the change is performed on only the affected parts. We use values of primary keys (PKs) or RowIDs of updated data in ORDB to indicate which elements should be updated. The PKs in ORDB originate from ID attributes. For elements which do not provide ID attributes, the values of RowIDs, which are automatically generated by the database system, are recorded to appropriately typed elements at the stage of populating data into the tables. Hence the values of these RowIDs can be indicated by the values of the RowIDs kept in ORDB.

When data in the ORDB is updated, the table name, PKs and values of PKs of the updated data will be returned and then the paths in the XML update command are converted to XPath expressions. The conditions in XPath expressions are based on the returned objects to indicate the positions in XML documents which will be updated. Since XPath has no capability for updating, we propose functions which serve as operators for updating XML documents.

5   Preliminary Conclusion and Future Work

As stated earlier, research in the area of updating XML is not fully developed. Thus we propose a potential way for updating XML via traditional databases. However, the mapping of XML onto simple RDB structures loses structural clarity, while object-oriented databases (OODBs) have limitations in representing constraints. Hence we map from XML to an ORDB. To eliminate redundancy, non-redundant data are kept in multiple documents and are linked by an rlink mechanism, mapping to an ORDB. We proposed an XML update language and techniques to translate XML update language into SQL. Finally, the change in ORDB is propagated to XML documents. A major benefit of updating XML through (O)RDB is that the task of preserving constraints can be pushed to the database engine.

In further work, we will first investigate how to handle the order of elements in XML documents when elements are inserted or deleted. Then we implement the translation of the update language and propagate the change in an ORDB to XML documents. Finally, we will conduct a performance comparison of updating one XML document containing redundant data via an ORDB in the manner of native XML database with that of updating linked XML documents containing non-redundant data via an ORDB. For the future work, we will propose mapping XML to an ORDB based upon XML Schema and focus on updating the structure of XML via ORDB and handling concurrency aspects such as lock levels.

References

1. Abiteboul, S., Quass, D., McHugh, J., Widom, J., Winer, J.: The Lorel query language for semistructured data. *In* Proceedings of Int. Journal on Digital Libraries. (1997) 68–88
2. Amornsinlaphachai, P. and Rossiter, N. and Ali, A.: Translating XML update language into SQL. http://computing.unn.ac.uk/pgrs/cgpa2/. (2004)
3. Chamberlin, D.: Influences on the Design of XQuery. XQuery from experts: A Guide to the W3C XML Query Language. Addison-Wesley. (2003) 143
4. Chamberlin, D.: XQuery from experts: A guide to the W3C XML query language. Addison-Wesley. (2003)
5. Fernandez, M., Kadiyska, Y., Suciu, D., Morishima, A., Tan, W.: SilkRoute: A framework for publishing relational data in XML. ACM Transactions on Database Systems. (2002) 1–55
6. Klettke, M., Meyer, H.: Managing XML Documents in object-relational databases. Computer Science Department. University of Rostock, Germany. (1999)
7. Rahayu, J.W., Pardede, E., Taniar, D.: On using collection for aggregation and association relationships in XML object-relational storage. ACM Symposium on Applied Computing. Nicosia, Cyprus. (2004)
8. Shamkante, B., Navathe, S.: A proposal for an XML data definition and manipulation language. VLDB Conference. Hongkong.(2002)
9. Tatarinov, I., Ives, Z., Halevy, A.Y., Weld, D.S.: Updating XML. SIGMOD Conference. Santa Barbara. (2001) 413–424
10. W3C: XQuery: An XML Query Language. http://www.w3c.org/TR/xquery. (2003)
11. XMLDB: XUpdate. http://www.xmldb.org/xupdate/xupdate-wd.html (2002)

Image Retrieval
Using Weighted Color Co-occurrence Matrix*

Dong Liang, Jie Yang, Jin-jun Lu, and Yu-chou Chang

Institute of Image Processing and Pattern Recognition,
Shanghai Jiao Tong University, Shanghai 200030, China

Abstract. Weighted Color Co-occurrence Matrix (WCCM) is introduced as a novel feature for image retrieval. When indexing images with WCCM feature, the similarities of diagonal elements and non-diagonal elements are weighted respectively based on the Isolation Parameters of the query and prototype images. After weighting, the similarity of relevant matches to the query image is strengthened and the similarity of non-relevant matches to the query is weakened. The experiments show the effectiveness of WCCM based method.

1 Introduction

Color Co-occurrence Matrix (CCM) [4-7] is a kind of commonly used color feature representation in image retrieval, but indexing image with CCM feature will ignore the shape information. Modified Color Co-occurrence Matrix (MCCM) [7] was proposed to overcome this disadvantage, where the similarities of diagonal elements and non-diagonal elements are taken into account respectively with equal weights. However, equally weighting on the similarities of homogeneous regions and non-homogeneous regions is not a good choice. For example, if a query and a prototype consist of few homogeneous regions, the similarity of homogeneous regions should play a more important role in similarity measurement, when they all consist of many small regions, the similarity of non-homogeneous regions should play a more important role. In this paper, Weighted Color Co-occurrence Matrix (WCCM) is proposed as an image feature. In which, the similarities of homogeneous regions and non-homogeneous regions of CCM are assigned with different weights based on the visual complexity of the query and prototype image.

The rest of this paper is organized as follows. Section 2 describes the WCCM feature. Experimental results are shown in Section 3 and conclusion is made in Section 4.

2 Isolation Parameter and Weighted CCM Feature

Let M be a co-occurrence matrix of image I, the MCCM feature vector is given by:

$$F^I = \left(M_D^I, M_N^I \right) \tag{1}$$

where M_D^I and M_N^I are diagonal elements and non-diagonal elements of CCM respectively. The similarity between the query Q and prototype I is:

$$S^{MCCM}(Q,I) = 0.5 S_1(Q,I) + 0.5 S_2(Q,I) \tag{2}$$

* Project supported by Key Technologies R&D Program of Shanghai (03DZ19320).

M. Jackson et al. (Eds.): BNCOD 2005, LNCS 3567, pp. 161–165, 2005.
© Springer-Verlag Berlin Heidelberg 2005

where $S_1(Q,I)$ and $S_2(Q,I)$ are the similarity of diagonal and non-diagonal elements respectively. We can see that for MCCM feature, the similarities of diagonal elements and non-diagonal elements are given same weights that mean the visual complexity of image is not considered.

Here we propose weighted CCM (WCCM) feature for image retrieval. In matching stage, different weights are assigned on the similarity of homogeneous region and non-homogeneous region based on the visual complexity of image content, which is denoted by Isolation Parameter [8]:

$$p_k = \sum_{i=1}^{N} U_k(i) \Big/ N, \; U_k(i) = N_s(f(j)=f(i))_{j \neq i} \Big/ N_k \tag{3}$$

where $p_k \in (0,1)$, N is the total number of pixels in image, k is the size of template, in our experiments $k = 0.01 \times N$. N_k is the total number of pixels in k-neighbors of pixel (i), $N_s(f(j)=f(i))_{j \neq i}$ indicates the number of pixel which has the same value as pixel (i) in k-neighbors, $U_k(i) \in (0,1)$.

If k is defined, Isolation Parameter is only relevant to image visual complexity. It is small when image consists of many small regions, and big when image consists of few homogeneous regions. Fig.1 shows the Isolation Parameters of different images, from right to left, the image becomes more intricate, and the Isolation Parameter becomes smaller. From this figure, we can see that Isolation Parameter is in correspondence with the complexity of human visual perception.

Fig. 1. The Isolation Parameters of different images. (a)0.207, (b)0.386, (c)0.578, (d)0.915

In matching stage of WCCM, the similarity between the query Q and prototype I is:

$$S^{WCCM}(Q,I) = w_1 S_1(Q,I) + w_2 S_2(Q,I) \tag{4}$$

w_1 and w_2 are obtained based on the Isolation parameters of image Q and image I. In this paper, a threshold $p_T = 0.5$ is defined. If $p_k \geq p_T$, we think image consisting of few homogeneous regions and if $p_k < p_T$, we think image consisting of many small regions. There are three instances:

- $p_k^Q \geq p_T$ and $p_k^I \geq p_T$, we strengthen the similarity of homogeneous region:

$$w_1 = 2 - abs(p_k^I - p_k^Q), \; w_2 = 1 \tag{5}$$

We can see that the closer between p_k^Q and p_k^I, the bigger of w_1, and then the bigger of $w_1 S_1 (Q,I)$, thus $S^{WCCM}(Q,I) > S^{MCCM}(Q,I)$, which means that the prototype I becomes more relevant to the query Q on WCCM feature than on MCCM feature.

- $p_k^Q < p_T$ and $p_k^I < p_T$, we strengthen the similarity of non-homogeneous region:

$$w_1 = 1, w_2 = 2 - abs\left(p_k^I - p_k^Q\right) \qquad (6)$$

In the same way, $S^{WCCM}(Q,I) > S^{MCCM}(Q,I)$, which also means that I becomes more relevant to the query Q on WCCM feature than on MCCM feature.

- $p_k^Q \geq p_T$ and $p_k^I < p_T$ or $p_k^Q < p_T$ and $p_k^I \geq p_T$, we weak the similarities of both homogeneous region and non homogeneous region:

$$w_1 = w_2 = 1 / \left(1 + abs\left(p_k^I - p_k^D\right)\right) \qquad (7)$$

We can see that w_1 and w_2 are less than 1, $S^{WCCM}(Q,I) < S^{MCCM}(Q,I)$, I becomes more non-relevant to the query Q on WCCM feature than on MCCM feature when they have different content complexity.

From the analysis above, we can see that the weighting is like a non-linear mapping. After weighting, the prototype images that have the similar color and visual complexity become more relevant to the query image and the images with the different color and visual complexity become more non-relevant to the query image.

3   Experimental Results

The image database used consists of 2103 images, which was collected from the Internet and Corel dataset, the commonly used image database in image retrieval [1-3, 10-12]. The database has 60 semantic categories, each category consisting of 11-60 images. In this paper, the HSV color space is used and color (hue) is quantized to 16 colors because 16 bins are sufficient for proper color invariant object retrieval empirically [10]. When indexing image, we randomly select images from each category as the queries, and return top 11 images to the user. Retrieval accuracy [3] and Average-retrieval-rank [7] are used as the performance criteria.

In order to demonstrate the effectiveness for WCCM algorithm, we compare WCCM based method with MCCM based method [7] and SCH based method that is superior to the cumulative histogram and Color Moments [9]. Fig.2 shows the performances using different features. In this figure for two criteria, WCCM based method outperforms the other features based methods.

Fig.3 gives retrieval results for one query with different features. In which, SCH, MCCM, WCCM based methods return 4, 8, 9 relevant images respectively. We can see that non-relevant match of the third and eighth positions in MCCM based method are pushed back to the fourth and eleventh positions in retrieval result of WCCM based method, and non-relevant match of the ninth position is pushed out of top eleven. At the same time, relevant match of the eleventh and tenth positions in MCCM based method are pushed forward to the third and sixth positions in WCCM based method, and one relevant match out of the top eleven in MCCM based method is pushed forward to the seventh position. We can see from fig.3 that some relevant images become more relevant to the query on WCCM feature than on MCCM feature and instead, some non-relevant images become more non-relevant on WCCM feature than on MCCM feature.

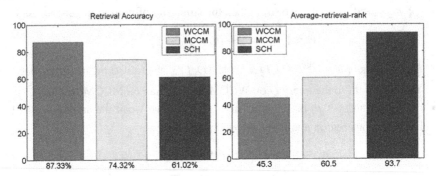

Fig. 2. The performance using different features

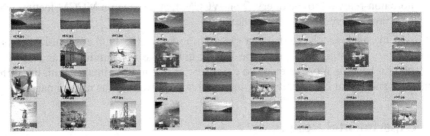

Fig. 3. Retrieval results using different features. (left for SCH, middle for MCCM and right for WCCM, the top-left is the query image)

4   Conclusion

A novel feature Weighted Color Co-occurrence Matrix (WCCM) is proposed. When indexing images, the similarity of homogeneous region and non- homogeneous region are assigned different weights based on the Isolation Parameters of the query and prototype. After weighting, relevant matches become more relevant and non-relevant matches become more non-relevant. The experiments show the superiority of proposed feature in comparison with MCCM and SCH feature.

References

1. Y.Rui, T.S.Huang, M.Ortega, S.Mehrotra, Relevance feedback: a power tool for interactive content-based image retrieval, IEEE Trans. On Circuits and Systems for Video Technology, 8(5), (1998) 644-655.
2. M.Flickner, J.Sawhney, etc.: Query by Image and Video Content: the QBIC system, IEEE computer. Vol. 28, (1995) 23-32

3. Xiaofei He, Oliver King, Wei-Ying Ma, Mingjing Li, Hong-Jiang Zhang, Learning a Semantic Space From User's Relevance Feedback for Image Retrieval, IEEE Trans. On Circuits and Systems for Video Technology, 13(1), (2003) 39-48.
4. V. Kovalev, S. Volmer.: Color Co-occurrence Descriptor for Querying-by-Example. Multimedia Modeling. (1998) 32-38.
5. Qiu, Guoping, Color image indexing using BTC, IEEE Transactions on Image Processing 12(1), (2003) 93-101.
6. Qiu, G., Constraint adaptive segmentation for color image coding and content-based retrieval, 2001 IEEE Fourth Workshop on Multimedia Signal Processing (2001) 269-274.
7. Seong-O Shim, Tae-Sun Choi.: Image Indexing by Modified Color Co-occurrence Matrix. IEEE International Conference on Image Processing. Vol 3, (2003) 493-496.
8. Luo Yun, Zhang Yu-Jin, Gao Yong-Ying.: Meaningful Regions Extraction Based on Image Analysis. CHINESE JOURNAL of COMPUTER. 23(12), (2000) 1313-1319.
9. Zhang Y J, Liu Z W, He Y.: Color-based Image Retrieval using Sub-range Cumulative Histogram. High Technology Letters. 4(2), (1998) 71-75.
10. Gevers, T. Smeulders, A.W.M. PicToSeek: combining color and shape invariant features for image retrieval, IEEE Transactions on Image Processing, 9(1), (2000) 102-119.
11. Ko, Byoungchul Byun, Hyeran, Extracting salient regions and learning importance scores in region-based image retrieval, International Journal of Pattern Recognition and Artificial Intelligence, 17(8), (2003) 1349-1367.
12. Hoiem, Derek Sukthankar, Rahul; Schneiderman, Henry; Huston, Larry, Object-based image retrieval using the statistical structure of images, Proceedings of the 2004 CVPR, V2, (2004) 490-497.

Street Address Correction Based on Spelling Techniques

Patricio Mois, Marcos Sepúlveda, and Humberto Proschle

Computer Science Department
Pontificia Universidad Católica de Chile
Av. Vicuña Mackenna 4860, Santiago, Chile
{pemois,marcos}@ing.puc.cl

Abstract. In the 90's, Geographic Information Systems started having a re-markable demand, since they are an innovative technology that allows visualizing information in a spatial way, along with its geographic distribution. Digital maps enterprises offer a variety of services, among them stand out the ratification of addresses: to check clients' databases for detection and correction of wrong entries, and then to validate the integrity of every new record that is inserted. This work details the development of an algorithm that improves the process of ratification using spelling techniques, with the goal of minimizing the human intervention required in the process, without sacrificing quality. The benefits are better response times and reduction of service costs.

Keywords: Text Retrieval, Text Processing, Spelling, Geographical Information Systems, Levenshtein.

1 Introduction

The automatic correction of errors found in strings started being strongly developed back in the 1960's [1]. The incredible increase in size experimented by databases along with the need for more reliable and accurate information has motivated the development of new algorithms and techniques within the scope of this discipline called *spelling*. The correction process usually implies building a series of possible corrections and a ranking of them, so one can be chosen [2, 3, 4]. For the detection and correction process, a so called lexicon or dictionary (a set of strings that are accepted as correct in the universe in which the search is performed) is used.

Companies have one or more computer systems that store and handle information. One type of information typically stored is the address (e.g., client address), which might have one of the following errors: a single entry with all the information of the address together, a street names misspelled, incomplete or abbreviated street names, or addresses with invalid numeration. These errors can be the source of many problems for companies and nowadays they are hiring services of normalization and ratification of addresses. The normalization service consists of processing an addresses database, targeting to normalize the address structure. The service of ratification consists of verifying that an address really exists. These services are given by organizations that have lexicons of addresses for certain counties, cities or countries, making it possible to detect and correct errors.

In this work, a novel algorithm is presented to improve the ratification process with the goal of diminishing to a minimum the human intervention needed in the process,

M. Jackson et al. (Eds.): BNCOD 2005, LNCS 3567, pp. 166–172, 2005.

improving the response times, reducing the service costs, and achieving high percentages of precision (the ratio between the number of correct items retrieved and the total number of incorrect and correct items retrieved) and recall (the ratio between the number of correct items retrieved and the total number of correct items that could have been retrieved). The proposed algorithm combines two spelling techniques and has been tested using a real database of clients, provided by a recognized Digital Maps company, verifying a set of approximately 10,000 records.

2 Analysis of the Correcting Addresses Problem

This work is focused on addresses of the city of Santiago, Chile and neither the city nor the country will be considered. In Chile, an address is composed of three relevant elements: the street name, the housing number, and the county where it is located. The street name can be split into a prefix, the street name itself, and a suffix. In this work, it was defined that a prefix is a word that makes reference to a type of street (e.g., Avenue, Road, Street) while a suffix suggests geographical orientation (e.g., North, South, East, West). Even though the structure of an address may differ between one country and another, since this work focuses on the correction of the street name, the solution presented here should be easily adapted to other address structures. The other components of addresses (number, county) are used mainly as searching filters.

This problem is more complex than correcting words in a text because:

- Each of the three elements (name, number, county) must be correct independently from the others and the union of the three must also be recognized as a valid entry.
- Many of the words that form a street name are repeated in several addresses (for example, avenue) and therefore are not useful for correcting an invalid entry.
- Since street names contain one or more words, it is necessary to consider that the omission or addition of one or more words will frequently happen.
- A lot of abbreviation is frequently used. Even if one cannot consider an abbreviated word to be misspelled, an address that has abbreviated words will differ from the ones stored in the lexicon.

This work focuses mainly in the correction of street names because an erroneous number does not give any type of information that allows correcting it, and in the case of the county, their universe is rather small, so the errors are negligible and easy to fix. When a street name is analyzed, there are four possible scenarios:

1. It is complete and correct
2. It is complete, but incorrect (misspelled)
3. It is incomplete or has additional words, but each word is correctly written (omission or addition)
4. It is incomplete or has additional words, and some words are wrongly written (omission or addition, and misspelled)

3 Proposed Algorithm

The developed algorithm consists of applying sequentially two techniques of correction, one of them pointing out to the correction of misspelling errors and the other one to the omission or addition of words.

The input provided by the user corresponds to a finished address, meaning an array formed by three fields: a Street_Name, a Street_Number and a County_Name. Independently of the method used, as soon as a correction is found, the algorithm proceeds to validate that correction with the Street_Number and the County_Name. This validation checks that the counties of the input and the correction are the same and that the Street_Number exists for the particular street in that county. If not, it is checked whether the Street_Number is between the minimum and maximum housing numbers for that street in that county. If so, the correction is considered valid because it is possible to geographically reference that point. If the counties do not coincide, the number check up is performed, but considering the correct county is the one corresponding to the Street_Name proposed as correction. If these crosschecks fail, the address is identified as incorrect.

3.1 Technique Based on Distance

The first technique is Based on Distance (BoD hereafter) and uses the metrics of distance to obtain a correction while facing a typographical or cognitive error. This technique is not very useful for errors of omission or addition of a word, since the distance that results between two street names in the absence of a word is significant.

For the development of this technique, we will use the algorithm of Levenshtein [5]. To calculate the Levenshtein Distance (LD) between two words, the following recursive formula is used [5]:

$$d(0,0) = 0$$
$$d(i, j) = \min\{d(i-1, j)+1, d(i, j+1)+1, d(i-1, j-1)+c(i, j)\}$$
$$where \tag{1}$$
$$c(i, j) = \begin{cases} 0 & if \quad i = j \\ 1 & if \quad i \neq j \end{cases}$$

LD corresponds to d(M,N), where M and N are the lengths of both words.

The key for achieving a correction in a prudent time consists of forming a set with possible correction candidates, as small as possible. This set must be broad enough as to assure the correct street should be contained in it and, on the other hand, must be sufficiently small to assure a low processing time. Kukich [6] mentions that several investigations show that few errors are made in the first letter of a word (not more than 7%). This is a good general filter that does not depend on the entry string. Thus, when an incorrect street is detected, a set is formed with all the words that begin with the same letter than the incorrect street. This set has excellent possibilities of containing the correct address and diminishes the lexicon at least in 20 times.

Knowing that this part of the algorithm is focused on correcting errors and not omissions, it is convenient to define a maximum distance between two words so one of them can be considered a correction of the other one. This maximum distance is defined as 25% of the street name length, with a minimum of 3. Additionally, if the entry is of length M, the possible correction of length N, and the maximum distance of correction MD, one proceeds to calculate LD if and only if $MD \geq |M - N|$

The lower bound for the LD between two words is the difference in length between both of them. Therefore, if this constraint is not fulfilled, it implies the word does not qualify as a possible correction [7].

The algorithm returns the street name that has a smaller distance with the entry string. If there is more than one word with the minimum LD, all of them are returned, leaving to the user the task of selecting the correct one.

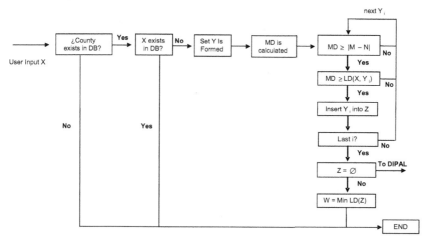

Fig. 1. Flow Chart for the technique Based on Distance

3.2 Modified N-Gram Technique: DIPAL

This technique was developed using N-Gram theory, but with a fundamental variation: N Grams are of variable length and each Street_Name might have more than one N Gram. Each of the words that form the Street_Name are considered a valid N-Gram if and only if the length of the word is greater than 3 and it does not belong to the prefix and suffix set. These conditions are imposed to reduce the number of candidates that do not add value.

In the street database, each Street_Name has a unique identifier for each of the counties in which it exists. Each set of {Street_Name, County_Name} has a primary key, which will be called Street_Name_Id. Using this key, a table with the following structure was constructed: {Street_Name_Id, Word, County_Name}.

This table, named DIPAL (in Spanish DIccionario de PALabras, word dictionary), is the essential element in this correction technique. Its construction involves processing each of the street names in order to recognize qualifying words and store them in DIPAL, along with its corresponding Street_Name_Id and County_Name. This process is applied to each of the street present in the lexicon. Disregarding a few exceptions (streets that do not fulfill the constraints, e.g., Sea Avenue), each street should create at least one entry in DIPAL.

The algorithm starts by parsing Street_Name in order to detect and eliminate all prefixes and suffixes. Next, a query is run over DIPAL in order to select all the Street_Name_Ids corresponding to each of the parsed words. For each of the parsed words, a dataset with each of the returned Street_Name_Ids is stored. Of all the

Street_Name_Ids obtained in the previous step, it must be decided with which of them gives the best correction. This is done by constructing a table of length P x (1+Q), where P is equal to the amount of different Street_Name_Ids that were obtained and Q corresponds to the number of words that returned al least one Street_Name_Id. The first column of the table is formed by the Street_Name_Id. The cell i,1+j is equal to 1 if the Street_Name_Id i is a member of the dataset j and 0 if not.

Searching in DIPAL for the street George Smith produces the following records:

Word	Street_Name_Id	County_Name
George	1040	Santiago
Smith	1041	Santiago

Word	Street_Name_Id	County_Name
Smith	1022	Santiago
Smith	1041	Santiago

Then, the following table is constructed:

ID	D1	D2
1040	1	0
1041	1	1
1022	0	1

We then look for the Street_Name_Id that shows the best chances of matching the Street_Name. It is possible to appreciate in the example that this Street_Name_Id is the one that shows more number ones in its corresponding row. Thus, the one that is probably the best correction in this case is the Street_Name_Id 1041. This search might result in more than one single result. If so, all solutions are returned.

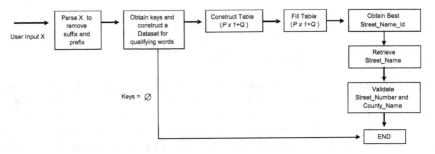

Fig. 2. Flow Chart for the DIPAL Algorithm

4   Results

The test database (nearly 10,000 records) and the lexicon (about 2,000,000 addresses) were provided by a local Digital Maps organization, DMAPAS. In this work, correction refers to two possible outcomes. The first one is a full address that was modified, either by changing its Street_Name or its Street_Number. The second one is an address that is properly identified as uncorrectable. To define an address as uncorrectable, either the street name has insufficient information (for example, it's only a prefix or suffix) or the street name and county are correct, but it is not possible to geographically reference the address. Table 1 shows the results of the test.

All judgments of what were good and bad corrections were done by manually inspecting each of the corrections. To calculate recall, 213 records were not considered because after evaluating each of the 698 addresses that failed to be corrected, it was determined that those had no chance at all of being corrected.

Table 1. Main testing results

Total Records Analyzed	9790
Error free records	4445
Records with errors	5345
Good corrections	4372
Total corrections	4647
Not corrected records	698
Not corrected records with no possible correction	213
Precision	94.1%
Recall	85.2%

Both of the algorithms performed differently (Table 2). BoD corrected nearly 16% and its precision was only 87.8%. DIPAL corrected 57% with precision of 96%. It is pertinent to remember that this corrector performs both algorithms in a sequential manner, and the sequence establishes that DIPAL comes at last. So it is not that DIPAL outperformed the BoD technique because it came first; it just seems to fit better this particular problem. DIPAL performs better because a greater part of addresses have omission errors; also suffixes and prefixes are frequently omitted or abbreviated, which compromises the effectiveness of the BoD algorithm.

Table 2. Results of the Based on Distance and DIPAL algorithms

Based On Distance Algorithm		DIPAL Algorithm	
Total Records Corrected	724	Total Records Corrected	2665
Good Corrections	636	Good Corrections	2544
Precision	87.8%	**Precision**	95.5%

BoD and DIPAL corrected together 3889 records, the other 1258 corrections were verified at the beginning by means of a simply query, using the % wildcard in the second and last position of the string. For example, for the address "George Smith", the query would be as follows: *Select*From{Street_Name}Table where Street_Name like 'G%eorge Smith%'*. The first wildcard is used to avoid a full table scan; the second one to find any missing information at the end of the street name. This simple query managed to correct 484 records, with a precision of 86%.

In the remaining 774 addresses the street name was rightly spelled, but its identifying number did not exist exactly in that street. However, it was possible to geographically reference it or to correctly identify the address as incorrect.

5   Conclusions

In this work, we have presented an algorithm that aims to correct errors found on street addresses, guaranteeing that the three elements that constitute an address (street name, street number, and county) are valid independently and also jointly.

The proposed solution consists of applying sequentially two correction techniques, each of them focused on correcting different types of error. While the BoD algorithm was constructed to correct misspellings, the purpose of DIPAL is to correct word omissions or additions. DIPAL outperformed BoD because omissions and abbreviations showed a higher frequency than misspellings and because street names with two or more words are more common than street name with one word. On the other hand, since DIPAL will not operate well if there is not at least one correct word, if the street name is formed by one word only and it has been misspelled, BoD would be more useful. A future goal is adding to the algorithm a previous step that analyzes the street name and, according to certain patterns, decides which algorithm tries first.

Although recall still has ground for improvements, correcting 85% of all incorrect addresses seems pretty good since it would leave a small set of entries for manual correction, reducing the amount of man hours needed to batch process a complete database. On the other hand, precision was 94.1%. Although there may still be room for improvements, the results are highly satisfying.

References

1. Damereau, F. A.1964. Technique for Computer Detection and Correction of Spelling Errors. Communications of the ACM, 7, 3 171-176.
2. Tillenius, M. 1996. Efficient Generation and Ranking of Spelling Error Corrections. NADA report TRITA-NA-E9621.
3. Kann V., domeij R., hollman J., and tillenius M. 1998. Implementation aspects and applications of a spelling correction algorithm. NADA report TRITA-NA-9813.
4. Navarro, G. 2001. A Guided Tour to Approximate String Matching. ACM Computing Survey 33, 1, 31-88.
5. Shulz K.U. and mihov, S. 2002. Fast String Correction with Levenshtein-Automata. International Journal of Document Analysis and Recognition, 5, 1, 67–85.
6. Kukich, K. 1992. Techniques for automatically correcting words in text. ACM Computing Survey. 24, 4, 377–439.
7. French, C.J., powell A.L. and schulman, E. 1998. Applications of Approximate Word Matching in Information Retrieval. Proceedings of the Sixth International Conference on Knowledge and Information Management, 9-15. 1997.

Personalising Patient Information in the Real World

Ben Sissons[1], W. Alex Gray[1], Anthony Bater[2], and David Morrey[2]

[1] School of Computer Science, Cardiff University, Cardiff, UK
[2] Clinical Information Unit, Velindre NHS Trust, Cardiff, UK

Abstract. This paper describes the development and analysis of a prototype patient information system. The aim is to identify how a large, multi-provider clinical information system can be used to improve the way patient information is delivered, and consequently the quality of care given. Practical aspects of theoretical problems are dealt with and an emphasis is placed on providing a base for future extensibility as technology and NHS policy develops. Many issues identified by this project are typical of ongoing issues in British healthcare as a whole and are relevant to any seeking to expose the information held in medical databases to patients.

1 Introduction

Velindre NHS trust is a specialist cancer hospital with a history of exploring how information technology can be used to improve patient care. Over the past decade, the Trust has been working, successfully, with other South East Wales healthcare providers to develop a large, inter-organisational information system for storing and utilising healthcare data. More recently the Trust has been working in collaboration with the School of Computer Science at Cardiff University to improve data gathering, access and maintenance procedures for this expanding clinical information system. With the current trend towards greater patient involvement in healthcare provision, it was decided that the latest collaboration should explore the role this system can play in providing patients with good quality information to facilitate this process.

This paper explains how a prototype patient information system was developed to improve current processes and explore what was required of any full working system. The necessity of the project, the way in which current procedures were improved and the barriers that were encountered to any complete implementation are explained.

2 The Project in Context

Reviews and audits by governmental and independent bodies have repeatedly highlighted the pivotal role information plays in improving healthcare provision and patient satisfaction. Patients are increasingly expressing a desire to be better informed and have more say in their healthcare process, rejecting the past, paternalistic, model of healthcare provision where doctors make healthcare decisions regarding uninformed patients. This power shift has contributed to a rise in litigation and complaints against healthcare providers, demonstrating a need for them to adapt to this new environment [1-7]. Patients having access to high quality sources of information and a say in their own care process can have benefits for healthcare providers. Such patients are likely to be less anxious, more co-operative and more satisfied when receiving treat-

M. Jackson et al. (Eds.): BNCOD 2005, LNCS 3567, pp. 173–178, 2005.

ment. It should be borne in mind however that poor quality information is just as liable to have an adverse effect on the care process [5, 6, 8]. The Welsh NHS has consequently placed great strategic emphasis on providing better patient information and involving patients in healthcare decision making [2, 9].

The explosive growth of the internet is considered likely to be part of the cause for the changing balance of power in healthcare. The World Wide Web provides a ready source of health information for the UK's increasingly computer active population. Due to the ease of web publication and the Internet's unrestricted nature, many concerns have been expressed about the likely quality of some health information it offers [6, 10-12]. It does, however, offer a fast, interactive way of obtaining the latest health information. Many sources of good information do exist on the Internet and it is in the interests of healthcare providers that patients locate and explore these, whilst avoiding the more dubious sources. Evidence also suggests that tailoring information to a patient's individual needs can further enhance its effectiveness [5, 13, 14].

2.1   The Project in Relation to Other Work

This project is concerned with how Velindre NHS Trust staff can guide patients to sources of high quality information that directly relate to each individual's circumstances. Many systems have been proposed that use health service provider's data stores to tailor information resources more specifically to individual patients. These range from simply inserting a patient's own details into general text, to restructuring the grammar of the document according to the demographics of each individual, for a more detailed review of such systems see [13]. Whilst many such systems have been proposed and tested, we have yet to encounter a fully operational, personalised Internet-based patient information system using NHS data. This project examines the issues involved in utilising confidential patient data to guide patient Internet access, by implementing a prototype system in a live NHS environment.

2.2   Information Provision at Velindre NHS Trust

In order to begin designing an improved, personalised information system the current system was first examined to discover what improvements were necessary. The review of current systems was achieved with the help of domain experts including clinical, and patient, information staff from Velindre and patient representatives. This section provides an overview of the current patient information procedures and then identifies what the domain experts perceived as the major problems with these procedures.

Current Patient Information Procedures. The majority of patient care takes place as a series of outpatient clinics and inpatient hospital stays, where the patient's progress is reviewed or care is provided. After a course of care has been decided, the patient attends an initial appointment where a consultant explains their condition and upcoming care to them. After this the patient meets with a specialist nurse who provides them with advice, and audio and written informational resources. Typically the patient is provided with a large amount of general information covering many aspects of coping with cancer. After this initial appointment specialist nurses and support charities are available to help but the onus is on the patient to seek further information. The main resource available after the initial appointment is the on site patient information centre. At the centre patients are provided with a list of recommended Internet sites, free Internet access and training on computer use.

All audio resources and leaflets go through a strict vetting procedure. For Internet resources trained information staff examine sites and add those that are deemed appropriate to a printed list. The list is available to patients via the information centre.

Problems Identified in the Current System. A number of specific problems were identified with current patient information procedures. Foremost amongst these were:

- The lack of consistency in the type and amount of information provided to different patients.
- Patients often being unable to take much information in at their initial appointment due to the traumatic nature of having their illness explained.
- A lack of specific information about what would happen at each clinic appointment a patient attended; this can lead to increased confusion and anxiety and possibly reduce the effectiveness of the care provided.

In addition, much of the information supplied to patients was generalized, not focused on the individual patient's condition. This left patients needing to sort through the information and decide what was relevant and irrelevant. In the patient information centre, for example, patients, who are often not computer literate, receive a list of web sites on all types of cancer and treatment, often having to locate those that relate to their circumstances by trial and error.

3   The System

This project sought to provide an easily implementable solution given the current conditions at Velindre NHS Trust that would address these issues. It was necessary for the new system to allow patients to access consistent, relevant information at their own pace. It was also important to provide patients with more, specific information on the treatments they would receive and what would take place at each appointment. The new system sought to adapt and enhance the current system rather than replace it, this was to decrease barriers to implementation and increase user cooperation and system acceptability. One part of achieving this is to use data from the patient record to tailor information to the individual patient's treatments and diagnoses.

3.1   Implementation

It was decided that the initial system would be a HTML web portal, providing users with a familiar interface and requiring no specialist software to access.

A web portal was built for patient information staff to catalogue information resources that they decided were of sufficient quality. The information resources were composed of web sites providing specific information on different diagnoses and telephone numbers or web sites where patients could obtain support. After deciding which patient types each resource was relevant to, the contact number or URL, together with a description of each resource, was stored in the database.

A parallel web portal was then built for patients to access information based around an appointment diary. When a patient logged in, giving a valid username and password, the system retrieved the details of all their valid appointments and diagnoses. Diagnoses were automatically hyperlinked to a list of all the information relevant to each patient's circumstances, and a list of applicable support resources was created from the catalogue maintained by patient information staff. Each appointment the patient was to attend was described using details retrieved from the database, such as location and consultant, and then hyperlinked to a web page explaining what would take place at the clinic. The resultant index web page was then served to the patient. General information resources could also be selected from lists without the need to log in, allowing relatives and carers of patients to make use of them.

3.2 Results

A prototype system was successfully implemented and then evaluated by a selection of end users and domain experts, including patient representatives and information staff. Initial results indicated they were very pleased with the system and all involved were enthusiastic. All those who evaluated the prototype agreed that it was likely to solve the problems identified above in a manner satisfactory to both patients and staff.

3.3 From Exploratory to Live System

This section provides an overview of how a live system can be created from the prototype. It lists the barriers that stand in the way, suggests how these may be overcome and outlines what is needed to complete the system.

Barriers Encountered. In general few barriers were discovered to implementing a system such as this. No real technological barriers were encountered. It was found that plenty of tried, tested and easy to use technology existed to accomplish all tasks. The real obstacles encountered arose from organisational policy and the sensitivities of making patient information available to patients themselves.

Information Quality. The Trust's information system was designed to be, and is, used by health professionals to store administrative and clinical data. An overhaul of the current database and information policies is needed to achieve and maintain sufficient data quality for a project such as this. In addition many data items, such as diagnoses, are phrased in ways that would only be meaningful to health professionals. Work is therefore needed to prepare the data set for public exposure.

Access to Information. In order for the system to function confidential patient information would need to be made available via the Internet, although only to the patient themselves and in a secure environment. Current institutional policy dictates that all patient information must be kept within the bounds of the NHS intranet. Access to the intranet is only available to authorised users and patients are not considered authorised users. This is a substantial barrier to giving patients Internet access to their own data and thus to tailoring information to a patient's needs.

A further area of difficulty, although not a barrier, is the burden identifying the quality of Internet resources places on information staff. It is desirable that this process be automated or the burden shared with other institutions. Although quality assessment tools and standards do exist, research is still ongoing in this area with many issues and gaps that still need to be addressed [6, 10, 12]. It is desirable that once the system is up and running any advances in this field be incorporated. For a more complete overview of the issues involved in such quality assessment see [10].

3.4 Next Steps

Currently it would be feasible to put a working system into place on site in Velindre by using limited, groomed portions of the database and offering patients supervised access on the NHS intranet. This would be a temporary solution however, composed of 'work arounds' and would be a serious limit on the utility of the system.

Whilst improving the quality of data held will, likely, demand substantial resources and change, this project has only provided one example of how poor data quality is likely to impact the future utility of the Trust's information system. For this reason the necessary processes of documentation, review and change have already begun.

Proven technology exists to make patient information secure on the Internet, for more details see [15]. It is, therefore, feasible to implement a more flexible security strategy now. NHS security policies are currently being re-examined as part of a drive to give patients access to their own medical records [2, 16] but time scales are unclear.

With either temporary or permanent solutions to these problems in place, the next stage of the project is to gain ethical approval for extensive testing and evaluation with a larger group of patient users. Subject to the success of this stage, and further ethical approval, the system could then be released into the live environment.

This system, once in a live environment, is intended as a basis for future expansion. Possibilities currently being examined include allowing patients to record and share feedback on treatment, the use of ontologies and text mining techniques to create an information digest, a multi-lingual version of the system and further tailoring information to, for example, the needs of different cultural groups.

4 Conclusions

The creation of a prototype generated a great deal of enthusiasm from both domain experts and potential users involved in testing. This demonstrated that there was a clear need for such a system, though the only true test of exact requirements would be to set a system up in a live environment and run a large-scale trial with patients. Barriers must first be overcome, however, and the project may have created higher levels of expectation than it is currently able to satisfy.

This paper has illustrated how real world projects such as this can face difficulties that are not dealt with in many theoretical systems. These issues have been examined and both temporary and long term solutions given. Once a system such as the one proposed here is in place, precedents will be set for overcoming the barriers encountered and future work can build upon this without these obstacles.

References

1. The Review of Health and Social Care in Wales. 2003, Welsh Assembly Government.
2. Informing Healthcare – Transforming healthcare using information and IT. 2003, Welsh Assembly Government.

3. Improving Health in Wales – Structural Change in The NHS In Wales. 2001, Welsh Assembly Government.

4. The Expert Advisory Group on Cancer to the Chief Medical Officers of England and Wales: A policy framework for commissioning cancer services – A report by the Expert Advisory Group on Cancer to the Chief Medical Officers of England and Wales (Calman Hine report). 1995, Department of Health.

5. McPherson, C.J., I.J. Higginson, and J. Hearn: Effective methods of giving information in cancer: a systematic literature review of randomized controlled trials. In: Journal of Public Health Medicine, 2001. Vol. 23(3): pp. 227–234.

6. Sastry, S. and P. Carroll: Doctors, patients and the Internet: time to grasp the nettle. In: Clinical Medicine, 2002. Vol. 2(2): pp. 131–133.

7. Neal, A.J.: Clinical Oncology: Basic Principles and Practice. 2003, London: Arnold.

8. Improving Supportive and Palliative Care For Adults For Adults With Cancer. 2004, National Institute for Clinical Excellence.

9. A Strategic Direction for Palliative Care Services in Wales. 2003, Welsh Assembly Government.

10. Risk, A. and J. Dzenowagis: Review of Internet Health Information Quality Initiatives. In: Journal of Medical Internet Research, 2001. Vol. 3(4): pp. e28.

11. Ziebland, S., et al.: How the internet affects patients' experience of cancer: a qualitative study. In: British Medical Journal, 2004. Vol. 328(7439): pp. 564–+.

12. Coiera, E.: Guide to Health Informatics. 2003, London: Arnold.

13. Bental, D.S., A. Cawsey, and R. Jones: Patient information systems that tailor to the individual. In: Patient Education and Counseling, 1999. Vol. 36(2): pp. 171–180.

14. Jones, R., et al.: Randomised trial of personalised computer based information for cancer patients. In: British Medical Journal, 1999. Vol. 319(7219): pp. 1241–1247.

15. Chadwick, D.W., et al.: Using the internet to access confidential patient records: a case study. In: British Medical Journal, 2000. Vol. 321(7261): pp. 612–614.

16. Grinod, B.: The Future of NHSnet. 2000, NHS Information Authority.

Republishers in a Publish/Subscribe Architecture for Data Streams

Alasdair J.G. Gray and Werner Nutt

School of Mathematical and Computer Sciences,
Heriot-Watt University, Edinburgh, EH14 4AS, UK

Abstract. We present a publish/subscribe framework for integrating data streams published by distributed producers. We introduce the idea of *republishers* which merge a set of data streams, either from producers or other republishers. The resulting hierarchy of producers and republishers can then be used to answer consumer queries over the streams. We discuss how to compute query plans to create such a hierarchy and the maintenance of these plans when the set of streams changes.

1 Introduction

Often streams of data are generated at many distributed sources, and are required by users who are also distributed, e.g. pollution or traffic monitoring. We propose to understand the management of these streams as a data integration task [5]. In such an approach, producers would publish a data stream while consumers would subscribe for data by posing a query over a global schema. This idea has been partially implemented in the R-GMA Grid information and monitoring system [2]. Another approach, being followed by the StreamGlobe project [6], is to use a P2P environment. However, it is unclear as to whether any guarantees are provided for the correctness of the answer streams.

In order to allow our data integration system to scale to a large number of data sources, and subscribers, we have introduced the concept of a republisher. These are components which merge a set of data streams, either from producers or other republishers, and make the merged stream available. This allows for more efficient query answering.

Queries over data streams are long lived, and during their lifetime the set of data sources can change. As such, the plans used to answer these queries become out-of-date because they rely on a producer or republisher that no longer exists, or do not cover some new data stream. We present mechanisms by which query plans can be updated whenever the set of data sources changes.

The rest of this paper is organised as follows. In Section 2 we describe the mechanisms previously developed for publishing and querying data streams [1]. Then we discuss the new techniques for planning republisher queries in Section 3 and for plan maintenance in Section 4. An extended version of this paper [4] gives further details of the planning and maintenance techniques.

M. Jackson et al. (Eds.): BNCOD 2005, LNCS 3567, pp. 179–184, 2005.

2   Publishing and Querying Relational Data Streams

We assume that there is a global relational schema against which consumers and republishers pose their queries. The attributes of a relation in the global schema are split into three parts: key attributes, measurement attributes, and a timestamp attribute. As an example, taken from a grid monitoring application, consider the relation ntp ("network throughput") with the schema

$$\text{ntp}(\underline{\text{from}}, \underline{\text{to}}, \underline{\text{tool}}, \underline{\text{psize}}, \text{latency}, \text{timestamp}),$$

which records the time it took (according to some particular tool) to transport packets of a specific size from one node to another. The underlined attributes make up the primary key of ntp, while latency is the measurement attribute.

Each specific set of values for the key attributes of a relation identifies a channel through which data can flow. For example, for the ntp relation, the subtuple ('hw', 'ral', 'ping', 512) identifies a channel through which measurements made with the ping tool for packets of 512 bytes originating at Heriot-Watt University (HW) and going to Rutherford Appleton Laboratories (RAL) can flow.

A data stream can be seen as a sequence of tuples. We have identified various properties that a stream may have: duplicate freeness, i.e. a tuple only appears once; disjointness, i.e. the same tuple cannot appear in two streams; and weak order, i.e. for each channel tuples appear in chronological order. We have adopted the notion of weak order as our streams will be published by distributed sources, which makes it difficult to guarantee chronological order when merging two streams.

Producers describe the streams that they publish by a query on the global schema, called a descriptive view. We limit these views to selection queries on a single relation in the global schema where the selection condition may only refer to the key attributes of the relation, i.e. a producer publishes a set of channels. Consider that there is a tool measuring the time taken for UDP messages to be sent from HW to RAL. Using the example ntp relation, we would register the producer S_1: $\sigma_{\text{from}='hw' \wedge \text{tool}='udpmon'}(\text{ntp})$. Later on, we will also consider the following producers with their views S_2: $\sigma_{\text{from}='hw' \wedge \text{tool}='ping'}(\text{ntp})$, S_3: $\sigma_{\text{from}='ral' \wedge \text{tool}='ping'}(\text{ntp})$, and S_4: $\sigma_{\text{from}='ral' \wedge \text{tool}='udpmon'}(\text{ntp})$. The set of four producers together record the latency in both directions between HW and RAL, using both the PING and UDPmon tools.

Republishers also publish a data stream. However, this stream is generated by posing a continuous query over the global schema. It is this query which describes the contents of the republisher's published stream. For our example on the ntp relation, we will consider three republishers. One for all of the measurements originating at HW, which would register the query R_1: $\sigma_{\text{from}='hw'}(\text{ntp})$, and likewise one for RAL with the query R_2: $\sigma_{\text{from}='ral'}(\text{ntp})$. We will also consider a republisher that republishes the entire stream for ntp, which would register the query R_3: $\sigma_{true}(\text{ntp})$. In Section 3 we will consider how to compute query plans to generate these answer streams. We refer to producers and republishers collectively as publishers.

A continuous query is one that returns a stream of answers. We limit these queries to arbitrary selection queries over the global schema. However, the global schema contains no data, so we have developed a registry [1, 2] whose rôle it is to act as a "matchmaker" (cf. [7]) between the queries and the descriptive views of the publishers. In doing so, the registry computes a query plan from which answer streams can be generated that contain the tuples to answer the query, based on the current configuration of publishers. For our example scenario, we will consider a consumer interested in latencies for messages starting at HW with a packet size of at least 1024 bytes. The corresponding query over the global schema is $q = \sigma_{\text{from}='\text{hw}' \land \text{psize} \geq 1024}(\text{ntp})$.

We will now illustrate the query planning techniques for consumer queries which were developed in [1]. These techniques compute query plans which guarantee to generate answer streams that are sound and complete w.r.t. the query, duplicate free, and weakly ordered.

The first step is to identify which publishers are relevant for the query. A publisher is relevant if (i) it can provide some channels which the query asks for, and (ii) all of the measurements for a channel are provided by that publisher. The second criterion ensures that all answer streams generated by the plan are weakly ordered. The set of relevant publishers for q is $\{ S_1, S_2, R_1, R_3 \}$.

Next, we compare the publishers according to what they can provide to the query. A publisher which can only provide a strict subset of what another republisher can provide is dropped so that we are left with the maximal relevant publishers. We do not allow a producer to override another publisher as there is no guarantee that its answer stream is complete w.r.t. its descriptive view. However, republishers are complete by construction. For q, this gives us the set $\{ R_1, R_3 \}$ since the view of the producers are logically weaker than that of these republishers. However, R_1 and R_3 are equivalent in what they can provide the query.

Finally, to provide some built in robustness to our query plans, we group the maximal relevant publishers so that we only need to choose one of a group of equivalent, w.r.t. the query, republishers. We represent the query plan as a pair. For q this is $(\{ \{ R_1, R_4 \} \}, \emptyset)$, where the first component consists of groups of equivalent republishers and the second would consist of maximal producers. Full details of how to compute and execute these query plans can be found in [1].

3   Republishing Data Streams

Republishers pose a query over the global schema and publish the resulting answer stream. As such, they merge together small "trickles" of data into more useful data streams. These streams can then be used by other global queries to make query answering more efficient, as only one publisher needs to be contacted.

A straightforward approach would be to construct query plans for republishers using the techniques developed for consumer queries. However, this can lead to cycles of republishers in the hierarchy that are disconnected from the producers. This is due to the consumer planning techniques favouring the most general

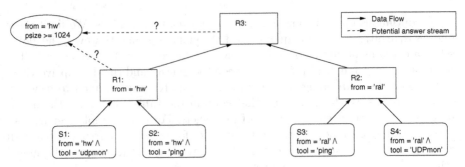

Fig. 1. Publisher hierarchy for a publisher configuration consisting of S_1, S_2, S_3, S_4, R_1, R_2, and R_3

data sources. These disconnected cycles of republishers are undesirable since a consumer that relies on such a republisher contained in a cycle will retrieve no answers, and thus would no longer be complete w.r.t. their query.

In [4], we argue that the following four requirements are essential for any planning mechanism for republishers: (i) Correctness i.e. the plan for each republisher should be sound and complete for the defining query as well as duplicate free and weakly ordered, (ii) Cycle Freeness i.e. the hierarchy should not contain any cycles, (iii) Uniqueness of the Hierarchy i.e. for any publisher configuration it should only be possible to derive one hierarchy, and (iv) Local Query Planning i.e. a republisher requires no information about the plans of other republishers.

These four properties can be maintained by suitably adjusting the definition of relevance. For a republisher R to be relevant for the query of another republisher R' we require that R supplies a strict subset of the channels that R' wants. By applying this new definition of relevance for republisher queries, to the example publisher configuration introduced in Section 2, results in the hierarchy illustrated in Fig. 1. The solid lines in the figure represent data flowing from the producers through the hierarchy. The dashed lines represent the choice the consumer has in retrieving its answer stream, i.e. either from R_1 or R_3.

4   Plan Maintenance

A query over a data stream is long lived, it continues to return tuples until explicitly ended. However, in a publish/subscribe system, components can be added or removed without notice. Thus, the query plans of both consumers and republishers must be maintained to reflect any changes in the configuration of publishers. We shall use the ongoing example to illustrate some of the points arising. Full details of the query plan maintenance techniques can be found in [4].

One possibility would be to compute the new query plan from scratch. However, it is likely to be more efficient to (i) identify when at all a query plan is affected by a change, and (ii) to amend the query plan, whenever this is possible,

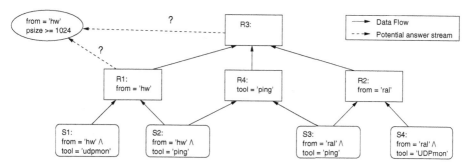

Fig. 2. Publisher hierarchy after the republisher R_4 has been added

based on the information contained in the old query plan and the change to the configuration.

We first note that we only need to consider query plans for which the publisher, which is being added or removed, is maximal relevant. We also note that the case of a producer being added, or removed, is straightforward. We will now extend our running example to illustrate the cases of adding, or removing, a republisher.

We first consider the effects of adding the republisher R_4: $\sigma_{\text{tool}='\text{ping}'}(\text{ntp})$. By using the query planning techniques of Section 3, we compute the query plan $(\emptyset, \{ S_2, S_3 \})$. The new republisher R_4 is a maximal relevant publisher for R_3, so we must consider if we need to update R_3's query plan. We note that R_4 is not equivalent to either of the other two maximal relevant republishers. Thus, the query plan for R_3 is now $(\{ \{ R_1 \}, \{ R_2 \}, \{ R_4 \} \}, \emptyset)$.

The publisher hierarchy resulting from these changes is illustrated in Fig. 2. We notice that the general republisher R_3 now has three sources even though the previous two would still cover all the data available. We have chosen this approach because (i) it maintains the criteria identified for a publisher hierarchy (Section 3), (ii) it is computationally difficult to show that R_1 and R_2 cover the entire set of channels, and (iii) the state would not be stable, if for example a new producer for a new site using the `ping` tool were to be introduced.

As the final part of our example, we will consider dropping republisher R_1 from the configuration. This affects the query plans of republisher R_3 and the query q. First we shall consider how to adapt the plan of q. We note that R_1 is equivalent to R_3 for the query, thus we simply drop R_1 from the query plan leaving us with $(\{ \{ R_3 \} \}, \emptyset)$.

For the republisher R_3, there is no republisher equivalent to R_1. Therefore, when R_1 is removed the query plan is no longer complete. We must patch the "hole" left by the removal of R_1. This is achieved by adding the producer S_1, giving us the query plan $(\{ \{ R_2 \}, \{ R_4 \} \}, \{ S_1 \})$. Producer S_2 is not added as the channels provided by S_2 are covered by R_4.

The resulting hierarchy is shown in Fig. 3. We note that the line from R_3 to the consumer is no longer dashed as there is no equivalent republisher to choose between now. The consumer must contact R_3 to retrieve its answer stream in the most efficient manner.

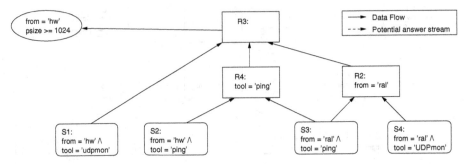

Fig. 3. Publisher hierarchy after republisher R_1 has been removed

5 Conclusions

In this paper we have extended our earlier work on integrating data streams [1] such that (i) hierarchies of republishers can be formed and are well defined, and (ii) query plans can be updated whenever there is a change in the set of available data sources. We have argued that the creation of publisher hierarchies are desirable as they make query answer more efficient, and feasible for a large number of publishers and subscribers. This need for a hierarchy of merged data values has also been identified in the MDS Grid information system [3], however their hierarchies have to be created and maintained manually. An important piece of future work is to develop methods to switch between query plans whilst ensuring that the subscribers receive sound and complete answer streams.

References

1. A. Cooke, A.J.G. Gray, and W. Nutt. Stream integration techniques for grid monitoring. *Journal on Data Semantics*, 2:136–175, 2005.
2. A.W. Cooke, A.J.G. Gray, W. Nutt, J. Magowan, M. Oevers, P. Taylor, R. Cordenonsi, R. Byrom, L. Cornwall, A. Djaoui, L. Field, S.M. Fisher, S. Hicks, J. Leake, R. Middleton, A. Wilson, X. Zhu, N. Podhorszki, B. Coghlan, S. Kenny, D. O'Callaghan, and J. Ryan. The relational grid monitoring architecture: Mediating information about the grid. *Journal of Grid Computing*, 2(4):323–339, December 2004.
3. K. Czajkowski, S. Fitzgerald, I. Foster, and C. Kesselman. Grid information services for distributed resource sharing. In *HPDC10*, pages 181–194, 2001.
4. A.J.G. Gray and W. Nutt. Republishers in a publish/subscribe architecture for data streams. Technical report, School of Mathematical and Computer Sciences, Heriot-Watt University, Edinburgh, EH14 4AS, UK, 2005.
5. A. Halevy. Answering queries using views: A survey. *The VLDB Journal*, 10(4):270–294, 2001.
6. B. Stegmaier, R. Kuntschke, and A. Kemper. StreamGlobe: Adaptive query processing and optimization in streaming P2P environments. In *DMSN 2004*, pages 88–97, 2004.
7. G. Wiederhold. Mediators in the architecture of future information systems. *IEEE Computer*, 25(3):38–49, 1992.

Author Index

Lecture Notes in Computer Science

For information about Vols. 1–3467

please contact your bookseller or Springer

Vol. 3517: H.S. Baird, D.P. Lopresti (Eds.), Human Interactive Proofs. IX, 143 pages. 2005.

Vol. 3516: V.S. Sunderam, G.D.v. Albada, P.M.A. Sloot, J.J. Dongarra (Eds.), Computational Science – ICCS 2005, Part III. LXIII, 1143 pages. 2005.

Vol. 3515: V.S. Sunderam, G.D.v. Albada, P.M.A. Sloot, J.J. Dongarra (Eds.), Computational Science – ICCS 2005, Part II. LXIII, 1101 pages. 2005.

Vol. 3514: V.S. Sunderam, G.D.v. Albada, P.M.A. Sloot, J.J. Dongarra (Eds.), Computational Science – ICCS 2005, Part I. LXIII, 1089 pages. 2005.

Vol. 3513: A. Montoyo, R. Muñoz, E. Métais (Eds.), Natural Language Processing and Information Systems. XII, 408 pages. 2005.

Vol. 3512: J. Cabestany, A. Prieto, F. Sandoval (Eds.), Computational Intelligence and Bioinspired Systems. XXV, 1260 pages. 2005.

Vol. 3510: T. Braun, G. Carle, Y. Koucheryavy, V. Tsaoussidis (Eds.), Wired/Wireless Internet Communications. XIV, 366 pages. 2005.

Vol. 3509: M. Jünger, V. Kaibel (Eds.), Integer Programming and Combinatorial Optimization. XI, 484 pages. 2005.

Vol. 3508: P. Bresciani, P. Giorgini, B. Henderson-Sellers, G. Low, M. Winikoff (Eds.), Agent-Oriented Information Systems II. X, 227 pages. 2005. (Subseries LNAI).

Vol. 3507: F. Crestani, I. Ruthven (Eds.), Information Context: Nature, Impact, and Role. XIII, 253 pages. 2005.

Vol. 3506: C. Park, S. Chee (Eds.), Information Security and Cryptology – ICISC 2004. XIV, 490 pages. 2005.

Vol. 3505: V. Gorodetsky, J. Liu, V. A. Skormin (Eds.), Autonomous Intelligent Systems: Agents and Data Mining. XIII, 303 pages. 2005. (Subseries LNAI).

Vol. 3504: A.F. Frangi, P.I. Radeva, A. Santos, M. Hernandez (Eds.), Functional Imaging and Modeling of the Heart. XV, 489 pages. 2005.

Vol. 3503: S.E. Nikoletseas (Ed.), Experimental and Efficient Algorithms. XV, 624 pages. 2005.

Vol. 3502: F. Khendek, R. Dssouli (Eds.), Testing of Communicating Systems. X, 381 pages. 2005.

Vol. 3501: B. Kégl, G. Lapalme (Eds.), Advances in Artificial Intelligence. XV, 458 pages. 2005. (Subseries LNAI).

Vol. 3500: S. Miyano, J. Mesirov, S. Kasif, S. Istrail, P. Pevzner, M. Waterman (Eds.), Research in Computational Molecular Biology. XVII, 632 pages. 2005. (Subseries LNBI).

Vol. 3499: A. Pelc, M. Raynal (Eds.), Structural Information and Communication Complexity. X, 323 pages. 2005.

Vol. 3498: J. Wang, X. Liao, Z. Yi (Eds.), Advances in Neural Networks – ISNN 2005, Part III. XLIX, 1077 pages. 2005.

Vol. 3497: J. Wang, X. Liao, Z. Yi (Eds.), Advances in Neural Networks – ISNN 2005, Part II. XLIX, 947 pages. 2005.

Vol. 3496: J. Wang, X. Liao, Z. Yi (Eds.), Advances in Neural Networks – ISNN 2005, Part II. L, 1055 pages. 2005.

Vol. 3495: P. Kantor, G. Muresan, F. Roberts, D.D. Zeng, F.-Y. Wang, H. Chen, R.C. Merkle (Eds.), Intelligence and Security Informatics. XVIII, 674 pages. 2005.

Vol. 3494: R. Cramer (Ed.), Advances in Cryptology – EUROCRYPT 2005. XIV, 576 pages. 2005.

Vol. 3493: N. Fuhr, M. Lalmas, S. Malik, Z. Szlávik (Eds.), Advances in XML Information Retrieval. XI, 438 pages. 2005.

Vol. 3492: P. Blache, E. Stabler, J. Busquets, R. Moot (Eds.), Logical Aspects of Computational Linguistics. X, 363 pages. 2005. (Subseries LNAI).

Vol. 3489: G.T. Heineman, I. Crnkovic, H.W. Schmidt, J.A. Stafford, C. Szyperski, K. Wallnau (Eds.), Component-Based Software Engineering. XI, 358 pages. 2005.

Vol. 3488: M.-S. Hacid, N.V. Murray, Z.W. Raś, S. Tsumoto (Eds.), Foundations of Intelligent Systems. XIII, 700 pages. 2005. (Subseries LNAI).

Vol. 3486: T. Helleseth, D. Sarwate, H.-Y. Song, K. Yang (Eds.), Sequences and Their Applications - SETA 2004. XII, 451 pages. 2005.

Vol. 3483: O. Gervasi, M.L. Gavrilova, V. Kumar, A. Laganà, H.P. Lee, Y. Mun, D. Taniar, C.J.K. Tan (Eds.), Computational Science and Its Applications – ICCSA 2005, Part IV. LXV, 1362 pages. 2005.

Vol. 3482: O. Gervasi, M.L. Gavrilova, V. Kumar, A. Laganà, H.P. Lee, Y. Mun, D. Taniar, C.J.K. Tan (Eds.), Computational Science and Its Applications – ICCSA 2005, Part III. LXV, 1340 pages. 2005.

Vol. 3481: O. Gervasi, M.L. Gavrilova, V. Kumar, A. Laganà, H.P. Lee, Y. Mun, D. Taniar, C.J.K. Tan (Eds.), Computational Science and Its Applications – ICCSA 2005, Part II. LXV, 1316 pages. 2005.

Vol. 3480: O. Gervasi, M.L. Gavrilova, V. Kumar, A. Laganà, H.P. Lee, Y. Mun, D. Taniar, C.J.K. Tan (Eds.), Computational Science and Its Applications – ICCSA 2005, Part I. LXV, 1234 pages. 2005.

Vol. 3479: T. Strang, C. Linnhoff-Popien (Eds.), Location- and Context-Awareness. XII, 378 pages. 2005.

Vol. 3478: C. Jermann, A. Neumaier, D. Sam (Eds.), Global Optimization and Constraint Satisfaction. XIII, 193 pages. 2005.

Vol. 3477: P. Herrmann, V. Issarny, S. Shiu (Eds.), Trust Management. XII, 426 pages. 2005.

Vol. 3476: J. Leite, A. Omicini, P. Torroni, P. Yolum (Eds.), Declarative Agent Languages and Technologies II. XII, 289 pages. 2005. (Subseries LNAI).

Vol. 3475: N. Guelfi (Ed.), Rapid Integration of Software Engineering Techniques. X, 145 pages. 2005.

Vol. 3474: C. Grelck, F. Huch, G.J. Michaelson, P. Trinder (Eds.), Implementation and Application of Functional Languages. X, 227 pages. 2005.

Vol. 3472: M. Broy, B. Jonsson, J.-P. Katoen, M. Leucker, A. Pretschner (Eds.), Model-Based Testing of Reactive Systems. VIII, 659 pages. 2005.

Vol. 3470: P.M.A. Sloot, A.G. Hoekstra, T. Priol, A. Reinefeld, M. Bubak (Eds.), Advances in Grid Computing - EGC 2005. XXI, 1198 pages. 2005.

Vol. 3468: H.W. Gellersen, R. Want, A. Schmidt (Eds.), Pervasive Computing. XIII, 347 pages. 2005.